WATER
TRAILS
WEST

Also by The Western Writers of America
TRAILS OF THE IRON HORSE

WATER TRAILS WEST

By The Western Writers of America

Doubleday & Company, Inc.   Garden City, New York   1978

Chapter head illustrations by Andy Dagosta

Library of Congress Cataloging in Publication Data
Western Writers of America.
Water trails west.
Includes index.
1. Inland water transportation—The West—History—
Addresses, essays, lectures. 2. Transportation—
United States—History—Addresses, essays, lectures.
3. The West—History—To 1848—Addresses, essays,
lectures. I. Title.
HE627.W43 1978   386'.0973
ISBN 0-385-12709-X
Library of Congress Catalog Card Number 77–82973

Acknowledgments

Western Writers of America, an organization of professional writers, celebrated its twenty-fifth anniversary in June 1977 at the Cowboy Hall of Fame in Oklahoma City. At this national shrine to our western heritage there is now a permanent display of books produced by Western Writers of America, anthologies of short stories and original histories like *Trails of the Iron Horse* (Doubleday, 1975) and *Water Trails West*, which is the thirty-fifth WWA title published in the United States since 1953. Many of these WWA books have also appeared in British editions and have been translated into Spanish, Portuguese, Norwegian, German, and other foreign-language editions.

Water Trails West is an informal factual portrayal in text and pictures of how travel and transportation by water opened and developed the American West. It is a group project, each chapter painstakingly researched, written, and contributed by a member to WWA, a nonprofit organization whose purpose is to encourage high-quality achievement in the various fields of western writing.

Western Writers of America thank all of the contributors listed on the contents page for the text of their chapters and the illustrations they supplied, and we particularly thank:

Donald Duke, our WWA editor, for his patient help and valuable suggestions in organizing this project;

Harold Kuebler, our Doubleday editor, for his direction with both text and essential illustrations;

Debra Groisser, Doubleday & Company, for her editorial help and indefatigable search for needed pictures.

Acknowledgments

Photography was not widely used in the United States until Mathew Brady's coverage of the Civil War in the 1860s, so many of our illustrations are sketches and drawings by contemporary artists, published in earlier newspapers, magazines, and books. Western Writers of America owe special thanks to both their member contributors to this volume, as well as to many nonmembers, in locating these early pictures and photographs, and to the historical societies, museums, and individuals who granted permission to use them.

We thank the following institutions:

Arizona Historical Society
Beverly Historical Society
Bibliotec Nacional, Madrid
De Young Museum
Stella Foote Collection
Fort Hunter Canal Society
Louisiana Historical Society
Mariner's Museum
Minnesota Historical Society
Missouri Historical Society
Montana Historical Society
National Park Service
Nebraska State Historical Society

New-York Historical Society
New York Public Library Collection
Oklahoma Historical Society
Oregon Historical Society
Peabody Museum
Provincial Archives of Manitoba
Public Archives of Ontario
St. Louis Art Museum
State Historical Society, Missouri
United States National Museum
University of Washington, Special
   Collection
Washington Historical Society

We thank the following individuals for their gracious help:

Clarke Blair
Bill Burchardt
E. A. Hegg
Don Holm
C. M. Ismert
Ellis Lucia
D. F. McOuat
Mary Lou Pence

Robert Petrie
Archie Satterfield
Kay Saunders
Kay Stevens
John Douglas Smith
Volkert Veeder
George "Hooper" Wolfe

And, to Andy Dagosta, the artist who produced the vignette chapter-heading illustrations, our appreciation for a superb job.

If a name or two that should have been listed above was missed in the three years of correspondence that created *Water Trails West*—our thanks to you, too—with apologies!

August Lenniger
Anthologies
November 1977   WESTERN WRITERS OF AMERICA

Introduction

No nation ever faced transportation problems more staggering than those that confronted the United States during its first century. Inadequate and uncertain transit isolated the states and the few cities which clung together along the Atlantic coastline. George Washington's dream of a network of roads and canals was slow to materialize. Roads of any kind scarcely existed; in fact, in winter a Philadelphian might journey to Baltimore by stagecoach in five days—with a bit of luck! The relative ease of sea travel made New York closer to Europe than to the Appalachians.

Colonial travelers journeyed by Concord coach, horseback, or preferably, by boat between Boston, New York, and Philadelphia. Between New England towns they patronized the "Apple Tree Fleet" of schooners whose skippers took bearings from the many orchards along the shore. Ten days were necessary for news of President Washington's death to reach from Washington to Boston. Delegates often met difficulty and delay traveling from capital to capital for legislative sessions. Poor transportation hobbled the new American economy and the functioning of its government. Unity was next to impossible until people and news could move faster. In a dilemma, the Americans turned to one of their greatest natural resources— the inland waterways system.

The rivers had long been the main avenue of trade before the coming of Europeans. The Indians had used water transport for uncounted centuries, and after the white man had pushed into the West, trappers and fur traders moved about on the rivers and their branches, leading lives not much different from the red man. Then, after the Revolution, settlers began to cross the mountains and for them the rivers provided an easier way.

Introduction

Beyond the Appalachians lay the challenge of a vast wilderness—almost trackless, largely unexplored, and completely undeveloped. The United States population, in those years between 1790 and 1850, increased more than 500 per cent, and great numbers of new Americans moved into the West. Once they became both producers and consumers, an urgent need arose for means of conveying to the East the materials they wanted to sell, and for returning to the West manufactured goods. The existing transportation system by packhorse was inadequate. There were a few wagon roads, but travel by wagon was slow and expensive.

Following the War of 1812, the nation went canal crazy. Thomas Jefferson declared that "talk of making a canal of three-hundred-and-fifty miles through the wilderness—it is little short of madness." Yet a network of nearly 4,000 miles of artificial waterways was built in the eastern half of the country to provide a safe, adequate, and reasonably cheap system of transportation.

Canals like the Erie, Pennsylvania Main Line, and Chesapeake and Ohio helped end the isolation of great sections of the nation, and not only opened the market place for the farmer, but provided employment for thousands of men who built, maintained, and operated the canal packets. Overnight, cities mushroomed into thriving ports, and emigrants streamed into the towns to continue their way west by schooner or lake transport. Travel on the Erie Canal cut the in-transit time from New York to Buffalo from twenty to six days; the cost of moving a ton of freight dropped from $100 to $5.

The irony was that for all their success, the canals were threatened with obsolescence even before they began operating. The steam engine had been perfected and steam power was now pushing great vessels against river currents. Steam was also moving trains on rails and plans were drawn for a railroad to span the continent—just forty-nine years after Lewis and Clark had begun their overland journey through the raw wilderness to the shores of the Pacific Ocean.

At the time of the steamboat's arrival, the state of inland water travel in America was scarcely advanced over that of the Indian birchbark canoe. There was the flatboat, keelboat, barge, Mackinaw, or pirogue used for hauling freight and passengers during the great westward migration. The flatboat was one of the popular means of river travel. It was rectangular and boxlike, with sides, and drew less than two feet of water. The keelboat represented a considerable improvement over the flatboat. The keelboat was seventy feet in length and up to eighteen feet in beam. It was better built and had a roof for protection from the elements, and a pointed bow and stern which made it glide through the water.

Virtually all traffic proceeded one way—downstream—before the arrival of steamers. Only rarely was a keelboat forced back upriver by means of sail or towline. In this situation, a cordelle was used by a crew of some thirty men pulling the boat against the current. As for flatboats, they traveled only with the currents; when they arrived at New Orleans or any terminal they were sold for the wood they contained. The members of the crew had to make their way home as best they could, often walking the entire distance. The coming of the steamboats changed all that.

The steamboat was the darling of the inland waterways, the powerful, elegant symbol of man's ingenuity over old man river. Not always was it so. The first steam vessels clanked and hissed to the sounds of jeers, clung to sheltered rivers and bays as had the first sailing craft a century or more before. But soon steam came of age. Who the actual inventor of the steamboat was has long been a matter of debate. However, the *New Orleans* appears to have been the first steamboat on the western rivers, built in 1810 at Pittsburgh by Robert Fulton and Robert Livingston. Initial steamboat travel was on the Ohio and lower Mississippi rivers. The early vessels were small by later standards, seldom exceeding 120 feet in length with only a single deck and extreme shallow draft. Not unlike the ubiquitous stagecoach, the river steamer—restricted though it was to navigable waters—moved westward with the advancing American frontier.

The steamboat and steamboatmen bound the nation together and wrote one of the great American epics. In less than half a century, steamer routes were fanning out from Pittsburgh, the head of navigation on the Ohio, to the upper Mississippi, Missouri, Arkansas, Red, and the Rio Grande. The river steamer was the wilderness breaker that advanced trade. Steamboats were spreading emigrants out into the valleys of the Columbia, handling cargo and passengers on Puget Sound, and carrying gold seekers to their diggings in the Yukon. Even on the lower Colorado River, steamboats provided service sailings from Fort Yuma to river points.

During the 1850s the Missouri River became the crossroads of inland water travel in the country with St. Louis as the "Queen City." While the nation's railroads were slowly building west, the 5,000-mile network of rivers provided the life-giving contact with more than one third of the nation. It was during this period that steamboats grew larger and more luxurious, containing many decks with fine cabins and public rooms appointed with fancy furniture, crystal chandeliers, carpeting, and luxurious dining accommodations that would rival any New York restaurant. During this time the boats ran on schedules for a change, and speed soon became of paramount importance.

News of the discovery of gold in California in 1848 signaled the start of the first gold rush in the history of the world, and one of the greatest migrations of man in the history of mankind. Within the year 1849 alone, the new territory's population swelled fivefold as 80,000 men hurried to California in hopes of claiming a share of the golden riches. The story of the Argonauts (those who came to California to hunt gold during the gold rush of 1848–49) is a book in itself.

They came by land, and they came by sea to find gold. No story of the strike was too fantastic to believe. Men left their jobs and sold all their worldly possessions to finance the trip to California. Ships were suddenly needed in great numbers, and as fast as the vessels came to their home ports, they were put on the California run. Old hulks abandoned as unsafe for years were hauled out of the mud, patched up, and sent to sea overloaded with gold seekers. The traveler had his choice of two routes. He could make the long trip around Cape Horn at the tip of South America on a sailing vessel, or he could sail to Central America, cross to the Pacific (usually at the Isthmus of Panama but sometimes at Nicaragua), and take another ship to San Francisco. For the lucky who got a fine ship, a good crew and captain, the trip around Cape Horn provided the most practical. The trip across Mexico or South America was attempted, but few made it all in one piece.

While the Cape Horn route soon took second place to the trip across Panama after completion of the Panama Railroad, it remained the only way by which cargo could be brought to California. The demand for fast ships brought about the development of the California clipper ship.

The clippers were beautiful sailing vessels, with clean lines and a sharp bow. They were called clippers because they were built to clip through the waves. Because they were long and sleek and thin, they were known as the "greyhounds of the sea." These speedy craft cut the average time from New York to San Francisco from a tiresome voyage of six or eight months to a rapid run of 133 days. Clippers such as the *Flying Cloud*, the *Swordfish*, and the *Andrew Jackson* made it to San Francisco in ninety days. By the end of 1853 the situation in California was less frantic, and the clippers began to disappear from the seas.

The construction of railroads all over America soon reduced traffic on the waterways. To make matters worse there were several low-water years, slowing river traffic. Competition from a new form of river transport, the towboat and barge, began to make inroads into the packet lines' freight revenue. By the end of the nineteenth century the supremacy of the steel rail over the paddle wheel as a means of commerce was increasingly evident. Even along the waterways, the railroads enjoyed the superiority of greater speed, less distance, and near door-to-door delivery. The steamboat had come to be regarded as another nostalgic holdover from the romantic past.

This volume is not intended to be a technical treatise about canals, keelboats, or steamboats, but rather an endeavor to recapture the course our pioneer forefathers took as a means of advancing the westward movement on the waterways of the West. Had it not been for water transport at this critical time in our history, the growth of the United States might have taken a different turn and settlement delayed more than a quarter century. *Water Trails West* has been compiled by members of the Western Writers of America, an organization of professional writers of western topics, as a pleasurable way to do a bit of storytelling above and beyond their own avocation. I know each and every reader will enjoy his trip on the *Water Trails West*.

Donald Duke

Contents

Contents

1

The Great Canoe Trail

BY ROBERT MCCAIG

In the annals of North America the thrust of empire was west, always west. True, the conquistadors had probed from the south into the desert lands, but they quickly withdrew. They found nothing to equal the golden treasures of Mexico and South America—nor did they return until the latter part of the eighteenth century. True, on his final voyage in 1778, Captain James Cook touched briefly along the west coast of the continent and found the Russians operating but hardly entrenched on the northwest bays and islands. But these explorations were just that, exceptions to the rule that the well-populated and long-established eastern colonies were the wellspring of the movement toward the West.

Though the West was still unknown, the ledgers of history in the East already had many pages, some starred by the bold exploits of brave explorers, others smudged and blotted by accounts of rapine and murder and war. The breed of men which pressed inland from the Atlantic shores was impetuous, reckless, brave to a fault. Most were headstrong, greedy, often unscrupulous, but they were the kind of men it took to open the dangerous and hostile land, the right men, in the right place, at the exact right time. Their ambition sometimes brought them riches, or a kind of doubtful fame. More often it led them to hardship and peril and the anonymity of a lonely grave.

The highroads these men traveled in the three and a quarter centuries between Columbus and the *Santa Maria* and Peter Cooper and the steam locomotive *DeWitt Clinton* were the waterways of North America. Expansion and settlement and commerce were solely dependent on the lakes and rivers, the bayous and the creeks. Along the Atlantic seaboard in those days, and for a thousand leagues into the interior, forest lay thick and overgrown, nearly

Explorers by waterway. Painting by H. C. Edwards. Courtesy Peggy and Harold Samuels.

impenetrable. Progress on foot or on horseback was slow and tortuous, even where rudimentary trails did exist. Those trails followed the watercourses, crossing ridge and mountain by way of the water gaps carved by the streams over the eons as they swept toward the sea.

Many of the settlers and immigrants of the eastern seaboard came from the maritime countries of Europe, so it was natural for them to use the bays and rivers and lakes for transport. The ocean-going craft, sloops and

The Great Canoe Trail

Coureurs du bois *on Lake Superior. Painting by F. A. Hopkins. Courtesy Royal On-tario Museum.*

schooners and frigates, barks and barkentines, brought goods from Europe to the coastal cities and sailed back with cargoes of furs and forest products, dried fish and whale oil. On the coastal runs, into the smaller bays, up the wide rivers and on the lakes, sailed the sloops and snows and brigs, or scows and barges propelled by oars or scraps of sail. On narrower, rougher streams, men used smaller craft, skiffs and pirogues and rowboats, or that mainstay of travel in the far interior of the continent, the birch canoe. No other craft was so well adapted to the needs of the region as this Indian invention.

The explorers who made those first probing voyages into the coastal bays and estuaries of North America recognized immediately the marvelous virtuosity of this graceful vessel, so particularly appropriate for the specialized needs of the environment. There were limited uses for their gigs and wherries and rowboats, but the explorers, and the early settlers and traders who came soon after, chose the light, maneuverable canoe for their travel along the swift streams. The canoe was remarkably tough, easy to handle, light enough to be portaged for considerable distances, and turned

bottom up, it served as a comfortably waterproof shelter along the trail.

In the larger, slower rivers, and the wide lakes, sailing craft of fair size could be used, and were. But in the narrow, swift waters, or where portages were essential, the canoe reigned supreme. In the fur country north and west of the Great Lakes, beyond the St. Lawrence, it was the only transport. In their swift canoes the *coureurs du bois* penetrated deeper and deeper into this western region, where the woods runners trapped or traded for the rich fur of beaver and otter, ermine, mink and fisher, fox and wolf and bear, for which a greedy Europe seemed to have an insatiable lust, no matter what the price.

The disappointment of the earliest explorers, when they did not find the Seven Golden Cities of Cibola, or the land of the Great Cham, was greatly tempered when they were able to send back word to Europe of the treasure trove of fur in the northern lands. Forty-three years after Columbus, in 1535, Jacques Cartier sailed through the Strait of Belle Isle into a large gulf, and thence west into a great river which he named the St. Lawrence. Exultantly, he sailed upstream, sure that he had found at last the long-sought Northwest Passage. But some 540 miles up this great stream, his ship's progress was blocked by the Lachine Rapids, and he could go no farther.

It was sixty years later that Pierre Chauvin came to the St. Lawrence and established the first settlement at Tadoussac. Other settlements followed quickly, at Quebec "where the river narrows," settled by Samuel de Champlain in 1608. Three years later Champlain established a trading post at Mont Royal, on the island below those Lachine Rapids, which had blocked Cartier.

The great river had seemed to plunge so far and so arrow-straight from the heartland that Champlain renewed his hopes that this might yet be the fabled Northwest Passage. He and his men ascended by canoe that great tributary of the St. Lawrence, the Ottawa, following rumors that this stream might lead him to "the sea of the north." But when the party reached Allumette Island, it became apparent that this was not the right track, so sadly he went back downriver. Unknowingly, he had followed a route that one day would be a passage to the Northwest, even though it would never find China.

The French had no monopoly on exploration into the wide and narrow waters looking for the Northwest Passage. In 1610 that doughty English seaman Henry Hudson sailed through Davis Strait and discovered that great northern indentation which now bears his name. For two months he explored the shores of Hudson's Bay, but he lingered too long in the brief summer season, and his thirty-five-ton bark, the *Discovery*, was trapped by the freeze-up. The ship spent the winter tight-locked in the pack ice of James Bay. By breakup time the next June supplies had run low. There was a mutiny, and Hudson, his son, and seven others were dumped into a small boat and shoved away from the ship, never to be heard of again.

The information about Hudson's discoveries which finally trickled back to England, the great bay with its access to the heartland, led eventually to English entry into the tremendously profitable fur trade of northern Canada. In that same way Hudson's earlier voyages had led to the whaling and fisheries venture in Spitzbergen and the northern seas. Sixty years after Hudson, a group of influential Englishmen obtained a royal charter as the "Governor

& Company of Adventurers of England Trading Into Hudson's Bay." That was the beginning of the famed Hudson's Bay Company. On paper, the company's charter gave priority to the settlement of the Bay region and the pursuit of that chimera, the Northwest Passage. Common trade was merely secondary.

By the configuration of the land mass, and the circumstances of exploration and settlement, the thrust of commerce of New France was west and southwest. The commerce of the Hudson's Bay, or English, faction aimed south and west from York House, Churchill, and Fort Albany. Both trading operations began moving slowly outward toward Lake Winnipeg and the Red River, toward Athabasca and the Rockies. Sooner or later territorial overlap and commercial rivalry would be inevitable. Both factions must use those same bright-water roads, the lakes and rivers. Where both sides claimed some lake or river with the contiguous region, there would be war to the knife, and the hilt of the knife.

Canada's area is 25 per cent water, so it is possible even today to put a canoe in the Hudson under the George Washington Bridge in New York and by lake and by river cross North America to the Pacific, to the very shores of the Bering Sea. No portage en route would be longer than the thirteen-mile Methys Portage in northern Saskatchewan, and even that is broken by a lake a mile long. Peter Pond, the famous trader of the Nor'westers, crossed that portage in his pioneering travels. Even in the eighteenth century the facility of these water routes opened the door to the unknown West.

If knowledge of these western waterways had come sooner, they might have further bolstered the plans of John Ledyard, "The Great Traveler." Ledyard was an American, a sergeant of marines with Captain James Cook on that last voyage which brought Cook to the west coast of the continent. Ledyard conceived the idea of crossing North America from west to east on foot. He planned to start from Nootka (not knowing it was on an island) and to make his way from tribe to tribe until at the last he would reach the hunting grounds of his old friends, the Iroquois, and go on to the shores of the Atlantic. In 1787, under the implied aegis of Thomas Jefferson, he made an almost incredible effort to reach his starting point from Europe. He was two thirds of the way across Siberia when the secret police of

Portaging on a canot maître, *around 1867. Drawing by William Armstrong. Archives of Ontario.*

the Empress Catherine picked him up. In a horrible journey by *kibitka* the agents dragged Ledyard back across the steppes in six short weeks, and unceremoniously shoved him across the Polish border. It was plain that the Empress wanted no interlopers in her profitable fur trade to Unalaska and the west coast of North America. But knowing the geography as we now do, we see that Ledyard's "plan of a madman" might very well have succeeded, and he could have been one of the first travelers along the Great Canoe Trail.

As the years passed, there was an ebb and flow of the Canadian spheres of influence, always keyed to the transport routes of the lakes and rivers. The patterns changed like the shifting of a kaleidoscope, spun by the winds of war in distant Europe, coalescing and realigning with each falling of an uneasy peace. The shift of alliances occurred not only among the white men but among the red. Every twist, every change, in the tribal alliances, in the European coalitions, affected the lives and fortunes of the buckskin-clad *coureurs du bois* in the far forest. Economics of nations a wide ocean away meant bread and butter and life itself to these daring rovers.

But more and more these free spirits were declaring their intolerance of conditions forced upon them by absentee politicians. They wanted to be their own masters, they wanted a fair share of the profits from furs they had wrested in hardship and peril from a stubborn, inhospitable land. They began to ignore each stupid ukase thrust upon them by some powdered fop in a distant foreign court. The men in buckskin went their own way and killed their own snakes.

By the end of the seventeenth century, three quite definite spheres of influence had become established. The H.B.C. posts and trade routes radiated south out of York House, Severn, and Churchill. The French held sway from the frowning casemates of mighty Louisbourg Fortress along the St. Lawrence to Montreal, then south to Lake Champlain and to

Vincennes, and west toward Sault Ste. Marie and Michilimackinac. The British-Colonial sphere spread out from New York and Fort Pitt, controlling the Hudson and Ohio valleys, and south into the wilderness of Kaintuck. Along the vague perimeters of these areas there was constant friction. Further, there were enmities between various Indian tribes, often fomented by traders for their own selfish ends. Over all hung a growing restlessness and recklessness.

This precarious balance of forces were shaken in 1697, when the Treaty of Ryswick awarded to the victorious French the control of all the former British lands to the north. But they had not yet consolidated their holdings before the War of the Spanish Succession began, ending in a treaty in 1713 that returned all their former lands to the British.

Despite these changes, New France continued an aggressive policy of expansion. Their trade routes fanned out from headquarters at Montreal, up the Ottawa, into the Lakes. They made peace with those perennial troublemakers the Iroquois. They coveted the rich lands of the Old Northwest and the Ohio Valley, and moved successfully to take them, defeating General Braddock and his colonial forces and annexing a great chunk of new territory.

For a few years New France was the dominant power in North America. Then again faraway events shaped destiny. The Seven Years' War began, embroiling the armies and navies and resources of half the civilized world. Its holocaust spread to North America, and to Canada, and at its bitter end in 1763, the Treaty of Paris stripped New France of practically all its possessions east of the Mississippi. Every acre of ground, every subject of New France, white or red or brown, became subject to the British crown. Thus Britain dominated all of eastern North America until the American Revolution wrested away the lands and the peoples below the St. Lawrence and the Lakes.

One might guess that the ending of the national wars would bring with it commercial peace. Instead competition became more intense than before. The Hudson's Bay Company, the North West Company, its spin-off, the New North West Company, the free traders, and later the companies of John Jacob

Astor, all moved into an era of expansion. Their factors and agents moved farther and farther into the wilderness, establishing trading posts and trade routes. Men like the Frobishers, Simon McTavish, and Peter Pond struck out beyond all known boundaries in their search for fur and more fur.

It was in those halcyon days that the water highway was established that became the Great Canoe Trail. From Montreal, heading west, the brigades would go out in April or May, as soon as the ice melted along the St. Lawrence and the Ottawa. The big *canots maître*, loaded with trade goods and supplies, would start up the Ottawa, four or six canoes to a group or brigade. The brigades would leave a few days apart, those destined for posts farthest west leaving first. All departures were scheduled as closely as the available information and the state of the weather would permit, for the open-water season at Montreal is usually not more than seven and one half months.

Then in the autumn, as the leaves turned red and gold, and the air grew crisp with the first sting of winter, the brigades would come sweeping back down the Ottawa, their *chansons* ringing clear across the water. The *voyageurs* would unload the bales, sewn into red covers, or *parales*, each bale stenciled with cryptic symbols of weight and destination and content. The ninety-pound bales would be tossed into drays for the journey along the cobbles to St. Catherine Street. Then the *voyageurs*, in their plumed hats, their billowing shirts, and bright *Assumption* sashes, would grab their pay and head for the nearest saloon, to break their long thirst and blow in a few days the meager wages it had taken them all summer to earn. And the great birchbark canoes would bob empty along the berm of the levee.

It is often hard to determine whether form follows function, or function is dependent on form. In the case of the freight canoes these *voyageurs* paddled, the *canots maître*, there was a perfect wedding of form and function. No better vehicle could have been invented to travel the rivers and lakes and portages that comprised the western trails.

The *canots maître*, used on the main routes, was thirty-six feet long, about thirty-three feet over the gunwales, with an extreme beam of sixty-eight to seventy inches, and a depth amidships of thirty to thirty-two inches. Its weight, wet and empty, would be about six hundred pounds. These canoes were so strong, so flexible, they could survive runs through the wickedest of white-water rapids. They were fast and maneuverable.

The canoe frame was built up of cedar and spruce. The covering was the bark of the white or paper birch. This natural material was, in spite of its appearance of fragility, amazingly strong, flexible, and durable. It could withstand contact with logs and rocks, the strain of portages, and the heavy weight of their loads. If the bark skin was damaged, a repair could be made with a bark patch secured with spruce root and spruce gum, readily available in the forest.

The bark to cover a canoe was stripped from the birch in large sheets. Seams and joinings were calked with the gum of the black spruce, melted and mixed with powdered charcoal and a small amount of animal fat. The sewing or lashing to the canoe frame was done with the strong and extremely flexible roots of the black spruce. Occasionally some decorations might be added to the canoe, either with paint or by scraping a design down to the inner bark layer at the canoe ends. Often even this was omitted.

The design of the freight canoe evolved over a great many years, perhaps a century. In the day of New France the canoes were built at a yard at Trois Rivières, on a sort of crude assembly line. The factory would produce as many as twenty of these great craft in a year. Most of the work was done by Indian men and women under French supervision. Some time after the merger of the North West Company and the H.B.C. in 1821, the yard was closed, and thereafter the canoes were built by the Iroquois on individual contracts.

These large canoes were the backbone of the fur trade, that immensely profitable business where an investment of £800 could bring a return of £16,000 in a short time. The entrepreneurs made sure that their canoes were heavily laden, both going and coming. Small fir or spruce poles were placed in the bottom to distribute evenly the weight of the cargo.

The lading outward bound for the trading posts might consist of axes, shot, canoe awls, gunpowder, gun tools, brass wire, flints, lead, beads, breeches, blankets, combs and coats, firesteels and finger rings, guns, garters and powder horns, spruce gum and birchbark, hats, cartridge boxes, kettles and pans, knives, fish lines, hooks and net twine, mirrors, ribbons and needles, rum, brandy and wine, blue and red broadcloth, tomahawks and hatchets, tobacco, pipes, thread, vermilion and ochre, wax and oilskin, medals and chains, hammers, nails, and perhaps even false hair.

This comprised the commercial load. In addition, each crewman had one bale of private property. His food allowance was one and a half bushels of dried corn or peas and one-eighth keg of grease per man. The tarpaulins, or *parales*, used to cover the cargo were eight by ten feet, made of canvas with grommets around the edges for the lashings. The canvas was treated with ochre, oil, and wax to make it waterproof, and this gave the *parales* a distinctive dull red color. Including freight, supplies, and men, the load of each big canoe would be about eight thousand pounds. Thus a brigade of four *canots maître* would carry about twelve tons.

Usually the cargo was made up in ninety-pound bales, called *pactons*. Liquids were carried in nine-gallon kegs. Valuable materials were packed in *cassettes*, wooden boxes twenty-eight by sixteen by sixteen inches of dovetailed boards strapped with iron and a tight-fitting cover secured by hasp and padlock. The brigade officers often carried a leather traveling case containing medicines, ink and paper, and other personal materials. Provisions were kept in tins or pack baskets along with the cooking utensils. The bedrolls were of blankets or robes made up with a tarpaulin or oilskin ground sheet. The rolls were used in the canoes for pads or seats. The canoe equipment, called *agres* or *agrets*, included paddles, lines, setting poles, rope, mast and sail, and repair materials.

Sometimes *pactons* of pelts would be repacked in one-hundred-pound bundles at the transfer point from the smaller (twenty-five-foot) *canots du nord* of the outback into the thirty-six-foot *canots maître*. Two of these *pactons* would be a minimum load for a man across a portage, but a true *homme du nord* would scorn to carry that light a load. The *pactons* rested on the small of the carrier's back, secured by a tump line which ended in a wide leather band fitting the man's forehead.

A latter-day brigade of voyageurs, around 1900, fighting white water and rocks with poles and brawn on the Abitibi River. Archives of Ontario.

On top of his two or more *pactons* a keg might be placed, or a *cassette* or two. Where the trail over a portage was moderately good, loads of 270 pounds per man were common. The maximum recorded was 570 pounds portaged by one man. Thrust forward by the weight of their burdens, the *voyageurs* moved ahead at a brisk trot—they had to! Every man was expected as a rule to make more than one trip over a portage. The empty canoe was carried upside down, usually by four men.

As can be guessed, the canoemen on the fur trail had to be a special kind of man. Many of them were Quebec farm boys from the regions east of Montreal. Why they were willing to trade the decent food and comparative security of farm life for the hardship and travail of the *voyageur* is puzzling. No doubt there was a certain glamour attached to the sight of new places, and an *esprit de corps* among these *coureurs du bois*. A woods runner was marked as a man of extreme toughness and stamina, never to be confused with the "pork eaters" of the towns, the pen pushers and pelt stretchers of the larger posts and Montreal. The cockade in his hat marked this special kind of man, perhaps the thing that in more southern lands is called *machismo*.

This pride must have been their real reward, for the *voyageur* was paid miserably and overworked to the point of death. He was usually small in stature, for less human weight meant more room for fur. He grew old before his time. He died of strangulated hernia, of heart attack, of pneumonia, or he drowned in savage lake waves or the white water of rapids. Beside the almost inconceivable labor on the portage, the *voyageurs* were expected to paddle fifty miles a day, rising at 2 or 3 A.M. They would paddle for hours before breakfast, and end their day only when stopped by gathering darkness at 9 or 10 P.M.

In the days of the Nor'westers, the men were permitted to carry on some private trading, to bolster in some small manner their miserable stipend. But after the merger with the Hudson's Bay Company (H.B.C.—"here before Christ") this practice was considered an infringement on the profits of the company and was sternly forbidden. Thereafter many of the experienced *voyageurs* left the trade and were replaced by Metis or Indians in this employment, a life so brutal it would have made a galley slave shudder.

Typically, a westbound brigade would depart on a brisk spring morning after a blessing by the priest at Ste. Anne de Bellevue. But first the *voyageurs* of the four or five canoes, twenty-five or thirty men, would try to drink their entire trip allowance of eight gallons of rum or brandy per canoe. In theory, a supply of spirits would last the whole journey. After due time, the men would reluctantly stagger or be kicked into the canoes. They would paddle erratically to the beat of drunken songs across the Lake of the Two Mountains and turn up the Ottawa. They were never expected to cover much mileage that first day, nor could they. But early the next morning the *directeur* or *guide*, who was sometimes a factor or partner, would roust the men out. They would reload the canoes, for if the weather was at all inclement, the canoes would have been emptied and overturned for use as a night shelter.

The bowman, or *avant*, was the captain of the craft. The steersman, or *gouvernail*, and the *avant* received for their duties a small premium on their wages. The loaded canoes would be shoved off in the dim dawn light, and to the rousing strains of "Viva la Compagnie!" or some *chanson* from the Loire Valley, they would pick up the beat and drive upriver. The canoe would move at a fast clip, the men wielding long paddles, which, to avoid tiring

never had blades wider than four and a half to five inches. Usually the men knelt two abreast to paddle, with their backs resting against the thwarts.

The trail led up the Ottawa, past the Long Sault and Rabbit River. Here the portages began, and the work became more strenuous. Above Dog Lake there were many rapids and more than a few portages. Past the two-mile Pipe Portage, and Fort Quibon post, the route turned away from the "Grand Rivière" into the Mattawa. From here over the Height of Land the travel was backbreaking, rapid after rapid, portage after portage. The broad reach of Lake Nipissing provided one easy stretch, then came the run down the French River over rapids and between narrow banks. The full run from Montreal to Lake Athabasca would entail more than one hundred portages, and innumerable rapids to be run, of greater or lesser danger.

Where the French flows into Lake Huron, the canoes would hug the north shore of Georgian Bay as they moved west, for the heavy lading of these freight canoes brought their freeboard down to mere inches. High waves might swamp the canoes, lesser waves would splash into the craft and wet the cargo. Then

A typical Hudson's Bay Company post, Moose Factory, already long-established when this photo was taken in 1868. Archives of Ontario.

Canots du nord *running white water on Rupert's River. Archives of Ontario.*

the brigade must stop and dry the bales and equipment. Along the north shore the brigade would pass amid the islands, beyond George Island into Fraser Bay, then through the channel between Great Cloche and Manitoulin and into the Bay of Islands. The canoes would sweep past Bedford Island, Amedroz and Clapperton, past Aird and John, to the mouth of Blind River. They would come at last to the point where the Thessalon debouches into St. Joseph's Channel.

If the brigade was bound for Michilimackinac, or on to Chicago or Prairie du Chien, it would turn south here and go through the narrow passage of the Detour. They would cross dangerous open water to land at the Isle of Mackinac, that key trading post which gave forever its name of "Mackinaw" to the short warm jacket of plaid wool which is still standard outdoor wear in the woods.

If the brigade was bound for Sault Ste. Marie, it would hold on west, past Joseph Island, where a Nor'wester post would replace Mackinac, lost to the Americans at the end of the War of 1812. Passing through the narrow confines of the Soo, the deep-laden canoes would again hug the shores of Superior, probably passing inside of Michipicoten Island and

skirting that great inland sea past the Slate Islands. In the years between 1778 and 1803, the brigade would move along south, down the west shore, past the Pigeon River, to land at the "Great Depot" that was Grand Portage.

After 1804, the canoes would round the point of Silver Islet and cross Thunder Bay to the new Nor'wester post at Fort William, where the Dog River drops into Lake Superior. Fort William was to become the main post of the North West Company, the hub of all trade to the north and west, and eventually to the Oregon country itself. Its importance is shown by the fact that the big brass, the officers and partners of the company, would gather there for their important meetings on policy and strategy.

Whatever the appointed destination, Mackinac or Grand Portage, the Soo or Fort William, the brigade would make its rendezvous with its eastbound brethren, brigades of the smaller *canots du nord*, which had come down from Lake Winnipeg or Athabasca, from Rainy Lake or Lake of the Woods. Cargoes would be interchanged. The smaller canoes would be loaded almost to the gunwales with trade goods and supplies bound for the remote and isolated trading posts. Into the

Fort William on Lake Superior in 1852. Sir George Simpson's canot maître being launched. Drawing by William Armstrong. Archives of Ontario.

The smaller canots du nord navigated the rivers and streams whose rapids and shallow depths proved too formidable for the heavily laden canots maître. Pic River, Thunder Bay District, around 1906. Archives of Ontario.

canots maître would be loaded the bales of furs, each in its canvas covering, in hot weather stinking of dead flesh and crawling with vermin. Each bale would be marked with various symbols, the weight, the type of fur, the consignee, and so on. A typical bale would hold three hundred mink skins, stretched and dried, compressed into a ninety-pound *pacton* by a hand-powered screw press.

The news exchanged, it would be time for farewells, and after what small celebration they could manage, each brigade would turn and go, back toward its home base. Neither brigade would waste time, for they must get to their destination before freeze-up. The *canots maître* would retrace their outward journey, braving autumn storms, forced to portage around rapids they had run in the higher waters of the spring runoff, for now the streams were at their lowest. In good weather in wide waters some speed was gained by the use of a rudimentary sail to help the paddlers. In less clement weather it was the paddle alone. And as a stream grew shallower, the paddles came inboard and the setting poles came out. In still lesser waters the *voyageurs*

walked along the stream banks and "lined" the canoes, literally dragging them by means of *cordelles*. Too often they had to employ the last resort: by sweat and toil carry canoes and cargoes on weary backs along the portage trail until deeper water was found.

There are no accurate figures extant giving the volume of freight that moved along the Great Canoe Trail in its busiest years. It must have been considerable. Examination of fragmentary export figures, and more detailed British import figures, gives a count of bales by hundreds and pelts by thousands. Some of those peltries came out of Hudson's Bay, but most of them undoubtedly came to Montreal by lake and by river in the big freight canoes.

There was other traffic along the trail. Dispatches and orders to and from headquarters, officials on inspection trips, factors or employees being assigned or reassigned to distant posts. The top men of the Nor'westers, the McKenzies, the Macdonalds, and McTavishes of the company hierarchy, often made trips into the interior. Their brigades traveled in style, their swift express canoes lightly loaded, each with six or eight or ten

Voyageurs with craft heavily laden with supplies preparing to leave for the isolated camps and posts. This photograph was taken at Rupert's House in the early part of this century. The dwelling is little changed from the halcyon days of the fur-trade era. Archives of Ontario.

paddlers. There would be one canoe alone for the tents and bedding of the great men, another for their gourmet food and whiskey and fine wines. The daily runs would be easy, and there would be time out when the aristocrats felt the urge to bag a moose, or to knock down a few brace of grouse or waterfowl. To join an expedition with the big brass was prized duty for any lucky *voyageur*. Paddling in the brigade of one of the lordly directors was the next thing to a well-paid vacation.

Gradually the business changed. By the end of the eighteenth century most of the nearer lands were trapped out; the companies and the free traders reached farther and farther into the wilderness. Rivalries deepened, between the free traders and the companies, between the companies themselves, between the Canadians and the Americans. The bitter warfare between the North West Company and its spin-off, the XY Company, ended in 1804, only when death had removed the irreconcilable personal enmities of the old leaders. The merger of the two companies brought a common front against their great rival, the prestigious Hudson's Bay Company.

Rivalry and expansion increased traffic on the trail. At the time of the merger in 1804, the North West Company brought to it 117 trading posts and 1,058 employees. The smaller XY Company brought in about a third as many posts, factors, and other employees. Thus the Nor'westers created a formidable opponent for the H.B.C., which spurned an offer to join the merger. However, financial reverses, and the mounting cost of waging internecine warfare, began to tell on the great company. So under Thomas Douglas, Fifth Earl of Selkirk, the H.B.C. merged in 1821 with the North West Company, further increasing traffic on the trail.

In American territory south of the Lakes, the area now called "the Old Northwest," John Jacob Astor was building a fur empire. But there were few factories in the new republic to supply trade goods. Besides, the Indian tribes were strongly bound by tradition and preferred the superior English goods, such as "the genuine Hudson's Bay fuke with the brass dragon on the stock." So much of Astor's trade goods came by the trail, and very many of the furs they purchased went back the same way to the Montreal market. Some goods came, and furs returned, by boat up the Mis-

sissippi, but the mainstream remained flowing from Mackinac to Green Bay, down the Ouisconsin to the Mississip' and St. Louis.

It was in 1810 that Astor sent Wilson Price Hunt to Montreal to outfit a party and buy trade goods. Hunt, with Donald McKenzie and Ramsay Crooks, followed the trail, refitting at Mackinac and going on to St. Louis. There Hunt with a larger party embarked on the long journey up the Missouri, to cross the Rockies in the wake of the Lewis & Clark Expedition, five years earlier. After much travail and many vicissitudes, Hunt and his party reached Astoria, at the mouth of the Columbia, in 1811. The Hunt party had been the second string to Astor's bow, for Astor had sent the ship *Tonquin* around the Horn to establish the new post named in his honor. Hunt found the western rivers teeming with fur.

But Astor's promising venture was short-lived. The War of 1812 was fateful for the enterprise, and, in 1815, Astor's agents ceded the Pacific operation to the North West Company. His dream of monopolizing the western fur trade, and eventually the trade to China, was over.

It would seem logical that the supply ships which brought goods and tools and food to the Pacific operation of the Nor'westers, to Astoria and Fort Vancouver and Victoria, would furnish cheap transport for the coast furs. But it was a long way around Cape Horn or the Cape of Good Hope, and the unit cost proved too high. Thus for many years the rich furs from the Columbia and the Snake River country, from the Okanagan and the Peace and the Fraser, went by canoe and barge, by lake and river, filtering from the outback into Fort William. Then they traveled in the traditional *pactons* in the great freight canoes down the same familiar trail to the warehouses of Montreal.

Yet well before the middle of the eighteenth century the fur market, upon which the prosperity of the great trading companies depended, was beginning to collapse. Changes in styles, changes in human needs began to bring drastic changes as well in the fur business. Price drops began to hurt in 1837, and they dropped even more drastically as time went on. The fur markets faded quickly. The last rendezvous of the American Fur Company took place in 1839. Most of the great com-

The end of the era. One of the last of the freighting canoes of the Hudson's Bay Company. Archives of Ontario.

panies diversified into other lines of merchandise, not always profitably. Yet without the fur trade, the cornerstone of their business, profits proved so disappointing that the H.B.C. pulled completely out of the Oregon country in 1871.

As the fur trade shrank from a torrent to a trickle, so too did traffic on the Great Canoe Trail. With the coming of sail and steam to the Great Lakes, there was faster and cheaper transport of goods and furs. So when the transcontinental railroad was completed, one would expect the trail to be abandoned. But the old ways die hard, and the brigades went out year after year, managing to keep the freight cost per pelt competitive, going into the remote areas that only the canoe could reach. On the swift, narrow streams of the outback, the bush, nothing could replace the canoe, though now it was more likely to be a commercial canoe of wood and canvas than the graceful birchbark craft of the *voyageurs*.

Yet the end was inevitable. In the fading years of the nineteenth century the great *canots maître* became memories. Dams and locks blocked the rivers. Still, it was not until 1910 that the very last of the brigades swept down the Ottawa with paddles splashing diamond drops in the sunlight, to the beat of a *chanson* of the last *voyageurs*. Now the swift ships of the airways can cross in minutes the miles the *hommes du nord* needed days of sweat and bitter travail to cover.

The great freight canoes are gone now, and the rivers lie empty except for modern pleasure craft. But for three hundred years or more those canoes moved the men and supplies along the Great Canoe Trail, and down the bright-water roads of the far wilderness. They brought back sleek and shining furs to grace the costumes of kings and queens, princes and princesses of the royal blood, furs to bedeck gentlemen and pretenders, ladies and courtesans, churchmen and scoundrels, across the face of all the world.

It was the Great Canoe Trail which in many ways made possible the opening of the West. Though fur was the lure, to reach the fur the trail conquered a wilderness. From its base men went forth and found the West and mapped it, and set down the first feeble roots. The perils, the persistence of the traders and trappers opened the gates of the West for the gold seeker, the stockman, the granger who followed the invisible wake of the great canoes.

2

The "Father of Waters"

BY ROBERT T. SMITH

Tom Sawyer and Huck Finn, Marquette and Joliet, the *Natchez* and the *Robert E. Lee*, riverboat gamblers in lace shirts and minstrels "strummin'" on banjos mean the Mississippi, Father of Waters, the Big Muddy.

The Mississippi courses through the heartland of America. It unites the East and the West. It unites the North and the South. It unites America. It is the nurturer of great cities. It is a gentle giant that can change in a moment to a violent force capable of destroying everything in its path. Since its discovery, the Mississippi has fascinated, even enchanted, those who have come in contact with it. Dreamers built empires around it. Others, of a more practical nature, tried to conquer it. They built boats and barges to move up and down its length. They built arches of steel to bridge it. They built locks and dams to control its flow. In spite of all their efforts the Mississippi is still today the ultimate American river.

This is the story of that river and those who peopled it. The river cannot be separated from those who floated down it or steamed up it or lived along it. The magic word "Mississippi" evokes both the geographic fact and the people who surround it, and many, many other things as well. Especially, the Mississippi means the West, not the geographic West, but the psychic West which dwells deep in our innermost self. The river marks the edge of the frontier, the Middle border, the edge of the unknown.

Before the coming of the white man the Mississippi linked together a large Indian population. For the most part they farmed and lived contented lives in permanent villages near their fields along its banks. The river itself attracted only the most adventuresome of them. As Indians, they revered the spirit of the Great River for such a great natural force would surely have a very powerful spirit. The river could be a wrathful thing, but for the most part they were comforted by its reassuring presence. It provided food and an easy means of transportation. It also provided easy access to the restless white explorers who would eventually destroy their way of life.

Hernando de Soto came upon the Mississippi in May of 1541 during his four-year quest for gold. The river blocked his way, and after crossing it he gladly left it behind as he continued his search for a "golden city." Destiny drew him back, however, when on May 21, 1542, De Soto died on the banks of the river he discovered.

Luis de Moscoso, De Soto's successor, feared that if their commander's death were discovered by the Indians, it would touch off a fight which could destroy the small Spanish force he now commanded. He told the natives that De Soto, the great chief, had gone to meet with the other gods. A party was formed and in the dead of night they removed the conquistador's body from its temporary resting place. They wrapped the remains in chains and placed them in a hollowed-out log. Moscoso and his tiny group of carefully selected Spaniards rowed to the center channel of the river. To the chanting of priests, the log and its contents slipped quietly into the murky depths. The Mississippi had claimed its first white victim.

Moscoso led what was left of the expedition to Mexico in 1543. Of the more than 600 men who began the expedition, only 311 survived. They found no gold and failed to recognize the value of the discovery they had made.

De Soto's discovery of the Mississippi. Engraving from the painting by W. H. Powell. Courtesy of the New-York Historical Society, New York City.

It would be more than one hundred years before the Europeans would again demonstrate an interest in the Mississippi.

On June 17, 1673, Father Jacques Marquette and Louis Joliet entered the Mississippi from the Wisconsin River. The two intrepid explorers, one in search of souls to save, and one in search of empires to build, traveled by canoe as far south as the mouth of the Arkansas. Their sole passport for travel amidst the Indian tribes was a calumet, or peace pipe, which saved their lives on more than one occasion. Confident that the river emptied into the Gulf of Mexico, they hurried back to report their findings to the French intendant, Jean Talon, at Quebec.

Talon, however, had been replaced by Louis Count de Frontenac. The date was 1672. Frontenac chose Robert Cavelier, Sieur de la Salle to develop the Mississippi basin. La Salle built Fort Crevecoeur on Lake Peoria in 1680. Fort Crevecoeur, it was hoped, would be the base from which the Mississippi would be conquered. That year La Salle dispatched Father Louis Hennepin to explore the upper Mississippi.

Father Hennepin's exploration of the upper portion of the river greatly added to the knowledge of that part of North America. He discovered and named the Falls of St. Anthony and kept a detailed account of the geography and ethnology of the region. Hennepin and his two canoe men almost lost their lives when Sioux Indians captured them. After months of wandering and suffering extraordinary privations, they were rescued by the French explorer of the Northwest, Daniel Duluth on July 25, 1680. Later, all of Europe read of Father Hennepin's adventures and, as a result, European awareness of the upper Mississippi grew rapidly.

After many trials La Salle and his lieutenant, Henri de Tonti, began their trip down the lower Mississippi in the spring of 1682. The trip itself was uneventful and on April 9, 1682, they arrived at the mouth of the Missis-

La Salle claims the Mississippi Valley for France. Courtesy of the New-York Historical Society, New York City.

sippi. As was the custom of the day, they claimed the whole of the Mississippi basin for the king of France. La Salle named the entire territory Louisiana in honor of his king, and that name has remained to this day. For the next eighty years France would attempt to build an inland empire in North America with the Great Lakes and the Mississippi providing a transportation and communication backbone. French fur trappers, using canoes, made good use of the Mississippi and its tributaries. To serve them and to protect them, trading posts and forts were established which would eventually become great cities. New Orleans and St. Louis are only two of the many cities along the Mississippi which began as French outposts.

The typical riverman of the French epoch was usually a swarthy Breton who found himself well suited to life on the river. He frequently married into the Indian tribes and soon a new amalgam formed. The forts and trading posts were *très jolie*. The rough men would eat heartily and sing and drink to all hours of the night. Songs like "Allouette" survive to this day as a reminder of the days when trappers and traders sang them along the banks of the Mississippi at places like Kaskaskia or Natchez.

French control of the Mississippi River and Louisiana ended in 1763 at the close of the French and Indian War and for the next thirty-seven years Spain dominated the lower river and Great Britain the upper river. Spanish rule did little to change the character of the Mississippi and life along it remained essentially French. During the American Revolution, New Orleans became a supply center for American forces operating in the West. Oliver Pollack, the principal American agent in New Orleans, at first received secret aid from the Spanish governor and once Spain entered the war the volume of that aid greatly increased.

The Mississippi River, of course, was an important battle zone during the war. The Americans had to control the Mississippi. Without it they had no access to New Orleans. Without that access all the land west of the Appalachians would fall into British hands. Most of the people along the river were not particularly friendly toward the English. The French population still smarted from the English victory of 1763. Therefore, the Ameri-

cans found many willing to join in their cause. Two expeditions, both mounted from Fort Pitt in Pennsylvania, were concerned with securing the Mississippi for the Americans.

The first expedition fell under the command of James Willing and had as its ultimate objective British West Florida. Willing set out in January 1778 and plundered his way down the Mississippi. He reached New Orleans, where Pollack had arranged a friendly greeting from Governor Bernardo de Galvez. Willing's activities, however, aroused the British and a probing move into West Florida met with disaster. Willing found himself and his party bottled up in New Orleans, effectively neutralized.

Meanwhile, the second and more famous expedition under the command of George Rogers Clark moved on the upper Mississippi. Clark relied upon support of French settlers along the Mississippi and with their co-operation captured Kaskaskia and shortly thereafter Cahokia. The French alliance had brought both France and Spain into the war on the American side and that meant that all the Mississippi was in hands friendly to the American cause. The British were unable to wrest back the area from Clark and after the Treaty of Paris of 1783, which ended the long war, the United States was in control of all of the east bank of the Mississippi with an important exception.

Spain continued its possession of the Isle of Orleans and the city of New Orleans, until 1800 but most of the people who lived along the Mississippi in that period continued to be French or French-Indian. A smattering of Spaniards populated the lower river and around Arkansas Post a few Anglo-American fur traders had established themselves. This polyglot population made its living trading with the Indians or serving those who did trade by growing foodstuffs. Spanish and French planters cultivated sugar cane south of Natchez and cattle ranching was surprisingly prevalent in the southern Mississippi flatlands. Moses Austin operated a lead mine in Missouri as did others, but to a large extent all these operations were small and of local significance. American settlers brought about the real change in life along the Mississippi.

To a large extent the Revolutionary War was fought over the question of settlement in the Ohio Valley, and when the Americans

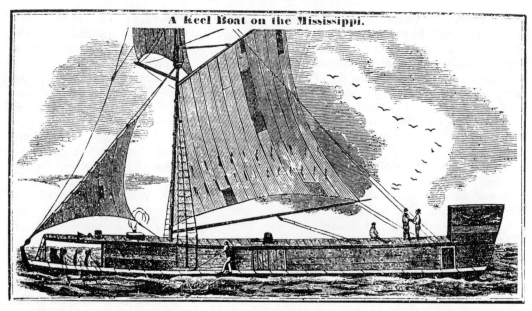

A Keel Boat on the Mississippi.

Keelboat on the Mississippi in Davy Crockett's Almanac. Courtesy of the New-York Historical Society, New York City.

won the war a vast flood of settlers moved into the West. In less than ten years after the signing of the Treaty of 1783 the Ohio Valley had a large population of farmers. Much to their consternation, they found trade outlets to the East far too restricted. The only way farm produce could be moved from the valley efficiently was by floating it down the Mississippi in either flatboats or keelboats.

The era of flatboats and keelboats began in the early 1790s and would last into the second decade of the next century when the more efficient steamboats would gradually replace them. During this same period the United States, Spain, and France wrestled for control of the river. The United States won in 1803 when James Monroe and Robert R. Livingston successfully negotiated the purchase of Louisiana from France. Now both sides of the river were American and the full development of its waterway could proceed.

For more than a hundred years the river had served as a practically deserted highway connecting a string of trading posts. It flowed through a sparsely populated region and river traffic was correspondingly sparse. As American farmers flooded into the Ohio River Valley, the Mississippi came alive. New Orleans became the great southern terminus for flatboats

and keelboats carrying produce and passengers from the Ohio Valley. Traffic picked up on the Mississippi; and as the importance of the fur trade diminished along the river itself, shifting farther west, many of the communities adjusted their services to meet the needs of these new and more numerous river people.

The keelboatmen and the flatboatmen were a hardy lot. For the most part they were usually only farmers off on a spree, but a few truly rough customers like the legendary Mike Fink earned their place in American folklore. They drank and fought among themselves and the townspeople along the river. Some of those who found the life of the river more attractive than farming became robbers or sharpers who preyed on river travelers of less experience. The nomads of the river soon gave it a dangerous reputation which on occasion it deserved. While the flatboats and keelboats would eventually be driven off the river by the competition from the steamboat, they continued to be a part of the river for many years.

This first steamboat to ply the Mississippi, the *New Orleans,* was launched in Pittsburgh in 1811 and after its historic trip to New Orleans in that year the river was altered dramatically. A series of earthquakes struck along large sections of the river, bordered by the present-day state of Missouri, destroying the famous Pawnee Bluffs, wiping out towns, and in general spreading havoc. In some places the river dropped more than forty feet, causing great waves to rush downriver. The frontiersmen who lived off the river sprang back quickly after the quakes subsided and the flood tides receded and in no time it was business as usual.

The War of 1812 delayed the impact of the steamboat on the river more than the earthquake the year before. The American economy stagnated during the war and the Old Southwest and Old Northwest east of the Mississippi saw relatively large amounts of fighting, mostly directed against the pro-British Indian population. The English, occupied by Napoleon until mid-1814, saved their principal effort against the Americans until that year. With Napoleon out of the way, the British commanders planned a major offensive, and one of the major objectives of that offensive was New Orleans.

The attack on New Orleans was part of a British grand design, which, if successful, might well have destroyed the young nation. The British knew that if they could seize control of New Orleans and the lower Mississippi, they could economically cripple the interior of the United States. They no doubt hoped that the largely French population of Louisiana could then be convinced to give their allegiance to Britain, who still maintained strong interests in the fur trade of the Southeast and the upper Mississippi Valley. The Battle of New Orleans, however, had no effect on the outcome of the war, for the Treaty of Ghent had been signed before the battle was fought. If the British had won, one wonders if they would have ignored the terms of the Treaty of Ghent and retained control of the city.

The story of that battle is one of the most remarkable tales in American history. Sir Edward Packenham and 7,500 British troops appeared in the Gulf of Mexico in the fall of 1814. President Madison ordered Andrew Jackson, the military commander in the Old Southwest, to New Orleans, where he hastily devised a defense. Packenham took his time and did not mount his main attack until the

Battle of New Orleans, January 8, 1815. Courtesy of the New-York Historical Society, New York City.

Mississippi flatboatmen, 1847. Painting by George Caleb Bingham. Courtesy St. Louis Art Museum.

morning of January 8, 1815. Jackson positioned his militia, numbering around six or seven thousand, behind cotton bales and waited in silence for the British Army to emerge from the heavy mist. The Americans heard the skirl of bagpipes and the beat of drums long before they saw the enemy. Jackson's men held their fire until the British were virtually on top of them. The battle lasted only half an hour and ended in total victory for the Americans. Andrew Jackson would use this victory to launch him into the presidency, and the Mississippi River would enter a forty-five-year period during which it would serve as the backbone of a transportation net which included virtually all of what is now known as the Middlewest.

Although the steamboat had been around for some time, not until 1816 would a vessel truly meet the requirements of river transport on the Mississippi. Henry M. Shreve, a keelboatman and river pilot, built the *Washington*

in 1816. The *Washington* included several improvements which would be incorporated in all the steamers that followed. Shreve moved the boiler of the *Washington* out of the hold, beginning a trend which would eventually result in all machinery being placed above the water line. This was a significant improvement as it allowed the boats to be built with the extremely shallow draft necessary for navigation on the shallow sandbar-filled western rivers. Cargo decks, boiler decks, and passenger decks were stacked above the water line, giving the impression of a floating layer cake.

The end of war also saw another invention, the cotton gin, make possible the lightning-like expansion of the cotton frontier across the deep South. An economic boom was on and the river would profit from it. By 1820 more than seventy-five steamboats operated on the Mississippi, and that number continued to grow as the cotton South grew.

Naturalist Thomas Nuttall made a journey down the Mississippi in 1819 and his account provides a good picture of the river in the early steamboat age. Even at this somewhat late date he found the river relatively devoid of population. In fact, he questioned somewhat rashly, "How many ages may yet elapse before these luxuriant wilds of the Mississippi can enumerate a population equal to the Tartarian deserts!" He found the river ". . . truly magnificent though generally bordered by the most gloomy solitudes, in which there are no visible traces of the abode of man." Shortly after he entered the river, boatmen cheated him out of five dollars on Wolf's Island. He reacted with outrage at the high prices charged for supplies at river towns such as New Madrid, which he described as an "insignificant French hamlet." His encounters with the Indians reflected the tragic state of their existence. He found most reduced to docile creatures whose only mission seemed to be to get more whiskey to feed a craving built up over the years by dealing with unscrupulous fur traders.

In spite of Nuttall's description of the Mississippi as devoid of significant population, some settlements such as Cape Girardeau and St. Louis on the upper river were taking on importance by 1820. St. Louis, in particular, had long been an important trading center and gathering point for traders operating on the upper Mississippi and the Missouri. The fur trade in the Rocky Mountain West headquartered out of St. Louis, where firms like the Missouri Fur Company and the Rocky Mountain Fur Company had their origins. St. Louis was a hard-living town, where mountain men rubbed shoulders with speculators fresh out from the East and seasoned French and Spanish traders like Manuel Lisa and the Choteaus. With the exception of the northern reaches of the river well above St. Louis, the stretch between the Ohio and the Arkansas was the most sparsely populated and during the years of the flatboats was most likely to serve as the hunting ground for river pirates.

Nuttall's journal reflected his fear of the river pirates. Some groups became large and powerful criminal syndicates, aided and abetted by corrupt government officials. The pirates would lay in wait along the loneliest stretches of the river for likely victims. Frequently they would disguise themselves as Indians. Only the growing population would put an end to their activities, for they shunned the more populated areas below the Arkansas.

The tone of Nuttall's description of the Mississippi changed when he reached what he called "the opulent town of Natchez." Prosperous plantations at Port Coupee impressed the naturalist, but he disapproved of the system of slavery which made that prosperity possible. Nuttall described the planters and their way of life as follows:

> These planters are nearly all of French or Spanish extraction and, as yet, there are among them but few Americans. Their houses are generally built of wood, with piazzas for shade in the summer. Notwithstanding their comparative opulence, they differ little either in habits, manners, or dress from the Canadians. Dancing and gambling appear to be their favorite amusements. The men as usual, are commonly dressed in blanket coats and the women wear handkerchiefs around their heads in place of bonnets. The inhabitants do not appear to be well supplied with merchandise, and the river is crowded with the boats of French and Spanish peddlars, not much larger than perogues [sic], but fitted up with a cabin, covered deck, and sails.

As Nuttall moved closer to New Orleans he noted that the banks of the river were referred to as "coast."

Nuttall's account became more animated as he approached New Orleans. The great city, then with a population of around 45,000, seemed to give off vibrations which aroused even this staid scientist. He reported that an almost uninterrupted line of "opulent" (a word which Nuttall returned to frequently) settlements continued from Baton Rouge to a point fifty miles below New Orleans. Coast front sold for $3,000 an *arpent* or about $75 an actual acre. The plantation owners grew sugar cane as a money crop, but oranges and other tropical fruits found favor among them as well. Eighty-six miles north of New Orleans a cattle-raising region supplied in 1819 more than twelve thousand beeves to the New Orleans market. Nuttall remarked of his admiration of the levees, which protected the towns from inundation, but saw no corresponding device which could protect the population from yellow fever or a slave revolt, two of the principal concerns of the region. There had not yet been a major slave revolt, but yellow fever had claimed five or six thousand lives in 1819.

New Orleans itself was still a city with

New Orleans in the 1820s after a drawing by Basil Hall. Courtesy of the New-York Historical Society, New York City.

rough edges. Nuttall commented, "Science and rational amusement is as yet but little cultivated in New Orleans." Gambling was the principal vice and the government was reduced to simply controlling it by a system of licensing which also provided funds for municipal expenses. As a man of letters, Nuttall regretfully reported he could find only three or four booksellers in the entire city. He also noted the large number of steamboats tied up along the levee waiting for the waters to come up in the river, and the nation to recover from the panic of 1819. The national economy did recover, and the South remained prosperous for the next forty years. Those forty years of the history of the Mississippi would be dominated by the steamboat.

The steamboat era would hit its zenith by the decade of the fifties. The steamboats had by this time become great floating palaces which moved up and down the Mississippi with stately grace, bringing excitement to every stop along the way. The riverboats carried with them a floating population of people who had been places and seen things which the mere mortals along the shore could never match. This was the age of riverboat captains,

who knew every sandbar in the river, and riverboat gamblers, who knew every ace in the deck. There were fancy ladies and fancy men, and boys like Mark Twain's Tom Sawyer and Huck Finn were drawn irresistibly to the river because of the romance it represented. That remarkable age would come to an end, however, with the outbreak of the Civil War as the river became a key to the conquest of the South.

Curiously enough, the South failed to recognize the importance of the river to their cause. The Mississippi and its tributaries would be the scene of a whole campaign of a very unique nature. The principal battle in that campaign would be fought at Vicksburg. New Orleans fell to Union forces in April of 1862, and the way lay open to Northern domination of the Mississippi. Until May, Southern defenders ignored Vicksburg, the only defendable point on the river. Through the efforts of General Mansfield Lovell, however, defenses were quickly prepared for the city. It was just in time. On June 28, 1862, several boats in Admiral David Farragut's river squadron steamed upriver.

The squat, ugly gunboats were designed

specifically for the river war. Because of their vulnerability to shore fire, it was necessary to clad them in iron. Because most of their fire would be directed against shore targets, they were armed with high trajectory weapons such as howitzers and mortars. This allowed them to deliver plunging fire on "dug-in" troops on the bluffs overlooking the river. Flotillas of small boats carrying infantry could easily attack the slow-moving heavy steamers. In fact, on one occasion on the shallow Arkansas, General Stan Waite captured a gunboat with a cavalry charge. To defend the boats against such attacks, gun ports were cut in the iron siding and marksmen were added to the gunboat's crew.

With great effort, Farragut's command forced its way through the batteries at Vicksburg and spent several weeks above the city before returning downstream to New Orleans. The Union controlled the river but could not make full use of it as long as Vicksburg remained in Confederate hands. It quickly became apparent that the capture of the city could be accomplished only by a combined land-river assault.

Upon taking command of the western armies, Ulysses S. Grant immediately grasped the importance of Vicksburg. He began his campaign to open the Mississippi in December of 1862. By this time General J. C. Pemberton commanded the Confederate forces protecting the now heavily fortified city. Grant's efforts to approach the city from his base at Memphis failed because of difficult terrain to the north of Vicksburg. In desperation he abandoned Memphis and crossed to the west side of the river. He moved to a point below Vicksburg and recrossed the river. Approaching from the east, he soon had the defenders trapped. Supported by the river fleet under the command of Admiral Porter, Grant tried to capture the city in three bloody attacks on May 22. He failed, and settled back to starve the defenders out. He did not have a long wait. Vicksburg fell on July 4, 1863. Five days later Port Hudson, the last Confederate base on the river, surrendered and the Union controlled the Mississippi. Denied access to the men and supplies of the West, the rest of the South eventually suffered the same fate as Vicksburg. Short of manpower and without

Flagship Benton *(at right) below Vicksburg. Courtesy Bill Burchardt.*

The famous riverboat Robert E. Lee *loading cotton. Courtesy of the New-York Historical Society, New York City.*

adequate supplies, Robert E. Lee surrendered at Appomattox on April 9, 1865. The war changed the South forever. The Mississippi became as much a symbol of the antebellum South as it once had been for the West.

Life along the Mississippi slowed in the last decades of the nineteenth century. The nation's attention focused elsewhere. The industrial Northeast attracted capital and the interest of the nation as well. Only the Far West vied with it for attention. The new pace exhausted one and all and only a short time after the South had been destroyed a feeling of nostalgia refocused attention on the antebellum South. Like most nostalgia movements, however, the remembered South differed in many ways from what had actually been the case.

The Mississippi became the principal element in that highly romanticized South that attracted the interest of many. Mark Twain, in book after book, perpetuated and in many ways created the Mississippi of the national consciousness. In *Life on the Mississippi* he told the stories of the riverfolk and their lives. In *Tom Sawyer* he portrayed an idyllic version of life in the small town of Hannibal on the

river in the years before the war. Finally, in *Huck Finn,* the river rose to allegorical meaning and entered into the minds of all America and the world forever.

The river remembered offered simplicity and an unhurried pace. The people who populated Hannibal and the other towns along the river didn't work in factories or speak with foreign accents. America was growing up in the second half of the nineteenth century, but Tom and Huck seemed locked in boyhood: a boyhood of river pirates, blood oaths, sharpers, and buried treasures. No one, not even Tom and Huck, could eternally avoid growing up and the river changed in spite of Twain, painter John Caleb Bingham, and others who tried to preserve it as a monument to the old South.

The realities of life along the Mississippi reflected the changing South and the changing nation. The southern economy was depressed and, as a result, commerce along the river stagnated. In the panics of 1873 and 1893, numerous boat operators went broke. Some tried to change their mode of operation by catering to special interests. Some boats specialized in luxury and provided lavish entertainment and cuisine. Gambling became a principal attraction along the river, for the boats operated free of local prohibitions against gambling. Nonetheless, it seems the boats were fighting a losing battle.

Railroads became a symbol of late nineteenth-century industrial development. The railroads spanned the Mississippi on steel bridges and in so doing reduced it to no more importance as an obstacle than the tiniest stream. The railroad went places where riverboats could not; the railroads could offer services the steamboats could not. In short, the railroads suited the age. The return to river transportation would not begin until the turn of the twentieth century.

With the coming of what historians call the progressive era, 1900–17, river transportation would gain new impetus. Progressives believed that government should play an active role in solving the problems of the people. In doing this the government grew enormously. Agencies expanded and each of them took on a life of its own, each trying to find new ways to serve the people. One of these agencies was the United States Army Corps of Engineers.

Early in the nineteenth century the Corps of Engineers had been given the responsibility of clearing waterways of snags and other obstacles in order to ensure safe river travel. With encouragement from progressive politicians the Corps of Engineers set out to actively promote river traffic by greatly improving the navigability of the river systems. This meant particularly the Mississippi and its principal tributaries. The corps built dams to regulate the water flow and provide cheap electric power, which attracted industry. They dredged and maintained safe channels, and the Falls of St. Anthony were handled by building a series of locks to lift barges up and over them. The

Modern-day Delta Queen *plies the Mississippi in traditional riverboat style. Courtesy Bill Burchardt.*

Mississippi became the testing ground where the corps developed the technology to manipulate other rivers like the Arkansas and the Missouri. Congressmen lent their support to such projects because it meant more federal money in their districts. At the same time, railroads found themselves under attack because of their identification with some of the seamier aspects of high finance in the late nineteenth century.

Entrepreneurs jumped at the opportunity they saw—a transportation net sitting there waiting to be used. Built and maintained by the Corps of Engineers, the navigable channels in the Mississippi and its tributaries offered them a real opportunity to make some money. Profits could be made easily as long as federal funds picked up the cost of maintaining the channels. Barge traffic expanded by leaps and bounds and by the 1970s profits to barge companies outstripped the railroads six to seven times on a percentage basis. Today, about one sixth of the goods transported in America travels by river, and for all practical purposes that means the Mississippi. Whether or not the Mississippi could continue to be an important link in the national transportation system without the heavy government subsidies, however, is a yet unanswered question.

In the 1970s a new use has been found for the Mississippi which echoes the attention it received in the late nineteenth century. Nostalgia buffs are again turning to the river to provide them with what they find missing in modern life. Businessmen once again have been quick to capitalize on this trend. Sternwheelers are churning up and down the Missis-sippi as they did a hundred or more years ago, but this time as excursion boats for Americans trying to recapture a lost past. The boats offer a return to a leisurely way of life not often found in modern America. Ironically, the boats were built in the first place because they offered speed and dependability above all else. Amusement parks are springing up along the river with nostalgia themes, and river towns, including Hannibal, are staging historical pageants and refurbishing old buildings in hope of attracting tourists looking for a bit of the tranquillity that Mark Twain created.

Mention the Mississippi to Americans today and certain images invariably come to mind: the *Robert E. Lee* racing upriver on a moonlit night; riverboat gamblers in top hats and fancy lace shirts; the minstrel shows with banjo players and blackface comedians; and, of course, Mark Twain himself in a crumpled white suit and a string tie. This never-never land has been created time and time again in motion pictures, on the stage, and now on television, but it was only a very small part of that river's grand story. The true drama was in the clash of empires that dominated the Mississippi's history for the two and one half centuries from its discovery in 1542 by De Soto to the Battle of New Orleans in January of 1816. In a way, all that followed was anticlimax. The use of a river as a trade route for agricultural produce was only temporary. Iron rails replaced the river, and on them America left behind the Mississippi and the simpler days of agrarian America.

3

The Arkansas River and the Red

BY BILL BURCHARDT

In 1816 the pirate Jean Lafitte came prowling up the Arkansas River. His given reason—to search for gold—seems unlikely. It was. His pose as a prospector was a cover for a Spanish mission. The Lafittes, Pierre and Jean, had aligned themselves with Royalist Spain. They were hired in the campaign to confound Spanish subjects, in what one day would become the United States Southwest, who were in the process of throwing off the royal Spanish yoke.

Anticipating rebellions, the royal monarch Ferdinand VII wanted the frontier country bordering on the Arkansas River to be mapped. The maps were for the later use of Spanish officers sent into the area in command of soldiers to put down contrivings and uprisings. Jean Lafitte, wearing the alias "Capitán Hillare," with a French cartographer, Major Arsène Lacarrière Latour, a hireling of the Spanish crown, came peregrinating up the river, mapping the countryside as they came.

The pirate Lafitte and Major Latour were latecomers. There is no way of knowing when river navigation of the ancient Arkansas and Red rivers began. On the banks of the Arkansas, hard against ultramodern Mayo Lock and Dam of the McClellan-Kerr navigation channel, are the remnants of the prehistoric Spiro mounds. The Spiro civilization was a sister of the Maya; perhaps country cousin would be a more comparable relationship. The Spiro temples to the gods, built on pyramids of earth, were primitive counterparts of the Mayan stone pyramids.

Among artifacts unearthed at Spiro, in eastern Oklahoma, are objects of adornment made from sea shells identified as having come from the gulf coast of Yucatan. These objects reached the Spiro site by river navigation, just as the culture itself was imported from the

Yucatan-Honduras region. Farther south, on the Red River, are the archaeological sites of Avoyelles Parish, the oldest known ceramic complex in Louisiana. They endured some eight hundred to two thousand years ago.

These ancient, indigenous people were master builders of the dugout canoe, called by the French *pirogue*. Made on the Arkansas from giant cottonwood logs, on the Red from equally huge cypress logs, these vessels were capable of covering vast distances and carrying much cargo. They were true progenitors of the great cargo barges that ply the river today.

The downriver cargo of the pirogue, furs, hides, foodstuffs, and herbs of the region, were to remain the same for more than a century. A major upriver pirogue cargo presaged change for the indigene, for in the pirogue came the European explorers. After De Soto and La Salle, Henri de Tonti, one of La Salle's men, in 1686 established Arkansas Post on the bank of the Arkansas a few miles upstream from its confluence with the White River. Juchereau de St. Denis came upstream to establish Natchitoches on the Red River in 1714. He may have been the first Frenchman to see Oklahoma.

By contrast, some of Oklahoma's earliest explorers came downriver. The Arkansas was then navigable to within eight days of Santa Fe, three days of Taos, and when the Mallet brothers left Santa Fe in 1740 they came down the Arkansas to the Mississippi. Among other explorers, de la Harpe had traveled up the Red River into Oklahoma from his grant in Louisiana in 1718. Lieutenant James Wilkinson, second in command of Captain Zebulon Pike's expedition, which named Pikes Peak, descended the Arkansas from its Great Bend in central Kansas as an offshoot of the Pike expedition in 1806. In 1819 the U. S.

Government sent a force under command of Major Stephen H. Long to search out the sources of the Arkansas and the Red. In that same year the great naturalist Thomas Nuttall ascended the Arkansas for the purpose of describing the flora and fauna of the region.

The Indian people these explorers encountered were, in Louisiana, the Attakapa, Chitimachas, Tunicas, and Caddoes; in Arkansas, Quapaws and Caddoes; in the Oklahoma River regions the Wichitas, Taovayas, and Caddoes. The Frenchman Chouteau later persuaded the Osage chieftain Clermont and 1,500 of his people to move into the Three Forks country of northeastern Oklahoma. They were the industrious hunters who kept his trading post at Salina busy.

European exploration augered European settlement: first at Arkansas Post, then spreading up the Arkansas to Little Rock; first at Natchitoches, then at Fort St. Louis de Carlorette, then Post Rapide, on the Red. As the settlements spread, trade increased. The pirogue became inadequate. Thus came the flatboat, the keelboat, the steamboat.

The first steamboat to ascend the Arkansas arrived at Arkansas Post at ten o'clock on the night of March 31, 1820. The vessel was the *Comet*. Under the command of its master, Captain Byrne, it had made the trip from New Orleans in eight days. Its coming raised the curtain on the drama of riverboating, an exciting era, but before we can appreciate the action we must comprehend the character of these two rivers.

The Red River rises on the Llano Estacado where it reaches into New Mexico from the Texas panhandle. The river creates the colorful *barancas* of the Palo Duro Canyon. It flows eastward to become the border between Texas and Oklahoma. Entering Arkansas but briefly, it flows south to Shreveport, Louisiana, on southeasterly to Natchitoches, thence to Alexandria. On downstream it follows an old meander of the Mississippi—though it flows northeasterly, the opposite direction the Mississippi flowed when it used this old channel. Twice more before its confluence with the Father of Waters the Red uses former Mississippi channels, through Sugar House Chute and Upper Old River.

The Kiamichi and Ozark streams which enter the Red make a giant river of this formerly lazy, broad stream. Above Shreveport, navigation of the Red has always been ex-tremely hazardous. Two factors, the undependable depths of water and the Great River Raft, were responsible. Prior to this century, steamboats of light draft regularly plied the river to Oklahoma's Fort Towson. Often they came on upriver to Fort Washita, especially after the removal of the Great Raft.

The Great Red River Raft was a mass of sunken driftwood, logs, and stumps virtually filling the channel of the river for 165 miles from Natchitoches. Kentuckian Ben Milam, later killed in the Texas revolution against Mexico, was the first steamboat captain to ascend the Red past the Great Raft. His steamboat, *Alps*, made its torturous way through the Raft in 1831. The man responsible for removal of this vast obstruction to navigation was Captain Henry Shreve, from whom Shreveport takes its name. Following his initial survey in 1833 he began work with his snagboats and in five years cleared the channel, opening navigation to Fort Towson, 720 miles above the mouth of the Red.

It required constant work to prevent rebuilding of the Raft. Every seasonal flood uprooted and swept out vast reaches of timber from Red River shores. These huge trees were carried downstream to become snags, or sawyers, to lodge on a sandbar, or where some point of land projected into the stream. A "snag" buries itself in the river bed, its trunk and branches broken off in sharp points, standing firm as a rock, out of sight beneath the water's surface, and angled to take the bottom out of the steamboat which strikes it. A "sawyer" becomes fastened to the bottom of the river by its roots, its trunk and branches left free to move up and down with the action of the current. Temporarily immersed, one of these monarchs of the forest would come lifting out of the water directly in the course of a steamboat. Its branches would slowly rise high in the air, bowing and scraping politely, a terrifying sight causing an early river poet to write:

> *I have been*
> *where the wild river's will*
> *has dashed me on the sawyer . . .*

An uprooted tree borne downriver until it lodged on a sandbar or point of land entrapped others. Thousands of these fallen trees, tossed by the flood, would pile up in great masses, extending for miles upriver, often completely blocking the channel. Such a

Early morning, and a touch of fog on the Arkansas River. From the pilothouse of the Border Star. Photo by Bill Burchardt.

"raft" of jagged trunks, gnarled, naked branches, and bleaching roots created the most desolate scene imaginable.

Another prevalent danger to navigation, the cutoff, was formed when the flooding river cut a new course across a point of land. These new channels were usually too shallow to navigate, and became the graveyard of many a steamboat whose captain was unwary, unfamiliar with the normal course of the river, or too easily tempted to risk the shorter route through the untried channel.

One political candidate of the times was quick to appropriate these river terms to his own advantage. He told his constituents that he was a man who "would come at the truth by a 'cutoff,' would separate and pile up falsehood for decay like the trees of a 'raft,' do all this with the politeness of a 'sawyer,' and with the unyielding principles of a 'snag.'"

The Arkansas River rises in the Rocky Mountains, its early beginnings cutting the Royal Gorge near Canyon City, Colorado, flowing then past Pueblo, La Junta, the site of Bent's old fort, and Lamar, to enter Kansas. There it passes Garden City, Dodge City, swings northward to Great Bend, southwest through Wichita, Arkansas City, and into Oklahoma, where today it forms a string of great lakes.

The first of these is Kaw Lake, under con-

struction. The river forms the south boundary of Oklahoma's Osage County and a dam near Tulsa impounds it in Keystone Lake. Where the river passes Tulsa a series of low-water dams are planned to create riverfront parks. At Muskogee are the famed Three Forks where the Arkansas, the Verdigris, and the Neosho (Grand) rivers join. The Verdigris is now a navigable barge canal, maintained at a nine-foot depth, as a part of the McClellan-Kerr Waterway.

From the Three Forks at Muskogee, the Arkansas River and the McClellan-Kerr Waterway are one and the same. Following the old course of the Arkansas south through Webbers Falls, the river enters beautiful Kerr reservoir, continuing through the country of the Five Civilized Tribes, past the ancient Spiro mounds, and into Arkansas at Fort Smith.

There it proceeds north past Van Buren, east into the lovely lake at Dardanelle, then through the old river towns of Russellville and Morrilton, and rolling on down to Little Rock. In 1833 an army report stated, "At Little Rock is seen the last rock which is visible upon the river. From that point to its mouth, the Arkansas runs entirely through an alluvial country . . . the course of the river is remarkably devious, numerous places appear where 'cut-offs' have been formed. There are shoal bars which obstruct navigation, particularly 'Dog Tooth Bar' about four miles below Little Rock.

"About 25 miles above the proper mouth of the Arkansas there is a channel leading from it to the White River, about eight miles above its mouth, which is usually designated by the local name 'The Cut-Off.' In this cut-off the water flows indifferently from the Arkansas to the White River, or from the White to the Arkansas, whichever river happens to be the highest." The report points out that steamboats navigating the Arkansas always use this cutoff to enter the Mississippi or, if bound upstream, enter the Arkansas from the Mississippi, via the White River and its cutoff. The report concludes, "Some of the best pilots on the Arkansas have never seen the last 25 miles of its course." The same is true today. The McClellan-Kerr Waterway does not follow the Arkansas to its mouth but takes the shorter route north through the mouth of the White into the Mississippi.

We have mentioned the most famous

skipper on the Red River, Captain Henry M. Shreve, a Pennsylvanian whose father had been a colonel in one of George Washington's regiments. Henry Shreve had earned a small fortune in the keelboat trade as a very young man and undertook to be the first to ascend the Mississippi in a steamboat—of his own construction. Steamboats prior to Shreve's did not generate sufficient power to travel upstream. Shreve succeeded though his enterprise was interrupted by a period of service with Old Hickory, Andrew Jackson, at the Battle of New Orleans. General Jackson commissioned Shreve a captain. The great work of Captain Shreve's life was clearing the rivers for navigation. He removed the Great River Raft from the Red with powerful snagboats, again of his own construction. He blasted underwater rock ledges and boulders, unmoored and disposed of islands and sandbars, and removed overhanging trees which obstructed the banks. When Henry Shreve died, it was reported that he did not leave much of earth's possessions, having used his own money to finish projects which the government's appropriations failed too soon.

Captain Phillip Pennywit, master of the steamboat *Facility*, would be the most famed captain on the Arkansas River. Born in Virginia's Shenandoah Valley in 1793, he became a river pilot early and built the first steamboat to be constructed at Cincinnati, naming the craft for that city. His *Facility* was the first steamboat to ascend the Arkansas to Fort Gibson, arriving there in February 1828. From that time, Little Rock's *Gazette* is replete with news of the comings and goings of Captain Pennywit's craft. The *Facility*, often towing keelboats, transplanted many Cherokees, Choctaws, Chickasaws, Seminoles, and Creeks from their dispossessed homes in the South to their land in Indian Territory.

There is no knowing how many tons of gunpowder and lead, sugar, coffee, stoves, hardware, candles, rope, rice, medicine, roots, herbs, tobacco, shoes, hats, molasses, indigo, sieves, tubs and pails, cigars, churns, coffee mills, washboards, bedsteads, mattresses and other furniture, guns, scythes, stoneware, lime, putty, bolts of linen, cashmere, shirtings, drills, sheeting, jeans, shirts, shawls, towels, cotton yarn, blankets, pepper and cloves, cav-

CAPTAIN PHILLIP PENNYWIT,
Arkansas River

Captain Phillip Pennywit and advertisements of steamboat sailings on the Red and Arkansas rivers. From The Chronicles of Oklahoma, *published by the Oklahoma Historical Society.*

Two light-draft steamboats at Webbers Falls on the Arkansas River in the 1860s. Courtesy of the Oklahoma Historical Society.

alry boots, opera boots, machinery, and sutlers' stores were transported upriver by Captain Pennywit's *Facility* and his later and larger steamboat the *Waverly*. In exchange, his downriver cargoes were raw materials, hides, furs, bacon, cotton, corn, and grains. It was Captain Pennywit's *Facility* that brought Captain, later General, Sam Houston to Fort Gibson for his years with the Cherokees between his fall from grace in national politics and his successes in creating the Republic of Texas. Captain Pennywit spent his retirement years in Van Buren, where he is now buried.

As the mid-nineteenth century passed, the Arkansas and Red rivers were busy with steamboat traffic. The Louisiana Historical Quarterly lists 823 steamboats licensed for the Red River trade during those years. While there were not that many on the Arkansas, it too was a busy river. Many of these vessels were cotton boats, sometimes of incredible capacity, and most steamers carried at least a few bales when bound downriver during the cotton-shipping season.

The *Daniel O'Connell* arrived at New Orleans in June 1874 from Campti, Louisiana,

with, among other cargo, thirty-one bales of cotton and an alligator seventeen feet long. The *Sam Howell*, while en route to New Orleans from upper Red River carrying seven hundred bales of cotton and thirty thousand hides, caught fire and was destroyed at Blanton's wood lot. The *Lelia* burned on Red River, July 28, 1865, with 381 bales of cotton aboard. The *Hallette*, Captain G. W. Rea, Red River Line, was built to carry two thousand bales of cotton. *La Belle* sank on Red River near Orleans landing December 13, 1873, with a cargo of 2,699 bales. The *Henry Frank* held the record for transporting the largest load of cotton, 9,229 bales.

Then, as now, the river was for fun, too. There were showboats like the *Banjo*, in the mid-1800s carrying her minstrel show to the Gaiety Theatre in Shreveport. And travel, for fun. Before the steamboat, travel was hard, backbreaking work. It was no fun to haul on the towrope of a keelboat. The earlier keelboats had to be pulled by *cordelle*, pulled by hard-pressed men stumbling along through the tangled timber and mud on the bank. Land travel was no better, with its rocking stagecoaches and jolting wagons. The need of prying these vehicles out of axle-deep mud or over rocky mountain trails, threatened with wolves and panthers or outlaws laying in wait to rob or murder, made such a thing as a "pleasure trip" beyond the imagination prior to the steamboat. No one considered travel for fun, unless they were a fool or a humorist.

The steamboat changed all that. On board a steamboat one could travel among cosmopolitan company. A traveler could take his ease lounging on deck, sipping a drink, or playing cards in the saloon. One could cover in a few days the same distance that would have taken weeks overland. With the steamboat, to isolated communities came such luxuries as whiskey, polished leather shoes, and white flour. With the steamboats came the planters, moving their household furnishings and slaves, clearing wilderness areas to create plantations in the west. With the steamboats came much pleasure, and but one ominous portent. Steamboating was hazardous. Exploding boilers, dangers from navigation, and fires were so numerous that the average life of a steamboat was only four years. The *Black Hawk* on December 27, 1837, exploded her boilers at the mouth of Red River, blowing off all her upper works forward of her twin paddle wheels.

The *Maggie Hays* exploded her boilers February 11, 1870, near Helena, Arkansas; twenty lives were lost. *Lioness* was destroyed when she caught fire en route to Red River; the cargo of powder stored in her hold exploded. *John D. Perry* caught fire and burned at De Vall's Bluff, Arkansas, April 6, 1869. Steamboating records contain hundreds of such accounts. Captain Frank Kendall, in the Arkansas *Gazette*, April 5, 1872, lists 117 steamboats which sank in the Arkansas River alone, from snagging, exploding, bursting, or collision.

We must mention just a few of the really unusual steamboats on the Arkansas and the Red. The *Robert E. Lee*, famed for winning the greatest of all steamboat races, with the *Natchez* from New Orleans to St. Louis, also traded on the Red River. The river column of the Shreveport newspaper notes, on August 10, 1870, that the *Robert E. Lee* arrived the previous day towing a barge loaded with a cargo of jugs. The *William Garig*, much later, in 1904, won a race with the *Delta Queen*. The *Delta Queen*, then operating on the Sacramento River, is the most widely known steamboat in

river traffic today. Most steamboats on the Arkansas and the Red also operated on other national rivers. The *Mollie Moore*, for example, in the Red River trade, gave up her life on the Missouri River, where she caught on the bank near Chamberlain, South Dakota, slid into the river, and sank.

Another "unusual" boat was the *Peninah*, which had the first "wildcat" whistle on Red River. It frightened farmers and their teams. The *Trader*, on the Red in 1855, was said to be able to carry more freight on less water than any other boat of her day. The *Lizzie Hamilton* left Shreveport on August 16, 1886, with a load of watermelons to be used in floating her over sandbars. The *Julia Randolph*, making a weekly trip between New Orleans and Jefferson, Texas, was the "fastest sternwheeler ever to leave New Orleans."

The *John T. Moore* had the finest cabins of any boat on Red River. In contrast, Captain J. K. B. Rea of the *Jennie* said his boat was so small she had a drygoods box for a cabin. The *Franklin Pierce* sued to have her name changed to *Texana* after she acquired a reputation of being unlucky. The *Cotton Valley* had a bad reputation. She tended to sheer away from her rudder and collide with boats coming upstream. The *Era* carried 4,500 bales of cotton, 700 head of cattle, and four classes of passengers. She was noted for her huge cabin and Texas deck, and published a daily newspaper on board.

Many rivers of this region were navigable, the Ouachita, Kiamichi, White, St. Frances, and others. The *City of Camden* held the record for making the fastest time between New Orleans and Camden, Arkansas, then the head of navigation on the Ouachita. One of the most widely traveled steamboats on all the western rivers was the *De Smet*, named in honor of Father De Smet, a Jesuit priest and Catholic missionary among western Indians. The *De Smet* burned June 12, 1886, near Newport, Arkansas.

The stories of the forts along the Arkansas, Fort Smith, Fort Coffee, and Fort Gibson —and Fort Towson and Fort Washita on the Red—are so interwoven with the story of the removal of the Five Civilized Tribes from their ancestral homes in the southern states that there is no way to separate them. The essential reason for all these forts, except Fort Coffee, was to intervene in the bloody fighting between the Five Civilized Tribes and the

Still plying the waterways, the venerable Delta Queen *in a recent race with the* Border Star, *held at the port of Little Rock on the Arkansas River. Photo by Bill Burchardt.*

Plains Tribes of the West. The Cherokees began removing from North Carolina and Georgia as early as 1810. In their new home in Indian Territory they came into immediate conflict with the Osage people. The Osages had long been at war with the Cherokees, Delawares, Shawnees, Caddoes, and Wichitas. These bloody intertribal vendettas made necessary the establishment, in 1817, of Fort Smith at Belle Point, where the Poteau River joins the Arkansas. Fort Gibson, in the Three Forks Country, followed in 1824.

Fort Coffee, on the Arkansas only twenty-five miles above Fort Smith, was established to bring an end to the nefarious business of selling whiskey to the Indians. Any craft suspected of carrying contraband was stopped there and searched. It was only partially successful. Steamboatmen devised skillful techniques of smuggling. Casks and kegs of whiskey were slung beneath the hull of the vessel by means of ropes and nets. Even the steamboat's captain was sometimes unaware that men in his crew were using his boat in smuggling.

Fort Towson was established on the Red River in 1824 as a result of trouble between the Choctaw people and the Comanches. Fort Washita, farther up the Red, followed eighteen years later as Five Tribes migrations continued, and the middle border Indian Territory became known as "Scalp Alley."

The southern states, Tennessee, Georgia, Alabama, Mississippi, Florida, continued to dispossess the Five Civilized Tribes, seizing their lands, then driving the Indian people westward over what became known as the "Trail of Tears." This grim time in United States history produced tragedies equal to the concentration camp slaughters in World War II. Indian people were forced westward in mid-winter, dying of disease and exposure by the thousands. Much of this forced migration was overland. But Indian people were also loaded on steamboats and shipped westward like cattle. On the steamboats they died from hunger, whiskey, bitter cold, disease, and in violent river disasters. The steamboat *Monmouth*, with 611 Indians on board, was proceeding at night through Prophet Island Bend on a course forbidden to upbound vessels. She collided with the *Trenton*, under tow by the *Warren*. The *Monmouth* was cut in two and sank almost immediately, with a loss of 311 Indian lives.

One account of an attempt to load a group of Creek Indians on board a steamboat states ". . . there was such a number sick that many of them died on the wharf before they could get on board. Some died immediately after they embarked and we had to bury them. This detained the boat some time." Another

account of such a landing: ". . . all the sick were brought to the spot in litters; a storm came up and the boats could not lay alongside the wharf. The storm lasted for two days. This rendered the situation of the Indians very unpleasant. . . ." The cold weather was ". . . so severe on the little children and old persons; some of them nearly naked. . . ." These people were forced to lie out on deck on wet or frozen canvas. Their distress wrung the heart of one compassionate officer who wrote, ". . . there was continued crying from morning to night among the children. . . . I used to encourage them by saying that the weather would moderate in a few days and it would warm, but it never happened during the whole trip."

During the peak years of Indian removal the columns of newspapers of the river ports en route to Fort Gibson on the Arkansas and

The Era No. 2 at dock in New Orleans, loaded with cotton from the Arkansas River valley. From the Louisiana Historical Quarterly.

Fort Towson on the Red were filled with items. In November 1832 the steamboat *Walter Scott* left Vicksburg with a thousand emigrants under the leadership of Nitakechi. They were landed at Arkansas Post with many others to await boats that could ascend the Arkansas. In January a thousand Choctaws were embarked on the steamboat *Reindeer* with a 170-ton keelboat in tow. The captain of the *Talma* said "he never saw any people conduct themselves better or appear more devout. They had morning and evening prayers and spent much of their time on board the boat reading and singing hymns."

These were not uncivilized people. They were Indian farmers who had owned the homes and property of which they were dispossessed in the South. On November 12, 1832, the *Heliopolis* and the *Thomas Yeat-*

man landed at Port Rock Roe on the Arkansas. Their arrival brought the number of Indian people there to 1,799. They were transferred to the *Archimedes* and *Harry Hill*, of lighter draft, to continue upriver. Newspapers noted the passage of the *John Nelson*, *Chippawa*, *Merchant*, and *Black Hawk*, carrying contingents of Indians.

The *De Kalb* passed Little Rock on November 22, 1837, with five hundred Indians on board, the *Kentuckian* on November 28 with two hundred, the *John Nelson* the next day. The *Fox* arrived at Little Rock on December 7 with 227 emigrants, reaching Fort Coffee on the twelfth. Captain Pennywit's steamer, the *Facility*, passed Little Rock in February 1828, with two keelboats in tow, carrying three hundred Creek emigrants to Fort Gibson. Sam Houston's arrival, aboard the *Fa-*

Reconstructed Fort Gibson, head of navigation on the Arkansas in the 1800s.

cility, at Fort Gibson in June 1829 is a part of the Indian removal story.

Houston had been married in Tennessee and separated from his bride on the same day. The marriage was later annulled—a mysterious scandal at that time, and unexplained to this day. Fleeing from the grief of this bitter experience, Sam Houston fled west to the wigwam of his adopted Indian father, Oo-loo-te-ka, chief of the Cherokees, with whom Houston had lived as a boy. Sam Houston then lived in the Indian Territory for more than four years, taking as his wife the beautiful Cherokee girl Tiana Rogers. Houston was a frequent river passenger while he lived at Wigwam Neosho, a trading post and frontier saloon he established near Fort Gibson. Houston attempted, without success, to aid the Cherokees in their problems with the United States Government. In 1832 he departed for fame in Texas, having tried to persuade Tiana to accompany him, but she preferred to remain in the Indian Territory. Jesse Chisholm, of the Chisholm Trail, was a nephew of Tiana Rogers. She now lies buried in the National Cemetery at Fort Gibson.

Many celebrities served or came by steamboat to Fort Gibson at the Three Forks. Washington Irving began his *Tour of the Prairies* there. Henry Wadsworth Longfellow is reputed to have written *Evangeline* at Fort Gibson. Nathan Boone, son of Daniel, headquartered there. Generals Matthew Arbuckle and Henry Leavenworth, and Colonels Stephen W. Kearney and Zachary Taylor, served there. Jefferson Davis, destined to become president of the Confederacy, and Robert E. Lee, to be general of the Confederate Armies, both served at Fort Gibson.

The Civil War brought bitter fighting to the Arkansas and Red rivers. Even before secession, the Confederacy seized all Union military posts on both rivers. In control of these water arteries, both were used by the South to supply their armies with beef, horses, salt, and cotton for cloth and uniform manufacture. Throughout the war, Union pressure on the rivers was unceasing. In September 1863 Union General Blunt succeeded in reoccupying Fort Smith. In 1864 a major federal campaign was launched to retake the Red.

Admiral David D. Porter's naval force of sixty steamboats spearheaded the campaign up the river, supported by General N. P. Banks' land forces. A major water engagement occurred when Admiral Farragut's flagship, the U.S.S. *Hartford*, captured the C.S.A. cattleboat *J. D. Clarke* at the mouth of the Red. The Union *Queen of the West* raided along the lower Red, capturing the *A. W. Baker*, *Moro*, *Berwick Bay*, and *Era No. 5*. The *Queen* was later run aground, captured by the C.S.A., outfitted as a Confederate gunboat, and finally sunk by federal naval forces in the Battle of Grand Lake.

The U.S.S. *Blackhawk* was Admiral Porter's flagship. Several iron-clad, tin-clad, and cotton-clad steamboats changed hands once or more, as Confederate ships were captured by federal forces and vice versa. At one point the Confederate ships *William H. Webb*, *Grand Era*, and *Doctor Baxter* were sunk at Shreveport to block the channel and prevent capture of the port by federal forces. One of the last river engagements of the war was the capture of the Union *J. R. Williams* by General Stand Watie and his Cherokee mounted rifles. The *Williams*, under way from Fort Smith with a load of commissary and quartermaster supplies for Fort Gibson, was ambushed at Pleasant Bluff in the Indian Territory. General Watie sank her with artillery from the shore and was in the process of looting her when Colonel John Richie and troops of the Second Union Indian Regiment appeared onshore and drove off the Confederates. Before retreating, Watie's riflemen set fire to the steamboat. Most of the supplies and the burning boat were lost, drifting off downriver. General Stand Watie was the last of all the Confederate generals to surrender, at Doaksville on Red River, on June 23, 1865, more than two months after Lee had surrendered to Grant at Appomattox.

River traffic boomed in earnest during Reconstruction days following the Civil War, but the railroads were a-building, and when the first M. K. & T. locomotive sounded its whistle crossing the Arkansas River trestle on Christmas Day, 1871, it signaled the end of the great steamboat era on the Arkansas and Red. The steamboats soon disappeared from the upper reaches of both rivers. Now, after many decades, river transportation has returned to the Arkansas, but it has changed.

There'll be no more characters like Zeb Marston, who founded Eagle Town at the mouth of the Mountain Fork on the far upper reaches of the Red River in Indian Territory. Zeb used to insist that the captain of the U.S. mail steamer *Emperor* stop at Zeb's "settle-

Admiral Porter's flagship Blackhawk *led the federal river campaigns on the Arkansas, Red, and Mississippi rivers in 1864.*

ment" each week and trade a barrel of whiskey for its value in cord wood. The *Emperor's* captain couldn't see why Zeb needed all that whiskey. It was too much trouble to stop at Zeb's cabin every week. He finally told Zeb so, and Zeb flew into a fury. "You talk about the trouble of leavin' me a barrel of whiskey a week! Here I am way out here where the drinkin' water is bad, I've got a sick wife and five children *and no cow!*"

There'll be no more incidents like that which befell Captain Armstrong. Acting Superintendent for the Western Indians, he was returning from New Orleans with $150,000 with which to make payments to the Cherokees at Fort Gibson. "I had succeeded in getting the specie in kegs, amounting to more than $100,000 of the total. I had a box of gold, and a box of dimes and half dimes." Sixty miles above Little Rock the boilers ex-

ploded and the steamboat burst. The box of gold was blown onshore, splitting in two. The box of dimes fell on the bow of the boat and split into pieces. The captain of the boat was blown onshore and dangerously wounded. The mate and the clerk were also disabled, and most of the hands were killed. The specie, in its "substantial kegs bound with iron hoops," floated off down the river.

Captain Armstrong reported, "By my own exertions, as is well known by those who witnessed it, I succeeded in recovering all the kegs of specie except for $61." Of the gold on the shore and the shattered box of dimes and half dimes, although the boat was a complete wreck and sank in less than an hour, he recovered all but $90.

"Had I been killed," he relates, "I have no doubt the greater part of the money would have been plundered, as were the dead and

Modern river traffic—barges at the port of Muskogee on the Arkansas. Photo by Bill Burchardt.

The modern Tulsa port of Catoosa, present-day head of navigation on the Arkansas River.

wounded of their watches, pocketbooks, and clothes. I saved the entire funds of the government with the exception of $151."

He concluded, "I was detained some days in a very uncomfortable situation, watching the money until a boat came along and relieved me. I shall obtain the proper certificates to relieve me from the loss—the amount is small and I have the satisfaction to know that my exertions made it so."

There will be no more steamboats like the *Dillard*, so shallow of draft that she was said to need only a "little dampness" for navigation. The shallow-draft steamers were essential for the upper rivers, where shoal waters often stranded boats aground for days or weeks, waiting for a rise to float them off. Webbers Falls on the upper Arkansas were seven feet high in the early days of steamboating, which meant the river must be flowing at least eight or nine feet deep for even shallow-draft steamers to pass upstream. Some of the captains were obtuse when confronted with low water. Captain Heckler of the *Trident* held the reputation of being able to run his powerful sternwheeler to Fort Gibson on less water than any other boat. When he went aground on a sandbar he would back up and attempt to "jump her over," slamming full tilt into the bar over and over again while the ladies in the cabin screamed with fright and the stewards hung on to the chandeliers to keep them from crashing against the walls.

The demise of the river steamer has relieved the world of one kind of tragedy, death by steamboat explosion. "Rich Joe" Vann owned a huge cotton plantation near Webbers Falls. One of the Cherokees dispossessed in Georgia and removed to the Indian Territory, he had risen by wit and work to become once more a wealthy man. In his passion for racing he became owner of one of the fastest quarter horses of his time. He named his racing mare Lucy Walker, then built a gorgeous sidewheeler steamboat which he also named *Lucy Walker*. He indulged his passion by challenging and racing every steamboat he encountered on the river. Said to be an insatiable driver of his Negro slaves on the boiler deck, he would swear and shout at them during the river races until they would feed the boiler fires slabs of bacon to heat the chimneys red hot.

On one of her trips the *Lucy Walker* went alongside the wharf to take passengers. As she moved again into the river in getting under way she erupted in one of the most frightful explosions ever to occur on any river. Legend promptly began to invent lurid tales to account for the explosion. The Lloyd's of London insurance investigation determined she had stopped her engine to repair a malfunction of machinery. While floating in the river current, the water in her boiler became exhausted. This caused the explosion. All of her passengers were lost or horribly wounded. All the crew were killed, including her owner and master, "Rich Joe" Vann.

The Arkansas River transports more traffic today than ever during the era of steam. Today's traffic is for the most part prosaic, cargo barges with their towboats. Some of the major river ports have a diesel-powered sternwheel or sidewheeler showboat or excursion boat featuring dramatic entertainment and/or traditional riverboat music, harking back in nostalgia to the days of the steamboat. Occasionally ascending the Arkansas is the *Delta Queen*, last of the great riverboats accommodating overnight cruise and excursion passengers.

The Arkansas River's McClellan-Kerr Waterway, with its eighteen modern locks and dams, is a wonder to behold, and beautiful to travel in any season. Along today's Arkansas you'll see dredges at work maintaining the channel, and coast guard craft patrolling. The Arkansas is kept free of dangers to navigation as it never was during the steamboat era, and the Red River is scheduled to be navigable again to Shreveport by 1983. You'll never sink from a bottom-ripping snag, or suddenly encounter a huge sawyer rearing up out of the depths of the river before you. The rivers are gorgeously scenic, and you no longer need navigate with the dread fear of an exploding boiler shattering the deck beneath your feet or tearing off the superstructure over your head. The Arkansas now is, the Red will soon again be, *Water Trails West*, better and safer than they ever were in history.

4

The Ohio River:
Throughway "For the West"

BY ROBERT WEST HOWARD

Scores of rivers roil runoffs from the average rainfalls of thirty-seven to sixty inches down the east slope of our Atlantic Seaboard mountains. Montreal, Bangor, Boston, New York, Philadelphia, Washington, Richmond, Charleston, Savannah were all founded at river fall lines or tidewaters. But down the west slope of these mountains, New York to Alabama, one river system sluices all of the runoff into "Mrs. Sipi."

The Senecas, masters of the vital Niagara gateway to the Upper Great Lakes, called this system "Ohio," meaning "great river." Between 1780 and 1860 it was the throughway "for the West" to both Southerner and Northerner, the grim laboratory and testing place for every form of transportation used in the Far West and the birthplace of folkways, legends, and phrases now considered "pioneer West."

The flatboat, broadhorn, ark, and amazing keelboat were all perfected at Pittsburgh and Wheeling between 1780 and 1800. The first steamboat in the West was built at Pittsburgh in 1811. During 1816, at Wheeling, Henry Miller Shreve designed and built the first of the shallow-draft "floating dishpan" steamers that became standard on Far West waterways. Thirteen years later, and again on the Ohio, Shreve designed the *snagboat* that opened and maintained ship channels on the Mississippi, Ohio, Missouri, Red, and Arkansas. By 1840 the quickest and by far the most comfortable route between the Atlantic and the Rockies, or Texas, was via the waterway network made navigable by Shreve's inventions plus the canals built to the Ohio.

All of this ingenuity, as ominous to nineteenth-century America as electricity-reciprocal engines-aircraft would be to its twentieth was

achieved in an environment as foreboding as any phase of Far West pioneering. Millennia of floods, tornadoes, and occasional earthquakes had shifted and reshifted the Ohio's channels. Variations in rock strata and contour along its 981 miles caused tight curves, sandbars, suddenly swift currents. Dead trees became the foundations for islets of timber, bramble, and muck that could strip the hull off a boat as easily as a fisherman guts a trout.

This array of deadly "*snags*"—the word is Scandinavian and means "sharp point"— would cause the invention of such riverman terms as:

> *Planter* A tree trunk firmly wedged into river bottom at one end but floating free at the other end.
> *Raft* A snag that completely, or almost, blocked a channel. (Shreveport, Louisiana, is named for Captain Shreve because his snagboat removed a "raft" 100 miles long that blocked navigation on the Red River.)
> *Sawyer* A snag so delicately balanced that a breeze could cause it to bob up and down.
> *Sleeper* A water-soaked log floating just beneath the surface.

Robert La Salle is assumed to have explored part of the Ohio Valley in 1670. It appeared on Joliet's map of 1674. Migrations into Kentucky, mostly by Virginians, began in the 1760s. The capture of British forts at Kaskaskia and Vincennes by George Rogers Clark and Virginia-Kentucky riflemen in 1778–79 contributed greatly to U.S.A. sovereignty in the Ohio Valley and its acknowledgment by Great Britain in the Peace Treaty of 1783. High taxes and mortgage defaults in

Henry M. Shreve pioneered transportation on the western rivers in the early 1800s and designed early shallow-draft steamers and the ingenious "snagboat" that made possible the clearing of tree-clogged waterways. New York Public Library Collection.

New England and the upland-cotton boom caused by Eli Whitney's invention of the cotton (en)gin contributed to the rush "for the Ohio."

Bitterness between the U.S.A. and Canada—most of our Loyalist refugees settled in Nova Scotia, New Brunswick, and Ontario—prevented much immigration up the Great Lakes until after the War of 1812. The Clinton-Sullivan Expedition of 1779 razed Six Nations' homelands in western New York and established Niagara Falls and Lake Ontario as the Loyalist frontier. This action opened a route to Pittsburgh and the Ohio headwaters via the Susquehanna and Allegheny valleys for New Englanders and New Yorkers.

The Pennsylvanians built the first trans-Appalachian cartway to Pittsburgh during the 1770s and, before 1750, Penn-Dutch craftsmen on the Lancaster-Harrisburg frontier designed the momentous red, white, and blue Conestoga wagon. (How and why its 1840s

adaptation was given the name of a Gloucester, Massachusetts, fishing vessel and called "a prairie schooner" remains a mystery!) Maryland and Virginia "talked big" about a Potomac-Ohio canal but flubbed it and relied on cartways to Pittsburgh or the Boone's Trace route through Cumberland Gap. Carolinians and Georgians could trek through the Smokies via the routes of the wild horse and wild cattle "crackers," then slither down to the headwaters of the Tennessee.

During 1778 General Clark had founded Louisville beside the river's most dangerous rapids, subsequently and somewhat grandiloquently known as "the Falls of the Ohio." In 1780 more than 300 craft reached Louisville. During 1788–89 the 500 plus drifting west from Pittsburgh carried an estimated 20,000 people, plus 8,000 horses, 2,400 cattle, 1,000 sheep, and 700 wagons.

The first family fortunes of Pittsburgh and Wheeling came from boatbuilding and provisioning. The vessels built for trappers, traders, and the first wave of pioneers were narrow barges, with gunwales high and thick enough to stop a fusillade of arrows or bullets. The windows in the slab-side hut atop the deck were just wide enough for a rifle barrel.

When the "Ohio or Bust" wagon trains began to squeal in, Pittsburghers designed the *ark*. This was a flatboat forty to seventy feet long and twelve to fifteen feet wide, with a hull that rose six to seven feet above the water line. A log cabin was built on the deck. Its roof had a level area between the eaves so that the family wagon and crates of chickens could be lashed there.

Two huge rudder-oars extended from front and rear to simplify the steering problem. Aside from these and a fendpole or two, the arks depended on river currents. They were too bulky to be rowed or sailed.

Livestock clattered aboard the ark via a gangplank that led to stalls, or pens, in the stern. Then the hinged stern was closed or barred. The cabin, serving as storeroom for bags, boxes, trunks, and the cherished rocker, dresser, commode from "back home," had bunks along one wall, a stone or brick fireplace along another, and barred windows covered with cloth or greased paper. (Window glass cost $5 a pane.)

The haplessness of the arks floating willy-nilly through the forests, individually and

The snagboat U.S. R. E. DeRussy in 1868.

without escorts, invited piracy. The death toll from pirate gangs on the Ohio, Mississippi, and Natchez Trace between 1785 and 1805 is estimated to have exceeded two thousand men, women, and children. Their most notorious haunt was Cave in Rock, near present Shawneetown, Illinois. There were ugly rapids and whirlpools upstream around the Wabash-Ohio junction. Pirates, stationed midstream in dugouts, posed as pilots and offered to "git you through them riffles downstream." They did the job deftly, if gruffly, then urged the ark's master to "put ashore at that cave thar, 'cause it be a wondrous thing to see and it's got the sweetest drinkin' water in two hundred mile."

Inside the cave, blinking at its white limestone shimmer, the immigrants were shot down by pirates hidden behind boulders. Bodies and boat were looted; corpses were carried downstream and tossed overboard; the boat was ferried down to the Cumberland or Tennessee and sold.

The most notorious of the pirates who used Cave in Rock were Micajah "Big" Harpe, Wiley "Little" Harpe, and "Slick Sam"

Mason. The trio terrorized between 1798 and 1803. The regional posses of volunteers called Rangers were the only law enforcers in the valley and were subject to the whims of district judges. The Harpes are reputed to have murdered more than one hundred before a posse cornered "Big" and "Little" on a Kentucky hilltop one August afternoon in 1799. A hulking six footer with a purply red face, jug-handle ears and snake eyes, "Big" snarled challenge and began shooting. The Rangers winged him, closed in, and began questioning. "He confessed the killing of Mr. Stump on Big Barren," a Lexington paper reported on September 10. "He also confessed the killing of 17 or 18 besides. They had with them eight horses and a considerable quantity of plunder, seven pairs of saddlebags. They cut off his head." The scowling head was carried to the junction of the Henderson–Madisonville road and jammed into a tree fork as a warning to all outlaws.

"Little" Harpe got away and stayed in hiding, probably in still-Spanish Louisiana, for a year. A few weeks later, Sam Wilson appeared at Cave in Rock with "daughters and

Illustration from a public broadside. Courtesy of the New-York Historical Society, New York City.

sons-in-law." They bullied the resident pirates into alliance as bartenders, waiters, cooks at "Wilson's Liquor Vault and House of Entertainment." Lavish signs went up over the entrance. Wilson became the genial "Colonel." The program of this combination saloon and brothel was knockout drops in the drinks, neat and orderly throat cutting, and downstream disposal of the bodies.

When Louisville merchants suspected foul play at "that Wilson cribhouse," a keel-boat crew was sent upstream to investigate. Folklore attests that Mink Fink was one of the crew. The keelers learned the truth, escaped, and returned to Louisville to organize a raiding party. But Wilson had friends in Louisville and fled. He reappeared on Stack Island in the Mississippi and used it as headquarters for ambushing travelers on the Natchez Trace. "Little" Harpe and his hirelings murdered Wilson in 1803 and brought his head into Natchez to collect a reward. Keelers identified Harpe. He was arrested, tried, and beheaded. Both the Wilson and Harpe heads were displayed on stakes along the Natchez Trace.

Meanwhile, keelboat owners had moved in and organized arks and flatboats into flotillas for the journey between Cincinnati and Cairo. The keelboat guardian stayed near the center of the procession so that its "half hoss, half alligator" crew could get at aggressors upstream or downstream. The technique may well have influenced the organization of wagon trains on the Santa Fe and Overland trails after 1825.

The combination of pirates, cutthroat pimps, and natural hazards along the Ohio made the keelboat and its crewmen Old West immortals, worthy of as much prose-poetry-art as the wagon trains, Mountain Men, stagers, and railroaders.

The keelboat was the express train of muscle-powered navigation in the West. Its design was based on the Durham, a craft originated on the Delaware to deliver ironware to Philadelphia from the Durham Furnace, upstream near Trenton. Its greatest asset, in the East, had been the "running boards" that hung out over each side of the deck. Each board was a foot wide and cleated. Using iron-tipped push poles twelve feet long, crewmen

"ran the boards" and pushed the boat upstream. (This Durham boat invention marked the first American appearance of the term *running board!*)

The first keelboats built at Pittsburgh, about 1775, averaged seventy feet in length with a ten-foot beam and were pointed at each end. The deckhouse had bunks, cargo space, and a tiny galley called the *caboose*. (This word was an Americanization of the Holland Dutch phrase *kabin haus*. Three generations later, railroaders would snitch the word for the crew car and lookout perch that still sways at the end of a freight train.) One-pounder cannon, rifles, cutlasses, and the crew's deftness with knives, gouging, rupturing, and "stomping" assured the keelboat serene passage at Cave in Rock and other plunder points.

The captain of a keelboat was the *patron*. The pilot was the *bosseman*. The lean, mean, and boisterous crewmen were *keelers* and they were paid $15 a month. The keeler's badge of office was a low-crowned broad hat of felted beaver. With this, usually, he wore skintight cotton breeches, dazzlingly striped blue, red, purple, green, a shirt of homespun, and a leather or homespun jacket. The dance callers at new Louisville and Cincinnati shrewdly

Cordelling. Courtesy of the Nebraska State Historical Society.

summarized the "half hoss, half alligator" personality requisite for a keeler when they chanted:

Dance, boatmen, dance
Dance, dance away.
Dance all night till the broad daylight
And go home with the gals in the morning.

The use of the running board and three other techniques established the keelboat as the only vessel that could make the round trip on the Ohio, Mississippi, and Missouri. The other techniques were *cordelling, bushwhacking,* and *warping.*

Cordelling was the grim, and sometimes deadly, process of towing the boat with a rope. (The Louisiana French word for rope was *corde.*) There weren't any mule teams or towpaths. After rigging the rope, a tow gang went ashore. Rattlesnakes were so numerous on rock ledges that two cordellers, carrying forked sticks, went ahead to toss snakes off the route. Occasionally, they would "whoop it up" by slithering a particularly fat and ugly rattler over the cliff and down onto the ship's deck, preferably at the feet of the bosseman, and howl joyously at "that damfine snake dance."

The cordellers scrambled through thickets, across swamps, and up cliffs. On the lower Mississippi, alligators charged out of the swamp grass. Wildcats and wolves snarled warnings. Black bears reared on hind legs to offer battle. Bees, yellowjackets, hornets zoomed from dead-tree hives; chiggers created agony from shins to armpits.

Bushwhacking was the trick of treadmilling the boat upstream, via the running board, by grabbing tree branches that overhung the channel.

Warping upstream was the drudgery of fastening a rope around an upstream tree and then hauling it in.

Even with these techniques plus push poles plus oars plus a sail, the keelboat averaged five miles an hour downstream and one mile an hour upstream. George Rogers Clark and his 175 Virginia militiamen built one of the Ohio's first keelboats at Pittsburgh in 1778. General Clark's "kid brother," William, and President Jefferson's personal secretary, Meriwether Lewis, used a keelboat on their momentous search to the Pacific in 1803–5. By 1810 more than three hundred keelboats served as expressmen, escorts, explorers, trou-

The legendary Mike Fink performing his favorite stunt of shooting a hole in a whiskey-filled tin cup perched on a friend's head. New York Public Library Collection.

badours, and hard-nosed peacemakers on the Ohio, Mississippi, and Missouri. During 1811 Manuel Lisa and a picked crew of twenty keelers established an all-time record by ascending 1,100 miles of the Missouri in sixty days, an average of nineteen miles a day.

Such a distinguished profession had to have famous graduates. Mike Fink, the legendary "Snapping Turtle," began his "half hoss, half alligator" career in 1798 and by 1803 was considered "the best bosseman on the Ohio." About 1815, growling that "It's too crowded down there," he moved to the Missouri. He is reputed to have been bosseman on the keelboat that carried Jedediah Smith, Hugh Glass, and "the kid" Jim Bridger on their first hunt to the Yellowstone's valley. A year later, John Barleycorn won. Fink attempted his favorite trick of shooting a hole through a tin cup perched on the head of a friend. He missed and killed the friend. An onlooker shouted,

Steamboats appeared on the Ohio in the second decade of the nineteenth century. They were an amazing sight to Sunday afternoon strollers. New York Public Library Collection.

"Deliberate murder!" beat Fink to the draw, and killed him. Folklore says "the king of the keelers" is buried in an unmarked grave near the ruins of Fort Henry at the Yellowstone's mouth.

David Crockett was a keeler for several years before the War of 1812 and some of his zanier yarn-spins originated on a keelboat deck or cordell path. The great Henry Shreve, a migrant from New Jersey, learned the Ohio's tricks as a keeler, fought his way up to bosseman and patron, and thus won enough confidence to be given the captaincy of the Ohio's second steamboat, the seventy-five-ton *Enterprise*, in 1815. Abraham Lincoln's puckish skills as a jokesmith and anecdotal philosopher were at least honed by contacts with keelers on his flatboat trips to New Orleans in 1828 and 1830.

By 1810 more than 1,082,000 Americans lived west of the Appalachians, and Indiana, Kentucky, Mississippi, Ohio, and Tennessee had statehood. The arks and barges got most

of them there via the Ohio; the rafts and flatboats they "rolled" into feeder creeks carried their harvests to Cincinnati, Louisville, distant New Orleans; the keelers, for all their feisty boisterousness, were their knights-errant.

The transition to machine power in western navigation was initiated in 1810–11. On August 17, 1807, Robert Fulton maneuvered the S.S. *Clermont* up the Hudson from Manhattan to Albany. Fulton's backer was Robert R. Livingston, the Hudson valley patroon who had served on the committee that drew up the Declaration of Independence and had recently negotiated the "cheapest real estate deal in history," the Louisiana Purchase. Livingston considered the steamboat the exclusive property of his family and his protégé, Fulton, and persuaded New York's legislature to grant him a monopoly for steam-powered craft on the state's waterways. During 1809, Nicholas Roosevelt, great-great-uncle of President Theodore Roosevelt and also an engine designer, negotiated a partnership in which he, Livingston, and Fulton would monopolize steam-powered navigation in the West.

That fall, Roosevelt and his bride, Lydia Latrobe, wagoned to Pittsburgh, rented a keelboat, and rode downstream to extol "steamboat prosperity" to merchants' associations at Cincinnati, Louisville, Cairo, St. Louis, and the Missouri shore boomtown, New Madrid. The merchants were dubious; keelboat patrons laughed. But Roosevelt returned to Pittsburgh and wrote recommendations to Livingston for a 116-foot craft with a twenty-foot beam. Livingston approved, fixed a construction budget of $38,000, and ordered Fulton to build a one-cylinder engine with a thirty-four-inch diameter that, as on the *Clermont*, would power paddle wheels placed amidships. For obvious promotional reasons, the vessel would be christened *New Orleans*.

The *New Orleans* was launched during May 1811. Conestoga wagons transported Fulton's engine. The summer-long outfitting included masts and sails "just in case." Roosevelt ordered the initial voyage to begin on August 26. His crew consisted of a captain, engineer, pilot, six deckhands, two maids, a waiter, a cook. The only passengers were Mr. and Mrs. Roosevelt and their massive Newfoundland dog, Tiger. Mrs. Roosevelt was eight months pregnant.

Halley's Comet again blazed in the night skies, and again provoked predictions of "Doomsday." Some downstream gawkers associated the ship's clank-hiss-splash with the comet. Indians nicknamed the vessel *Penelore*, "the fire canoe." The voyage to Cincinnati was an uneventful two-day run. Snags and curves into Louisville took another two days. There Roosevelt encountered the factor that would make the Fulton-type steamboat impractical for navigation in the West. The *New Orleans* required a deep channel; it could not run the shallow rapids of "the Falls of the Ohio." The downstream voyage must wait for heavy rains.

Roosevelt took deft advantage by bucking currents back to Cincinnati and proving that his vessel could outpace a keelboat on the upstream journey. The rains began in mid-November. Mrs. Roosevelt safely delivered her baby. On the last day of November, soundings indicated that water depths in the rapids averaged five inches deeper than the ship's

keel. An extra pilot was hired for the attempt. The passage was made without incident.

But, as though in fulfillment of Doomsday prophecies, the convulsions of major earthquakes began that night as the *New Orleans* lay at anchor below the Falls. Trapped by the Falls from returning upstream, Roosevelt decided to attempt the run for Natchez, despite evidence that riverbanks were cracked and ready to avalanche.

Anthracite was still a brash new fuel in the East. During the keelboat trip, Roosevelt had spotted several coal outcroppings along the Kentucky and Indiana shores, then dickered with farmers to dig out and stockpile enough for refueling his steamboat. The coal piles were waiting. The chunks gave off as much heat as wood, and lasted longer. This use of a new fuel initiated another regional individualism. Throughout the nineteenth century, Ohio steamers would burn coal. But the Mississippi's captains preferred wood, thus evolving the wood piles and "totes" immortalized by Rodgers and Hammerstein in "Ol' Man River."

The weeks of inching out of the Ohio and down the curlicue of "Mrs. Sipi" to Natchez were sheer terror. Mrs. Roosevelt wrote, "I lived in a constant fright unable to sleep or sew or read." Tiger, the Newfoundland, howled or moaned as he paced deck and cabins. The ship rocked, shuddered, thumped. Earthquakes and succeeding floods destroyed most of New Madrid, then created Reelfoot Lake, just south in Tennessee. Channels shifted. Islands sank; new ones oozed up at midstream.

Safe in New Orleans by mid-January, Roosevelt decided to limit the *New Orleans*' operations to the deep-water run between New Orleans and Natchez. Edward Livingston, brother to Robert R., had become an influential attorney in New Orleans so he lobbied a bill through the Louisiana legislature granting Livingston-Fulton-Roosevelt a steamboat monopoly within the state's waters. (His efforts to push through similar laws for Mississippi, Tennessee, Missouri, and other upriver governments were boo'd to speedy defeat.)

A snag ended the *New Orleans*' career near Baton Rouge in 1814. A few months later, while Andrew Jackson's frontiersmen built barricades against the British invaders,

Henry Shreve splashed his seventy-five-ton *Enterprise* up to a New Orleans wharf. Roosevelt and Edward Livingston appealed for a court order to impound the craft. General Jackson barked them off, and ordered Shreve upstream to race in guns and ammunition stored at Natchez. This chore finished, Shreve and his crew volunteered as gunners with Jackson's artillery, thus serving doubly in the victory of January 8, 1815.

During February, Shreve headed the *Enterprise* upriver. The ship averaged fifty-five miles a day, and reached Louisville within twenty-five days. That was three times as fast as the keelboat record.

Shreve was not satisfied. The upstream struggle convinced him that a radical new design was essential for the western steamboat. All that summer and fall he and a boatbuilder at Wheeling argued, cussed, beamed about designs for a shallow-draft steamer. The hull that took shape during the winter of 1815–16 was as dishpan-flat as a raft. A stout deck was laid just above the water line. The engine went atop this deck. The passenger cabins, pilothouse, and dining room were built on decks above the engine deck. Coincidentally, Shreve brooded about the potentials of the high-pressure steam engine recently developed by Oliver Evans, and finally decided to install one even though it made more noise than a fife and drum corps and would probably keep the boat in a constant shimmy.

Fully equipped, the boat grossed four hundred tons but rode the river as lightly as a swan. So she deserved the name of *Washington* and lived up to it by making the Louisville-New Orleans round trip in forty-five days.

Roosevelt and Livingston continued lobbying to have Shreve's boats seized or banned from Louisiana waters. But the state courts balked. A storm was brewing in New York, they knew. The gaunt towhead Kornelius Van Der Bilt, feisty operator of Manhattan-Staten Island ferries, was hollering "freedom of waterways" and had hired Daniel Webster as his attorney. New Jersey's legislature had joined the chorus by resolving that New York did not "own the Hudson River," so what the hell goes on? John Marshall and associates on the U. S. Supreme Court were listening. The argument involved the sticky, still unresolved mat-

Port of New Orleans in the steamboat era. From the sketch by A. R. Waud.

The Ohio from the riverside at Cincinnati at the turn of the century. New York Public Library Collection.

ter of jurisdiction of interstate commerce. So just at this time, decided Louisiana's politicos, the Roosevelt-Livingston potato was too hot.

The Ohio's boatbuilders beamed. By the end of 1817 there were a dozen steamboats on the river. By 1819 there were more than sixty. A steamboat navigated the Missouri in 1819; another churned the upper Mississippi in 1823. All of them were patterned on Shreve's dishpan design, so showered both decks and countryside with fiery embers spat out by high-pressure, horizontal-cylinder engines.

On August 2, 1824, Justice Marshall read the Supreme Court's majority decision that Congress had the power to regulate interstate commerce. "Steamboats," he thundered, "can no more be restrained from navigating waters and entering ports . . . than if they were wafted on their voyage by the winds, instead of being propelled by the agency of fire." The steamboat monopoly died. By the end of 1835 there were 684 steamers in the West, and 628 of them had been built in Pittsburgh,

Cincinnati, or Louisville yards. Some of them could rev up speeds of twenty miles an hour. But their boilers were iron, and when they blew, the ship went too. More than 120 died when the *Orinoko* exploded during 1838.

While some captains and owners connived to develop powerful corporations, such as the Cincinnati-Louisville Mail Line, Captain Shreve remained the creative pioneer. He made no effort to profit from his dishpan design, and was soon pondering a method for controlling snags, rafts, sawyers, and similar channel hazards. During 1828 he decided to invest much of his capital in a weird, totally new type of steamer.

The hull that took shape in an Ohio yard that fall had two sharp and narrow prows. Actually, it consisted of two hulls fastened together amidships. The V-shaped space between them was fourteen feet long and angled out until it was ten feet apart at the prows.

A derrick straddled the prows. Each derrick pole was thirty feet long, tapered from a diameter of two feet at the base. Suspended from the poles by pulleys was a huge iron claw. This could be used to swing snag logs aboard the boat. Cranked down until it extended into the water beyond the prows, it became a battering ram and grappler that enabled the pilot to pick "sawyers" and "planters" loose from their moorings, or bludgeon a channel through a sandbar. A crew of lumberjacks was stationed behind the derrick to turn snag logs into cordwood.

Captain Shreve called this invention a *snagboat* and named the first one *Heliopolis*, after the ancient Nile Delta "city of the sun." During 1829 the *Heliopolis* cleaned out a raft of snags that had imperiled mid-Mississippi traffic since the New Madrid earthquakes. Congress was so impressed that it created the post of Superintendent of Western River Improvements for Captain Shreve.

Although Shreve's inventions completed the roster of critical contributions to Far West navigation out of the Ohio, the "great river" continued to be the favorite throughway to the high plains, Rockies, and Pacific Slope until railroads gandy-danced in during the 1850s and '60s. Valley shipyards continued to produce the bulk of the 1,190 steamers operating on "western waters" in 1846.

When news of the nuggets discovered in Sutter's millrace loosed the Argonauts of 1849, the young Pittsburgh composer Stephen Collins Foster provided their favorite pop tune, "O Susanna." The gigantic teeth and femurs from Big Bone Lick, Kentucky, so intriguing to Thomas Jefferson and Meriwether Lewis, proved an important link in the decades of research that gave birth to paleontology . . . the massive discoveries of dinosaur and other prehistoric skeletons in Kansas, Colorado, Wyoming, and Montana . . . the perfection of the contemporary museum . . . the development of a National Park System . . . the twentieth-century search for petroleum.

The Civil War and railroads all but killed the river's traffic. A revival began during World War I and burgeoned through World War II. The surge has continued. During 1970 the Greater Cincinnati area reported its river shipping totaled "more than 136,000,000 tons."

Industrial smogs, the Orwellian monotony of ticky-tack suburbias, and highways have obliterated much of the stark grandeur of the Ohio. But Cave in Rock still glowers on the north shore near Shawneetown, Illinois, and the local name for the section of U.S. 41 between Sebree, Kentucky, and Evansville remains Harpe's Head Road. Brunswick stew, burgoo, persimmon pudding, groundcherry and grape pies perpetuate the zest of keelboat and steamboat fare, although most of the "country fried chicken" ballyhooed in valley towns sullies it. And still, on some of the leaf-bowered reaches west of Louisville, the prevailing westerlies can—if you listen properly—transform a patrol car's siren to the haunting "waaah" of a keelboat's cow horn, or mute the snarl of a truck to the contralto "chukety pow" of a steamboat splashing another load of immigrants toward western destiny.

5

George Washington's Dream: The Chesapeake and Ohio Canal

BY G. M. FARLEY

George Washington had a dream. While the first settlers were pushing their way westward into the Ohio Valley and beyond, he recognized the need of a navigable waterway from the Atlantic Coast to the Ohio River. He foresaw the growth of the young nation, and realized her potential, if suitable transportation could be provided. His original ambition was to open the Potomac River for commercial use.

About 1740, Colonel Thomas Cresap, a friend of Washington, made his way to the forks of the upper Potomac and built a fortified home against possible Indian raids. Eight years later, after recognizing the need of an organized effort to open the river for trade, he entered conjointly into an association with other interested parties and formed what was called the Ohio Company. This company soon became the most powerful of all pre-Revolutionary trade corporations, and made the first English settlement at Fort Pitt, which later became Pittsburgh, Pennsylvania.

The first commercial use of the Potomac above tidewater made by white men was by Cresap's company in 1749, the year King George II of England issued a charter to a half-million acres of land on the north of the Ohio River with the provision that the company must erect a fort on the land. Governor Dinwiddie became interested in the project and wrote, "I have the success and prosperity of the Ohio Co. much at heart." He became a shareholder along with Thomas Cresap and George Washington's half brothers Lawrence and Augustine.

Cresap immediately set out to explore this vast wilderness area using Nemacolin, a Shawnee Indian, as guide. The company built a storehouse at Will's Creek (Cumberland, Maryland) and ordered £4,000 worth of trading goods from London. The business prospered, and the stockholders were overjoyed. They brought their goods upriver by flatboat and canoe from Alexandria, Virginia.

In 1754, George Washington visited the commandant of the French forces on the Ohio during which time he studied the various possibilities and difficulties in using the Potomac River as a waterway to the Ohio Valley. Earlier, when surveying along the Potomac for Lord Fairfax, he had envisioned this as the most suitable passage, and now his convictions grew. Governor Sharpe of Maryland and Sir John St. Clair boated the river in January 1755 from Cumberland to Alexandria. The conclusion was that the river channel might be opened to navigation for the use of flat-bottom boats by the removal of the rocks which form Little Falls and Great Falls. The original idea was to use the river as far as Cumberland, and then perhaps find a portage through the mountain passes to the Ohio Valley. The Revolutionary War interrupted George Washington's dream. The Ohio Company collapsed about 1779.

With the surrender of Cornwallis at Yorktown in October 1783, independence for the American colonies was ensured. While waiting for the dismissal of the Army, Washington again turned his thoughts and energies toward his plan to find a navigable route to the West. In September 1784 he made a six weeks' trip through the Allegheny Mountains and returned to his Mount Vernon home to recommend a system of public improvements for the young nation. He offered a bill to the Virginia and Maryland legislatures which, in 1785, resulted in the "Potowmack Company," of which Washington was elected first president.

George Washington's dream two decades later, the restored C & O Canal at Oldtown, Maryland, as it looks today. Courtesy George "Hooper" Wolfe.

Washington's plan to open the Potomac to navigation did not prove feasible. The Potomac was too shallow in places, and at other places huge boulders formed impassable rapids. Short canals would be necessary. A tremendous amount of time, effort, and money went into the attempt at dredging the sandbars and removing the rock. Dams were constructed along the river to raise the level of the water, and short canals skirted the major falls. Some of these canals had to be blasted from solid rock. The builders had trouble in the form of acquiring competent labor. At times fever plagued the labor camps and many died or deserted. After more than $723,000 was spent on the project it was found that the boating season was limited to about two months of the year. The entire project was abandoned about 1830.

In 1816 the General Assembly of Virginia created a Board of Public Works, which, shortly afterward, suggested that a connection might be built between the waters of the Potomac and the Ohio. This, apparently, is the earliest official suggestion for a continuous canal from tidewater in the Potomac to the headwaters of the Ohio, and may partially have been brought to mind by the building of the Erie Canal. It was not until four years later that the General Assembly of Virginia requested an inquiry into the expediency of the 1816 proposal.

On December 27, 1820, a report was sent to the governor of Virginia that a canal from Georgetown to the Coal Banks above Cumberland was practicable at a cost of only $1,114,300.

In making this estimate a major difficulty was not taken into consideration. In many places the Potomac Valley becomes a narrow gorge confined by cliffs. Because of these cliffs the canal would have to be built, in places, on the very margin of the river, and in other places partly in the channel, exposing the works to the full force of the frequent and sometimes violent storms of the Potomac Valley.

For years Baltimore had opposed the

57

opening of the Potomac River to navigation on the strength that such action would deprive them of much of the western trade. To placate their disposition a proposal was made that a branch canal could be built connecting the Maryland city with the proposed Chesapeake and Ohio Canal. Feelings ran high between the two states with only slight interest from Pennsylvania, which was already involved in building the Erie Canal and would be affected but little by either the Potomac River or a canal along its course.

In 1823 a joint commission met in Virginia and adopted the name The Potomac Canal Company. In view of the enlarged purpose of the enterprise the name was changed to the Union Canal, and finally to The Chesapeake and Ohio Canal Company.

Virginia was the first to react to a proposal to open books for subscription to stock in the company by granting a charter on January 27, 1824. The following January, Maryland confirmed the act.

Through a period of controversy and amendments, a charter was finally granted with the object being "to establish a connected navigation between the Eastern and Western waters, so as to extend and multiply the means and facilities of internal commerce and personal intercourse between the two great sections of the United States. . . ."

A survey was made of the suggested route to the Ohio River which resulted in a two-part proposal:

1. The Chesapeake and Ohio Canal was to extend from tidewater in the Potomac to the mouth of the Savage River.

2. The Ohio and Erie Canal would extend from Pittsburgh through either Ohio or Pennsylvania to Lake Erie.

Pennsylvania's Erie Canal was already in operation when, on July 4, 1828, President John Quincy Adams turned the first spadeful of earth for the C & O Canal near Little Falls, Maryland. Adams experienced a moment of embarrassment when his spade struck a root and he was unable to remove any of the soil. Undeterred by such a trifling obstacle, the President stripped off and laid aside his coat and completed the task, much to the enjoyment of the spectators, and construction on the canal was officially started.

The Baltimore and Ohio Railroad was the canal's strongest competition. The same day John Quincy Adams broke earth for the beginning of the C & O Canal, ground was also being broken at Baltimore for the beginning of the railroad by Charles Carroll, the only survivor of the signers of the Declaration of Independence.

The question of which would succeed was not to be decided amicably. President Mercer of the Canal Company wrote in November 1828 that "this controversy will probably not retard our operations in the least degree." He was wrong, for even though the canal won the first legal battle, prolonged litigation, great expenditure of time and finances were among the consequences arising from the efforts of the Canal Company to slow the progress of the railroad.

Roadbeds could be leveled, crossties and steel rails could be laid much faster than a canal could be dug, especially when much of it had to be blasted through solid rock, and dams, aqueducts, and locks built. Even before ground was broken the Canal Company filed an injunction to prevent the railroad from locating its road between Point of Rocks and Harpers Ferry on land on which the Canal Company had laid previous claim. The court issued an injunction to prevent location of the railroad between these points. Thus began a long series of court battles that was to hinder the progress of both the canal and the railroad.

Both companies hired engineers, and surveys and joint surveys were made. An injunction was rendered against the Canal Company, a decision that was reversed in the Court of Appeals, and the right of way granted to the Chesapeake and Ohio Canal Company. The injunction against the railroad was continued.

In the course of time an alternative was worked out, but not without legal entanglements, until a bill was passed on March 22, 1833, providing for joint construction of the canal and railroad between Point of Rocks and Harpers Ferry. Even so, friction continued to mount and more investigations made until another compromise was reached. At one point the railroad found it necessary to use horses to pull the cars between the two points while the court was reaching a compromise.

Financial difficulties, as well as varied interests of individuals on each side of the dispute, caused constant confusion. By June 1834 there still remained seventy-eight miles of the canal to be built. Two years later both the

Harpers Ferry, West Virginia, 1860. C & O Canal can be seen on the far side of the river. Courtesy George "Hooper" Wolfe.

Chesapeake and Ohio Canal Company and the Baltimore and Ohio Railroad each received $3 million from the state of Maryland. This enabled the railroad to continue construction, which had ceased when it reached Harpers Ferry. By the end of 1841, due to near bankruptcy of the state of Maryland, not a laborer was at work between Dam No. 6 and Cumberland, and the situation remained in this state until passage of a further act in 1845. On March 10 of that year a bill was passed by which the liens of the state were postponed and deferred in favor of such bonds as were necessary to complete the Canal to Cumberland. Sale of these bonds enabled the company to renew construction on the canal and finally to reach Cumberland on October 10, 1850, a total of 185 and seven-tenths miles from the mouth of the Tiber in the city of Washington, D.C., to Cumberland, Maryland.

This was the terminal point of the Chesapeake and Ohio Canal, a partial fulfillment of George Washington's dream of a waterway to the Ohio. But his dream of a passageway was

to be realized, as the Baltimore and Ohio Railroad continues until this day.

There were better than seventy-five locks, eleven aqueducts, and nearly one hundred culverts on the canal. Each lock was a hundred feet in length, approximately sixteen feet deep, and fifteen feet wide. It took ten to fifteen minutes to pass a boat through a lock. The canal boats were ninety-two feet in length and fourteen feet six inches wide, which must have been an inconvenience in a lock with only three inches to spare on each side. The capacity of the boat was about one hundred twenty-five tons, and was used primarily for carrying coal from Cumberland, Maryland, to tidewater. However, their usefulness was not limited to transporting coal, but carried anything that could be manufactured or grown. Passengers found it a leisurely way to reach a destination, for the speed of the plodding mule teams rarely exceeded two miles an hour, and never broke the speed limit of four miles per hour.

In retrospect, life on the C & O Canal may seem glamorous, but it was neither easy

George Washington's dream of a westward passage was realized partially by the C & O Canal, and fully by the Baltimore and Ohio Railroad. Courtesy George "Hooper" Wolfe.

nor glamorous to those who spent long tedious hours tramping behind weary mules or those who were actually born on the canal boats. It was a hard life, sometimes filled with excitement, but more often a repetition of the days and weeks before. Some families lived aboard the boats, and their children were born there and raised in constant movement from one lock to another and from Cumberland to Georgetown.

Life aboard a canal boat was naturally confined to the deck or cabin of the ninety-two-foot boat. Young children were fitted with a "deck harness" and leash, and allowed to roam on top of the rear cabin deck in sight of the parent who steered the boat. Childhood was short. Most children began driving mules at the age of six or seven. There was little time for play as the boats were usually busy hauling freight from one point to another. The children felt that driving mules, walking barefoot along the dusty towpath, watching for snakes

and wildlife, meeting and passing other boats, was far better than being harnessed to the deck of the boat. Of course, during the three months that the canal was frozen over, the boats remained idle, and some of the families lived in homes. Some remained on the boats year-round.

The locks were in operation day and night. A lock tender was provided with a house and an acre of land for a garden. He would usually raise a few animals which could graze free on canal property. The lock tender was on duty twenty-four hours a day, and the cry "Lock ready! Hey-ey-ey, Lock!" while the steersman at the back gave blasts on a bugle was enough to bring a tender from his bed. When the water level had been adjusted to the direction the boat was traveling, he would signal with a lantern, and the boat would pass through the lock.

The canal was amply wide for two boats to pass and was done by simply passing the

A three-mule team on the canal in the early 1900s, driven by canal-boat owner Captain Tom McKelvey. Courtesy George "Hooper" Wolfe.

Generations of canal-boat children spent their youth walking behind the mules on the towpath. This scene is at Lock 44, about 1920. Courtesy George "Hooper" Wolfe.

Aqueduct at Williamsport, Maryland, 1905. Captain Mosby, the "Gray Ghost" of
Civil War fame, shelled and damaged the aqueduct, stopping all traffic on the canal
until repairs could be made. Courtesy George "Hooper" Wolfe.

Scenes such as this at Pinesburg, Maryland, 1920, will soon be repeated as restoration
of the canal continues and a newly built canal boat is readied for tourist travel. Courtesy George "Hooper" Wolfe.

towline over one of the boats. Walkways were built along one side of the aqueducts so there would be no need to stop or unhitch the mules, as was sometimes necessary at the overpasses.

Near Paw Paw, West Virginia, it was necessary to build a four-thousand-foot tunnel through a mountainside. It took nearly seven years to build the tunnel, working from both ends and using hand tools and black powder. The tunnel is approximately twenty-two feet wide, twenty-four feet high from the bottom of the ditch, and is still 100 per cent intact. Only one boat at a time could use the tunnel, which on some occasions precipitated difficulties. One such incident occurred in the early 1900s.

It was customary when two boats met at the tunnel for one of the boats to back off to let the other through. One day two captains, none the better for having imbibed too freely, entered the tunnel at the same time, and met near the center. Neither would back off, but demanded the right of way. Before long the tunnel was filled from both directions with boats, mules, and irritated boat captains. A fight broke out between the two captains involved. They were separated by their crews, but shortly afterward were at it again.

When time came for the evening meal, fires were lighted in the various boats. They used corn cobs for fuel, and soon the tunnel was filled with an unbearable smog. A neutral captain volunteered to go for a district supervisor, and a solution was found. Both captains were penalized, but allowed to continue working on the canal.

The C & O Canal followed a particularly scenic route. From Harpers Ferry, West Virginia, to Cumberland, Maryland, it follows opposite West Virginia's northern border, and more beautiful scenery is difficult to imagine. The canal paralleled the winding course of the Potomac River, sometimes in a wide valley with purple hills in the distance, and at other times the hills converged to form a narrow, scenic passageway for the canal, the B & O Railroad, and the river.

The C & O Canal was a major source of transportation during the Civil War. The nation's capital and the gun factories and foundries at Harpers Ferry needed the coal from the Cumberland area. A number of battles of minor importance took place along the waterway, especially in the Williamsport, Maryland, area, but a major temporary blow was struck when Captain John S. Mosby, the famous Gray Ghost of the South, shelled the aqueduct which crosses the Conococheague Creek at Williamsport. His cannon destroyed a portion of the west end of the structure, spilling the water into the creek, thus halting the transportation of needed materials for the Union cause.

An era passed with the abrupt closing of the waterway in 1924. The Baltimore and Ohio Railroad continued its service while the canal fell into disuse and serious disrepair. The United States Government purchased the canal in 1938, which includes a narrow right of way along the canal. It became a National Monument in 1960, and a National Park on January 8, 1971. Restoration of the lower division of the canal was begun by the National Park Service in 1940.

In the early 1970s the Park Service began to purchase the property between the canal and the river in an effort to restore the canal as nearly as possible to its original condition. The National Park Service has established some thirty-five campsites along the canal which are accessible via the towpath. There are also places for automobiles and campers, although the towpath as a whole is not open to motor vehicles, being reserved for hikers and cyclists. Hikers can walk the entire length of the canal, and during the warm months of the year many groups travel the old towpath, where so many years ago the thud of shod mule hoofs, the soft rustle of bare feet in summer's dust, and the call of the boat captains broke the silence to roll across the wide valleys and echo from the mountains and limestone cliffs.

Superhighways and railroads now carry on but the restoration of the canal continues. Eventually, interested persons will be able to ride on a newly built canal boat, towed behind a team of mules, and for a moment be transported back to a day when no one seemed to be in a hurry, and the world was a better place for it.

6

Westward with Lewis and Clark: The Great American Adventure

BY DON HOLM

On March 8, 1804, a detachment of U.S. soldiers of the 1st Infantry, under Lieutenant Stephen Morrell, crossed the Mississippi from Cahokia to St. Louis and marched to Government House. With them were Captain Meriwether Lewis, Morrell's friend and co-commander of the "Corps of Discovery," which was now encamped for the winter at the mouth of the Dubois, or Wood, River, opposite the Missouri.

This was a strategic moment for the young United States of America. Decades of geopolitics by the great European powers of those times, with the struggling but lusty American colonies caught in the crunch, were about to be resolved. No one fully realized it —except possibly Mr. Jefferson back in Washington—but the nation and the world would never be quite the same again.

The next day, Captain Amos Stoddard, officially representing the United States, who also was acting commissioner for the French Government, formally received transfer of Upper Louisiana from the Spanish Governor De Lassus on behalf of Napoleon. Then, on March 10, came the moment for which President Thomas Jefferson had waited, schemed, and intrigued for so long.

It was a crisp, windy spring day with the smell of damp earth and the river and wood smoke heavy in the air. Soldiers stood at parade rest. Villagers such as the powerful Chouteaus, who controlled the fur trade and commerce at this strategic *entrepôt*, lined the square. Around them mingled growing numbers of upriver Indians, come down to see the ceremonies and hopefully take presents from their new "father." There were trumpeted airs, barked commands, cadence of marching boots. Then, briskly, the French flag came down as

the halyards lowered. Captain Stoddard solemnly received transfer from himself as French representative to himself as U.S. commissioner. A brief loaded pause, a suspension of movement and sounds. More shouted commands, muskets barked, and great clouds of black powder smoke rolled up from the ranks.

Then, snapping crisply in the breeze, the seventeen-starred flag of the United States flew up the pole.

Saluting, Captain Lewis remained at at-

Meriwether Lewis. Courtesy Oregon Historical Society, Portland.

tention for the rest of the ceremonies. Relief from the tensions of the past months brought on sudden letdown and weariness. He, more than anyone else present, fully understood the historic importance of this moment. A neighbor of Jefferson's, an experienced frontier soldier, and for the past two years Mr. Jefferson's personal secretary, he was well aware of the planning, the events, and the incredible fortuitous coincidences that came into dramatic focus at these ceremonies on this day.

The continued existence of the united colonies as a nation absolutely depended upon western expansion, not just across Appalachia, but down the Ohio and Mississippi to New Orleans and seaports on the Gulf; and across the Mississippi, up the Missouri, and across the western or Shining Mountains to the Pacific or Great South Sea.

Caught in the international power struggle between England, France, and Spain, the struggling United States was hemmed in on all sides. Survival meant playing off the big powers against each other, and pushing westward trade and settlement as fast as possible. England, still smarting over defeat in the American Revolution and the loss of the colonies, wanted colonial status returned and conspired with and armed Indians and fur traders from the north to harass the frontiers. Spain, now decadent but fearing American pressures to the south and southwest, closed the port of New Orleans to American flatboat commerce and arrested anyone caught moving across the Mississippi without a license. France, under Napoleon, had grandiose ambitions, not only of recovering Canada from the British, but of taking over the entire continent. The staging area for this massive military operation was to be her Caribbean colony of Santo Domingo on the island of Haiti.

Jefferson had seen all this coming as far back as the signing of the Declaration of Independence. For years he had collected maps and scraps of information from travelers and adventurers. While Minister to France, he had continued his interest and his search for knowledge of the northwest coast and the interior of the North American continent. He had discussed various schemes for exploring from the West. He had even tried to interest George Rogers Clark, hero of the Revolution and older brother of William Clark, in leading such an expedition overland. As Secretary of

Wooden bust of Robert Livingston, Jefferson's Minister to France, who, along with James Monroe, negotiated for the purchase of the Louisiana Territory. Courtesy of the New-York Historical Society, New York City.

State, he had quietly lobbied and waited his chance. As President, his first act was to bring Captain Lewis, a trusted neighbor and brilliant officer, into his official family.

In 1800, Napoleon Bonaparte secretly forced Spain to return Louisiana to France as a prelude to his campaign to attach through America's "soft underbelly." That is, up the Mississippi, through the back door. Meanwhile, with New Orleans bottled up and no outlet for the western settlements, President Jefferson instructed his Minister to France, Robert R. Livingston, to try and negotiate with Napoleon for New Orleans, and the rumblings of insurrection in Santo Domingo under the black General Toussaint L'Ouverture, increased the urgency. Jefferson's friend James Monroe was sent to France to assist Livingston. On January 18, 1803, Jefferson sent a confidential message to Congress asking for

$2,500 to finance ostensibly a trade and literary expedition into the unknown western regions.

Napoleon at first heckled and held at arm's length the American negotiators. But when his Santo Domingo adventure cost him 50,000 lives, he realized that there would never be a French North America. To balance England's influence there, he had only one option left: place it all in the hands of the United States, where it would be more easily influenced by France.

Instead of just selling New Orleans, he offered to the startled U.S. ministers *all* of Louisiana, and for a mere $15 million—the greatest real estate bargain of all time.

Jefferson was ready. Captain Lewis and he had already been planning and preparing to explore the West in any event. The Louisiana Purchase just made it legal. The expedition, which began in secret, soon became an open secret as news of the Purchase swept across the frontier. Lewis mounted final preparations, which included many buying trips to Philadelphia, cram courses in celestial navigation, medicine, botany, geology, map-making from some of Jefferson's scientific friends, and writing to his old friend, William Clark, inviting him to share command of the expedition. At last, breaking away from Washington, he traveled to the eight-year-old government armory at Harpers Ferry to pick up arms and ammunition, including fifteen new Model 1803 rifles, which were later to become standard army issue. He also had made there the folding iron framework of what was probably America's first "kit boat." It was to be assembled in the wilderness and covered with bark or skins. He called it *The Experiment*.

He moved on to Pittsburgh, where he supervised the completion of a large keelboat and purchased two smaller pirogues.

The "keelboat" did not actually have an external keel, but was a development of the Colonial bateau-type river cargo craft. It measured fifty-five feet long, about twelve feet maximum beam, and drew three feet of water fully loaded. It was flat-bottomed, but with a pointed spoon bow and a squared-off stern so a large rudder could be hung. A single thirty-two-foot mast was carried stepped in a "tabernacle" so it could be folded down and used as a ridgepole for an awning. The square sail no doubt doubled as an awning when the boat

William Clark. Courtesy Oregon Historical Society, Portland.

was encamped or tied up. The keelboat had twenty-two oars and a great cabin aft. And later lockers were built along the gunwales for storage and so that when the lids were raised they formed breastworks for defense against attack. Swivel guns were mounted fore and aft.

The pirogues were typical flat-bottomed, planked canoe-type riverboats, but not the so-called Mackinaw boats of later river travel, which were flatiron shaped. The pirogues were identified as the red and the white boat, one with seven oars, the other six. They were taken all the way to the Great Falls and back.

In case Captain Clark could not accept the invitation, Lewis had permission to engage Lieutenant Moses Hooke in Pittsburgh as second in command. Had events turned out differently, it would have been known as the Lewis and Hooke Expedition today. But, at Pittsburgh, Lewis finally heard from Clark, who was delighted at the opportunity to join the adventure.

So, on August 30, Captain Lewis departed Pittsburgh, down the Ohio, now shrunken to its lowest level in four years. With him were eleven men, of whom seven were detached soldiers, three were young men "on trial," and one was a professional river pilot. It was hot and humid that autumn. The thermometer in the cabin often reached the high eighties. Days were filled with strenuous exertions, dragging the boats over the shallow riffles and bars and rowing through water stagnant with scum and the fallen leaves of buckeye, gum, and red sassafras. Frequent stops were made at river settlements, hiring and firing crew members, buying supplies, engaging teams of oxen from farmers. There was little time for sleep and for writing letters and making journal entries, but Lewis found occasional relaxation playing with his huge Newfoundland dog, Scannon, which he had purchased for the premium price of $20.

By the time the flotilla reached the Falls of the Ohio, where William Clark waited for him, the expedition had recruited nine tough young frontiersmen of Kentucky. When Clark came aboard, the first real military discipline began. While Lewis was the intellectual and the thinker, Clark was the better leader of men and the getter of things done. Moving on down the Ohio, they stopped at Fort Massac (called Fort Massacre by the men) and re-cruited a squad of regular Army volunteers, including some of the most dependable members of the expedition such as John Ordway and Patrick Gass.

Rounding the "Cape" at the junction of the Ohio and Mississippi, they poled, oared, and sailed upstream past Fort Kaskaskia, where the rest of the party was recruited, and on to the mouth of the Dubois River, just opposite the mouth of the Missouri, arriving on December 12. As the transfer ceremonies had not yet taken place, the party could not legally —or at least not without embarrassing incident—move across to the west side, which was still under the Spanish flag.

Captain Lewis went to St. Louis, leaving Clark to establish Camp Dubois and to begin the tough training and discipline that they hoped would whip those tough, unruly young men into an efficient military organization. Held to minimum complement because of logistics problems, the party would be on its own and facing unknown odds and uncounted enemies on its dash across to the Pacific and back. At night, in his quarters, Captain Clark doodled figures on paper. He estimated 3,050 miles to the Pacific. He was a thousand miles short—it was actually 3,958 miles. It would

The Jefferson Peace Medal—front and obverse sides. Courtesy Oregon Historical Society, Portland.

take 376 days of actual travel from Dubois to the Pacific or 562 days round-trip actual traveling time. The trip home would be an easy 186 days of traveling. The whole trip would cover nineteen months of travel or twenty-nine months of elapsed time. They would make 393 separate campsites along the route. Of the almost eight thousand miles ahead of them from the mouth of the Missouri to the Pacific and return, less that five hundred miles of it would be by land. It was to be more of a naval than an Army operation—or more properly an amphibious military expedition.

Now, March 1804, the formal transfer ceremonies were over and the urgency of the Lewis and Clark Expedition mounted daily. Lewis learned that the Spanish planned to intercept and arrest him if he moved even one mile in the direction of Santa Fe. There were rumors of the British conspiring with Sioux and Minnetares and supplying them with arms against the Americans and arranging to "buy hair." American settlers crowded the outposts along the Mississippi, waiting to spill over into the new territory. Fur brigades were being organized.

What with the training problems at Camp Dubois, there were additional supplies to get, watermen to recruit for the support team up as far as the Mandans, letters to write, personal, social, and political obligations. The rivers, especially the Missouri, were swollen and muddy, full of ice floes and debris. Lewis was needed to help Captain Stoddard, the first American provisional commander at St. Louis, get established. Clark had assisted Lewis in the inspection of surrounding military installations, and in setting up defense perimeters, and in short trips with Chouteau to placate some Indian outbreaks.

Finally, on Monday, May 14, 1804, in scattered rain showers, with a crowd of settlers in attendance, Clark ordered the swivel gun fired, and the boats shoved off at 4 P.M.

"I set out at 4 oClock to the head of the first Island in the Missourie 6 miles and incamped, on the Island rained." So Clark noted the occasion in his daybook, in his inimitable style and charming spelling.

The Great Adventure had begun.

The main party camped in the rain that first night on a small wooded island under the bluffs of St. Louis, departing the next day to breast the heavy current of the Missouri to St.

Charles, the settlement about twenty miles above, where Captain Lewis would meet him. There the villagers entertained the entire party, which included the permanent members as well as the support team of soldiers and *engages* who would handle the boats. There was much celebrating and perhaps too much whiskey and too many pretty girls, for the first of many courts-martial took place, which, to cool the ardent animal spirits of the crew, usually resulted in running the gamut or submitting to as many as a hundred lashes on the back.

These were all young men, and this was an expedition of youth bent on adventure as well as political and economic errands. The commander, Captain Lewis, was not yet thirty. His partner and second in command (although regarded by Lewis as an equal) was an old man of thirty-four. Youngest was George Shannon, then only a blue-eyed youth of nineteen. The rest of the permanent party were mostly in their twenties except John Shields, the blacksmith and gunsmith, who was an aging thirty-five. The permanent party also included Clark's black servant, York, who had been a member of the Clark family since birth and probably was about the same age as Clark.

In spite of the obstacles, it was one of the best-equipped expeditions in the history of exploration. In addition to delicate scientific and medical instruments, such as sextants, chronometers, and thermometers, there were complete kits of medical supplies put together by the most eminent physicians of the day, the finest military arms available—including one forty-shot repeating air rifle—and enough power and shot to last them to the Pacific and back with plenty to spare. The powder was packed in lead canisters, which were to be melted for shot when empty.

The expedition carried ironworking, gunsmithing, carpenter, and blacksmithing tools including an anvil. There were heaps of trade beads and gifts for the Indians, a flour mill, large supply of fishing tackle, books to read, maps, bound books of blank paper for keeping daily journals, writing paper and ink powder. There were barrels of salt pork, beef, and lyed corn, coffee, tea, lard, beans, flour, biscuits, soap, candles, wicks, cornmeal, molasses, whiskey, and 193 pounds of "portable soup" obtained from a cook, François Baillet at 21 North Ninth in Philadelphia, for which he was paid $289.50.

Branding iron of Meriwether Lewis. Courtesy Oregon Historical Society, Portland.

The staples were not to be used, of course, as long as there was fresh game to be killed, wild greens, fruits, and berries to be picked. The expedition's hunters were experts. Besides the 12,000 pounds of food brought along, they killed about 3,000 deer, 800 elk, 600 buffalo, 3 antelope, tons of waterfowl, fish by the hundreds, plus many bear, cougar, bighorn sheep, squirrels, beaver, badgers, and prairie dogs.

They also consumed wild berries and fruits, Indian corn, squash, watermelon, pumpkin, herbs and roots, coyote, wolf, and dog meat, horse meat, whale blubber, and even mushrooms, a food then unknown in the American diet and, fortunately for history, in this case only nontoxic varieties were sampled.

Although the captains avoided mentioning it in their journals, some of the men carried traps and caught beaver, which were as good as money on the frontier. Some of the men, especially Goodrich, were anglers and fished almost every day for both food and sport. Records of expedition purchases list among other things, hooks, jigs, and a sportsman's "flaske" and eight "stave reels" from the Old Experienced Tackle Shoppe at No. 32 Great Dock Street in Philadelphia.

In addition to being the hunting-est and fishing-est, the expedition was also the writing-est crew in the history of exploration. Besides the two captains, seven of the men kept journals, of which four survived. One, that of Ser-

geant John Ordway, is the only one extant that records the occurrences for every day of the trip.

The Missouri, even at the time of the Lewis and Clark Expedition, was a busy waterway of commerce and fur trade with the interior Indian tribes, at least up to the mouth of the Platte, which was regarded as the "Equator" beyond which a party took its chances. The corps met coming downstream, with the winter's haul of furs, dozens of dugouts and rafts manned by half-wild traders and trappers. Many of these were married to Indian women or had strong connections with some of the tribes. Lewis and Clark stopped them all and picked their minds for scraps of information, while encouraging them with a dram or two of whiskey.

Going upriver, the expedition endured unbelievable hardships. Usually they labored from daylight to dark on the oars, or if they were lucky they had the help of the sails. This was broken by frequent interludes when they had to wade ahead alongshore or in shallow water, often up to the armpits, hauling on the cordelles like beasts of burden. As the summer advanced, the sun became hotter and the mosquitoes thicker. Clouds of gnats tormented them. They had many close calls with rattlesnakes. They had only the muddy river water to quench their thirst, and this, along with exhaustion, brought on spells of dysentery and rashes of painful boils. On the water there were many hazards, such as sawyers which could spear a boat, or sandbars where a boat could turn sideways and broach. Great chunks of dirt caved in along shore. Channels changed overnight.

The lucky ones were the hunters, who ranged onshore with the horses, charged with killing game and bringing it down to the night camps. The captains often walked onshore to stretch their legs or to explore. Watch was always kept for Indians. At night camps were made on sandbars or islands if possible, and a regular guard mounted among the tired men. But they ate well and even had a little entertainment in the form of Crusatte and his fiddle, and dancing by the light of the driftwood fires.

High points of the cruel days and weeks they battled up the Missouri stand out in the journals—the first antelope brought in, the first buffalo shot and the sumptious dining on humps, the day more than five hundred fish were seined by Goodrich and others from one creek, the picking of tart and juicy wild plums, meeting a trader, sighting some Indians.

Literally foot by foot they fought their way up the river, past the Platte, into the dangerous territory, holding councils with all the tribes they met, passing the word about their new Father in Washington. The first of these councils was held August 3, just above the site of present-day Omaha. On August 20, Sergeant Charles Floyd died of a burst appendix. Patrick Gass was appointed to replace him. In September they ran the gamut of those warlike brigands of the woods who had moved west to terrorize the plains—the Sioux. The Sioux had taken over the middle section of the Missouri and either harassed or demanded tribute from all who passed.

The confrontation with the Sioux came in late September and the expedition's courage, boldness, and diplomacy got its supreme test. The captains refused to be intimidated, although the slightest flicker of weakness or hesitation could have resulted in a massacre of the little band by the overwhelming hoards of Sioux. The captains at the same time knew when to be conciliatory and spread some presents around in the right places. Both Lewis and Clark were old Indian fighters and knew how to read the signs. Besides they had such backup as George Drouillard, himself part Indian, a dead shot and a fearless fighter, as well as interpreter. They had four swivel guns all loaded and manned. They had the latest weapons from Harpers Ferry arsenal, they had men behind the lockers in the keelboat and deployed elsewhere. Had the Sioux attacked, there would have been a lot of wailing squaws in the camps that night—and the Sioux knew it. The expedition passed on in peace.

In late November, the expedition went into winter quarters among the Mandan villages at the Big Bend of the Missouri in what is now central North Dakota. Here they built a stockade with huts, named it Fort Mandan, and manned it like a military post as they prepared for the long hard winter. Here they found the young Indian girl Sacagawea, who had been captured years before from the western Shoshoni and who could help the expedition when they got to her homeland. To take her, they also had to take her master, the Falstaffian character Toussaint Charbonneau, a half-breed trader who lived among the Mandans.

At Fort Mandan the expedition was now 1,609 miles from their last winter quarters at Camp Dubois. It was to be a hard winter, when the temperatures dropped to forty below zero and game became scarce. But it was to be a busy winter. Not only was there the constant need for hunting, ranging out as far as fifty miles, but of defensive action against Sioux war parties, and preparations for the next phase of the journey in the spring. The captains had journals to copy, reports and letters to write, flora and fauna specimens to classify and pack for shipment home. They had politicking to do among the villages, information to gather, British intrigue from the trading posts in Canada to counteract, parties to attend and give. Christmas and New Year's were observed with special celebrations, the blowing of "sounden horns" and the special rations of rum and tobacco.

In early spring, when the ice began to break up, the keelboat was loaded for the return trip to St. Louis under command of Corporal Richard Worthington. He would take with him the temporary detachment of soldiers and the hired engages. Lewis had some of the men build cages to hold the live birds and small animals being sent back to Jefferson. The returning party would also take along an Arikara chief and his party to meet the President in Washington.

The permanent party, going upstream, shoved off at the same time, on April 7, 1805, in the two pirogues and six dugout canoes that had been hacked out of cottonwood trees. The expedition now numbered twenty-nine soldiers and officers, Charbonneau and Sacagawea and their two-month-old son, Baptiste, or Little Pomp; York, Clark's black servant; and Lewis's dog, Scannon.

The expedition moved up the Missouri, past the mouth of the Yellowstone, to the Great Falls during the spring runoff. They saw the plains come alive with grasses and wildflowers, and witnessed herds of antelope, elk, and deer, and of buffalo so numerous they sometimes took days to pass. They encountered the ferocious grizzly bear for the first time. At the Great Falls they had to make an eighteen-mile land traverse around the cascades. This was done by building wagons, with wheels made from rings of cottonwood trees.

Sacagawea with Lewis and Clark. Painting by L. Fred Russell. Courtesy Missouri Historical Society.

The wagons were also fitted with sails to take advantage of whatever wind came behind them.

Above the falls, Lewis had the men assemble the iron frame of his portable boat, *The Experiment*, which he had brought all the way from Harpers Ferry, and covered with elk hides. It sank when first loaded and launched and had to be abandoned.

The party continued through the Gates of the Mountains to the three forks near the present Bozeman. Had they taken Clark's Fork, which flows westward through the mountains to Pend Oreille Lake and thence via the Kootenay to the Columbia, they could have traveled the entire distance to the Pacific on water. But the captains had their minds fixed on finding the Shoshonis and buying horses. Taking the westernmost fork of the Missouri, they moved on up to the Continental Divide as far as they could, then cached the canoes and supplies they could not carry. By another of their many happy coincidences, they not only made contact soon after with the Shoshonis, but came upon a party that included Sacagawea's brother, Chief Cameawait. After a joyous reunion, horses and guides were obtained.

Crossing the Bitterroots to the Clearwater was a terrible ordeal and a race against approaching winter. Of all the hardships of the journey so far, this was the worst. But they made it and met up with the Nez Perce, who welcomed them, took charge of their horses, and served as guides for the next phase. The party made more dugout canoes on the Clearwater, then paddled down to the Snake, at the present site of Clarkston, Washington, and Lewiston, Idaho, and thence down the Snake to the Columbia, near the present Pasco, Washington. Here they met more friendly Indians, and continued on down the great Columbia River—the long-sought goal of President Jefferson. At the Dalles, they came upon one of the two great aborigine *entrepôts* on

William Clark's signature as carved on the side of Pompy's Pillar, near Billings, Montana. Courtesy Stella Foote Collection.

the Columbia, and found the Indians catching salmon and preserving the pounded and dried flesh for trade and winter use.

The downriver dash was fast, passing many villages of river Indians, through the great gorge of the Cascades, then the lush green western valleys, the Coast Range, and finally the island and slough maze of the lower Columbia, with its many permanent Indian towns and mild moist marine climate.

On November 7, they camped onshore, clinging to the wet steep cliff on the north side of the Columbia just opposite Pillar Rock, and Captain Clark was able to write in his rain-sodden notebook, "O the Joy! Ocian in sight!"

It was still twenty miles to the ocean, and many historians have disputed this statement, but most such detractors have never seen Pillar Rock, which today is a remote navigational marker. In Clark's day, there were no jetties on Clatsop Spit and the channels of the lower river were considerably different. With a typical winter sea breaking at the mouth of the Columbia, it would, indeed, be possible to see the surf from as far up as Pillar Rock.

After more hardships and some tense meetings with Indians, they selected a site on a sheltered river that emptied into the great bay of the Columbia on the south side. They built a stockade of logs, with storerooms, barracks, and quarters, and called it Fort Clatsop. It was finished in time for the Christmas celebration, 1805, the first American military post on the West Coast.

During the winter, friendly relations were maintained with the Clatsop Indians (who nevertheless failed to inform the captains that at least one ship had called 'at the mouth of the Columbia while they were there). A saltworks was established about twelve miles south on the estuary of the Necanicum River in what is now Seaside, Oregon. The captains spent the winter composing detailed descriptions of flora and fauna, of local Indians and their customs, catching up on journal entries, and making short trips to the ocean and the villages.

On March 19, 1806, the last elk hunting party returned, and the captains gave Chief Comowool a certificate of good conduct and a list of names of the party for the benefit of any ships that came in later. After a hard rain shower mixed with snow and hail, they completed packing for the homeward trip. The guns were repaired, the last of the meat stowed, and at 1 P.M. on March 23 the canoes shoved off. It was still early spring and the weather terrible. They made slow progress moving up the swollen Columbia. They suffered great hardships and even starvation getting across from the Columbia to the Nez Perce villages where they found their horses waiting for them as promised.

Again they had to struggle to get over the Bitterroot Mountains, making two starts before they succeeded in crossing Lolo Pass to Traveler's Rest on the Bitterroot River. It was the first of July before they put the Bitterroots behind them for good.

The corps was then split up for the next stage. Captain Clark and the main party would head south for the canoe cache, then cross over to the Yellowstone and go down that river to the junction with the Missouri. The others would head for the cache at the head of the Great Falls. There, Captain Lewis, with a small detachment of picked men, would take the horses and explore the headwaters of Marias River, the idea being to push the U.S. claims as far north as possible to head off the British. A detachment under Sergeant Ordway would take the canoes down the Missouri to the Great Falls, make the land traverse to the cache below the Great Falls, where the pirogues were hidden. If they failed to rendezvous with Captain Lewis, they would continue down to the mouth of the Yellowstone.

On July 17, Lewis set out on horseback

Pillar Rock, in the Columbia River, where Captain Clark first sighted the Pacific Ocean. Photo by Don Holm.

from the upper caches at the Great Falls, crossed over to the Marias, and rode up that river. On July 27, in an affray with a small party of Blackfeet Indians, they killed two, and drove the others off. Fearing reprisals, Captain Lewis and his party rode hard for the next sixty-five miles southeastward before stopping for a rest. Then they mounted up and rode another seventeen miles, stopping for two

hours more. On July 28, as they approached the Missouri, Captain Lewis heard shots. It was the Ordway party coming downriver. Another lucky coincidence.

The rendezvous at the Yellowstone was made in due course. Captain Lewis, during a hunt, was accidentally shot in the fleshy part of his rump by one-eyed Cruzatte, a painful injury that bothered him the rest of the way.

Lewis and Clark's saltworks, on seacoast, twelve miles from Fort Clatsop. Courtesy Oregon Historical Society, Portland.

In early August, the corps met coming upriver two intrepid Yankee trappers, Forrest Handcock and Joseph Dickson from Illinois. These were the first trappers to pass the Mandan villages after Lewis and Clark—and it was a miracle they had survived the Sioux and Arikara. Handcock was known to one of the expedition, John Colter, from his years under Simon Kenton. Handcock had moved west with Daniel Boone in 1799 and settled first at Boone's Lick. The two trappers went back down to Mandan villages with the expedition, and there Colter obtained permission to leave the party and join them in a trapping adventure up the Yellowstone. Colter remained in the Rockies until 1811, to become America's first Mountain Man, and the discoverer of the area that is now Yellowstone National Park and the Grand Tetons of Jackson Hole. Wrote Clark of this:

John Colter left early to go back up the Missouri with his new-found friends. The exam-

ple of this man shows how easily man can be weaned from the habits of civilized life to the ruder, but scarcely less fascinating life and manners of the wilds. Colter had been absent for over two years from the frontiers, and might naturally be presumed to have some anxiety or curiosity at least, to return to his friends and country; yet, at the moment when he is approaching the frontiers, he was tempted by a hunting scheme to give up those delightful prospects, and go back without the least reluctance to the solitude of the woods.

On August 17 the expedition shoved off for the final leg of the return trip, taking along one of the Mandan chiefs, Sahaka, who wished to visit the Great Chief in Washington.

On September 22, 1806, the party reach Fort Bellefountaine and were received by Colonel Thomas Hunt and Lieutenant George Peter with a seventeen-gun salute. The party quartered here for the night. The next day the party rose early and took the Mandan chief to the public store to buy him some civilized clothes. After breakfast they descended the river and landed at Camp Dubois, their starting point. Then they crossed back over the Mississippi to St. Louis, arriving at noon, with all the men firing their guns with joyous abandon.

The boats were unloaded and the baggage taken to storerooms. The captains accepted an invitation to stay at the home of Pierre Chouteau. The rest of the party were boarded around town while arrangements were made for discharges, final pay, and other business.

On September 24 the captains arose and began writing letters to the President, George Rogers Clark, General William H. Harrison, and to Charbonneau, whom they had left with the Mandans. Drouillard took the first of the letters going east across the river to Cahokia, where the post had been detained to await them. After dinner the captains went to the store to purchase goods and engage a tailor to make them suitable clothes.

The Great Adventure was over. Now would come the honors, the official receptions, the promotions, the notoriety.

But even before the party returned, news of the successful mission had spread to every state and territory and even to Europe. It excited the minds and passions and spirit of people everywhere—and especially the youth looking for challenge and purpose in life. The expedition had been one of those classic human endeavors that seems to strike a response in everyone. It was the landing of the *Eagle* on the Moon, 1806 version. It had all the elements of drama, suspense, adventure, danger, humor, pathos, tragedy, exotic spice. It was a great drama of motion, of fulfilling great expectations. *Wanderjahr!*

It was also the young America's first great epic national adventure. It was an uncommonly unique and successful military effort, accomplished with a handful of personnel on a shoestring budget (about $30,000 was actually spent). It was one of the best-organized, planned, and executed military missions of all time, and astonishing in that it had not one commander but in actual practice two of equal rank.

The mission was carried out with almost flawless precision and good judgment, losing only one man and that to an unavoidable illness. The party itself was a heterogeneous cross section of rough and ready frontier America, and included not only a black servant but an Indian women with a baby in arms, and a Newfoundland dog.

As a scientific expedition, the captains added about 160 new species of flora and fauna to the textbooks. They compiled dictionaries of Indian languages. They made celestial observations to pinpoint key geographic locations for later maps. They recorded weather phenomena.

Politically, the expedition tied the nation together between two oceans, and more than doubled its size. It linked the claims of Captain Robert Gray, who discovered the mouth of the Columbia in May 1792, to the Louisiana Purchase in 1803. It drove a wedge between the encroaching forces of the Spanish to the south and the British on the north. It touched off the great fur-trade era in the Rocky Mountains, and the later cattle-raising and mining and agricultural endeavors.

After it, there was no stopping the westward flood. Manifest Destiny became its name.

7

The Erie Canal

BY PHOEBE AND TODHUNTER BALLARD

His enemies, and he had many in the corrupt but dominant New York Regency that ruled the state, derisively called it Clinton's Ditch, fought it with laughter and legislative maneuvering for most of the eight years it took to pull it to completion. But DeWitt Clinton was never a personage to let harassment stop him. As boss of early New York's Tammany Hall, Clinton looked enviously at the thriving ports of Philadelphia and Baltimore, where all westbound freighting and immigration was unloaded from ships to begin the journey overland. He looked at Boston, the goods and people flowing from there throughout the northeastern region. He saw those ports growing richer and more powerful while his city lagged. He listened to the siren song of James Platt that a canal along the Mohawk River would be a fine campaign issue. And he dreamed his dream.

The Mohawk is the only water-level pass through the Appalachian mountain chain from the St. Lawrence to Alabama and east to west traffic was confined to a few primitive pathways. The people around Buffalo and the Great Lakes were increasingly dealing with Canada, which they could reach more easily than they could the lower United States, and fear was growing that all that territory could well be lost back to the northern neighbor. Only the very wealthy could afford the comparatively comfortable move westward up the Hudson to the St. Lawrence and thence west.

New York's harbor was excellent. As far as it went. The broad Hudson River stretched up its lovely valley between the barricading Catskills and Berkshires, navigable as far as Albany, and west from there the Mohawk followed its valley at the foot of the Adirondacks, slicing the state in half all the way to the

Great Lakes, which already carried heavy water traffic. But there was no continuum between the rivers. Ships could sail north to Albany, where they had to be unloaded and what they carried transshipped by wagon both north and west. Yet nature provided an ideal system that only needed connecting. The Hudson north, using Lake Champlain and its tributaries, could open the entire state to the Canadian border. The Hudson using the Mohawk could give access to the whole Midwest and beyond. Tied into the Lakes the waters could join the Mississippi, the Missouri, and at a single stroke make of New York City the finest and cheapest supply point for a great part of the continent. It was a heady concept. With such a combined water route New York could not avoid becoming the jewel of the eastern seaboard. DeWitt Clinton dreamed and plotted, connived and pushed. And kept at it against all odds.

Who was he? On his father's side he descended from a long line of Englishmen who had spent generations in Ireland to be qualified as Irish. His mother's side was Dutch, giving DeWitt entrée to the old patroon families of the Hudson Valley.

His political career began as secretary to his uncle George Clinton, then New York's governor, where DeWitt studied law. He was instrumental in organizing Tammany Hall, its ward healers, and hatchet men. As it burgeoned, opportunity offered and the Hall saw to it that DeWitt was elected mayor of New York, a powerful post. In that capacity he improved schools and initiated a number of polical reforms on one hand. On the other he introduced the spoils system that would lead to a long era of outrageous corruption. It was DeWitt who conceived the plan by which the

DeWitt Clinton. Courtesy of the New-York Historical Society, New York City.

Witt performed the legerdemain of becoming a senator while keeping his mayoralty position. From that vantage point he presented a memorandum to Congress asking that the national government assume the cost of constructing an Erie Canal. He met with a howl of protest led by Pennsylvania, Maryland, and Massachusetts as those states became terrified of a draining off of their ports' importance in moving goods inland. Still bitterly jealous of each other, they objected to the nation being forced to foot a bill that would benefit only New York.

Clinton pulled in his head there but he had no idea of abandoning his dream. Yet there was another stumbling block to going ahead in any other direction. The country had surveyors aplenty but there were no American hydraulic engineers able to design his ditch. Quietly, from his own pocket, DeWitt hired surveyors to seek out the best route by utilizing all the existing streams and lakes in his proposed paths. He also sent James Geddes and Benjamin Wright to England and Europe to study the old canals there and bring back plans.

When those results were in his hands he approached the New York State legislature asking that the state issue bonds to cover construction costs, bonds to be redeemed by tolls the canals would collect from all who used them. Again he met rejection from jealous and short-sighted politicians. The legislature, one of the most corrupt in the country, was under the thumb of the Regency, which in turn was controlled by Martin Van Buren and William Marcy, both old enemies of Clinton. Albany, the transshipment center for freighters who supplied the western counties, and the southern counties bordering Pennsylvania, rose in wrath. The proposed bond issue never got out of committee.

The stubborn Dutch strain in Clinton was equal to the challenge. Using his power base in New York City as a springboard, he ran for governor. Tammany Hall voted every man on its roles and every gravestone in the cemeteries. It helped that DeWitt had friends in high influential places. Gouverneur Morris, whose family was reported to be one of the wealthiest in the world, backed him. So did Jesse Hawley, an upstate newspaperman who wrote under the pen name Hercules in the Geneseo *Messenger*. In 1807 and 1808 he, rec-

city's block leaders and precinct captains, backed by the Irish police force, met the immigrant ships, marched the new arrivals to the nearest saloon for whiskey and lectures on the necessity of voting "right," then found them homes and jobs and froze them into the party.

Clinton loved his city but not entirely altruistically. He wanted to make it a metropolis outshining all others, and to that end he must have his ditch. From the time of the Revolution a web of canals had grown across the country as the most efficient paths by which to move large masses and weights of materials necessary to a rapidly industrializing nation. But Clinton's proposal was the most breathtaking yet, demanding almost four hundred miles of engineering and construction along the Mohawk where the natural water level dropped more than five hundred feet from its source at the Great Lakes to its junction with the Hudson. A second, less arduous link must be the Champlain route, each through very sparsely settled territory from which no immediate great income should be expected.

At that time United States senators were appointed by their state legislatures. With Tammany's growing power behind him, De-

ognizing the enormous benefit that Clinton's dream canal would bring to the whole area, argued the case eloquently in the press and mobilized all the representatives of the upper counties to work for Clinton's election. In spite of the Regency they won.

Clinton had also turned to General Philip Schuyler, one of the best-known and respected men of upper New York who held immense tracts of land both around Saratoga and in New Hampshire, and others in Ohio. During the Revolution, Schuyler had headed the Northern Command and, though he quarreled with everyone from Washington to Gates, he was loved as a war hero in the northern reaches. Harping on the great increase of revenues to be expected from his holdings, Clinton inspired him to form the Western Inland Navigation Company. As one result in 1796 Western Navigation wrung a token $15,000 from the legislature for a beginning.

But names, tokens, intentions were not enough. Sufficient ferment in favor of the canal had been generated to make it a popular issue, but Clinton was politician enough to know that if it languished like other proposals for any time the interest would dissolve. Some action was needed immediately, a start made that people could see. While he had the momentum he used the money to dredge and straighten a short section of the Mohawk itself. While nothing was built, the work did permit boats of sixteen tons weight to float from Schenectady to Seneca Falls for the first time.

The final route of the canal as surveyed used very little of the river proper, the surveyors disdaining the serpentine course of the channel. They laid out a straighter, shorter course, but before anything more could be done the War of 1812 interrupted and everything came to a halt until 1817.

Through those years factional arguments pulled one way and another. Clinton wanted the first main push to go east and west, but now that the canal loomed as a reality to be, one large segment of the legislature insisted that the Lake Champlain branch have a priority. Politics being the art of compromise, Clinton bowed and agreed that both channels should be built concurrently.

Another northern group was adamant that the canal stop at Irondequoit on Lake Ontario instead of continuing on the miles to Erie,

though this would have placed the lake connection east of Niagara Falls and defeated the purpose of opening Ohio and the western territories. Clinton held fast and won that round. His canal would push west from Albany to Lockport, thence south to Buffalo and an Erie basin lake terminal.

By abandoning the existing waterways, long overland cuts through high ground became necessary, as did much fill to cross gorges. The vast Montezuma Swamp must be bisected through its treacherous center. And locks were needed between Erie's level and that at the Hudson River—eighty-three in a distance of 363 miles.

Clinton's "Memorial," his final report on March 8, 1816, of what it all should cost, in millions, won him a grudging allotment of an extra $20,000. With that he had to be content for the time being. Then in 1817 the legislature opened the purse and voted him $7 million.

When the dust of infighting settled and work got under way for real, the great undertaking was divided into sections, each the responsibility of a different man and all of them under the Canal Commission appointed by DeWitt Clinton, himself the presiding member. The Buffalo segment and the lake terminus were entrusted to William Peacock. The canal from there east to the Seneca River would be built by James Geddes. From Seneca to Rome, Benjamin Wright would direct, between Rome and the Hudson, Charles C. Broadhead. The Champlain division was given to Colonel G. Lewis Garin, but we will not include that project here.

For the sake of showing immediate progress to keep enthusiasm high the digging was begun at Rome, where it was easiest, working both east and west through a sixty-nine-and-a-half-mile-long level. There would be a second Long Level of sixty-five miles around Rochester. The rest of the way was complex and none of the section heads were truly engineers. They learned as they went, and remarkably well, with Yankee ingenuity at its best.

West of Lockport, above Buffalo, the Lockport Five, a staircase of lock combines, must drop over the awesome Niagara Escarpment to permit traffic to descend from the Lake Erie water level to the next lower. With tumble bays to sluice excess water around the locks, the combines let down into the Deep

A typical quarry scene. Cutting Trenton limestone for use in constructing locks and aqueducts. Courtesy Fort Hunter Canal Society.

Cut, two long miles of canal to be hacked through solid rock with black powder and picks, an excavation of 1,477,700 cubic yards of the stubborn stone.

That project and another at the eastern end marked the coming of age of American engineering. In the fifteen miles around Albany to Schenectady twenty-seven more sets of locks must carry boats around the raging Cohoes Falls.

Between those extremes other inventiveness was needed. At Rochester the intersecting Genesee River must be spanned. An aqueduct was built atop a seventy-foot-high embankment, supported by nine Roman arches spanning the Irondequoit Valley for a stretch of 804 feet, the longest in America. The Mohawk itself was bridged by two other mighty aqueducts and wild Schoharie Creek crossed by a dam.

At Medina, between Casport and Albion,

the canal was to be crossed by a road running beneath the water. These and other spans were to allow farmers to move from one bank to the other. Overhead passages were also constructed but they were built so low that deck passengers had to bend double in their seats to avoid cracking their heads. Whence the old cry, "Low bridge, everybody down."

Then there needed to be feeders at the streams to open and close for keeping constant the water level of the main channel, and waste weirs to drain off excess flow when rains swelled the creeks. And side cuts, lateral boat connections such as the one at Little Falls where the highest single drop, forty and a half feet, was by-passed around the falls and traffic floated through the village itself.

Almost all this labor was performed by Irish recruited by Tammany Hall in New York, men fresh off the immigrant ships. Wages were four shillings and found plus the

The remaining section of the Schoharie Aqueduct built by Otis Eddy in 1841. Courtesy Fort Hunter Canal Society.

The north side of the Schoharie Aqueduct in an early stage of construction. Timber-faced sloping abutments prevented ice damage in winter. The temporary wooden trough carried canal boats over the creek. 1841. Courtesy Fort Hunter Canal Society.

Three-mule hitch towing east over the Scho-harie Aqueduct. Courtesy Fort Hunter Canal Society.

Jigger Boss, a half gill of whiskey for each man sixteen times a day.

They earned it. The Montezuma Swamp was a pestilential horror of snakes, mosquitoes, punkies, black flies, stinking mud, and a miasmic fever much like malaria. Untold thousands died there, while others perished in various construction accidents and still more lost their lives as new predatory communities grew along the channel. The watervliet side cut at the eastern terminus was the pay-off point and became a little Barbary Coast, with twenty-nine saloons in a two-block area. Its brawling accounted for a body a week dumped into the canal. Miraculously, the work advanced. Blasting, digging, filling, they punched through, without so much as a road to transport their materials until they made a corduroy one themselves.

They did not use Clinton's river and lake system but went up the hillside and made a land-cut channel, piling all they took out on the downward side, building up an embankment with a level towpath on top. Uphill they graded a heelpath on the berm and at crossovers they built cloverleafs much as are used on present-day highways to enable the tow teams to move from bank to bank. Craft heading in opposite directions could pass either by using the bridges or by the one heading downstream dropping its towrope slack, letting it sink, and the opposite boat riding over it.

Traffic did not wait upon completion. On October 22, 1819, when the first section opened, that between Rome and Utica, the chief engineer made the initial run in a record four hours. Behind him a flotilla crowded in like ducklings.

Grandest of all the canal craft were the packets, sixty to seventy feet long by eight wide, carrying passengers, mail, special freight, and perishables. Next in size and comfort were the corporation-owned Line Boats, also used in hauling both passengers and freight. Then came pure freighters, shanty houseboats, and the trouble-shooting Hurry-up Boats that rushed from point to point repairing breaches in the berm or towpaths and dragging off the "mudlarks," any craft that grounded. Probably, too, some experimented with the clumsy but capacious Durham Boats that had long been poled on the river, but they were not large enough to be practical on the canal.

Forty feet wide at the top, twenty-eight at the bottom, and four feet deep, the channel could soon almost be walked across from boat to boat. As the sections lengthened and the locks multiplied, the surface was further jammed by "squeezers," two-section freighters roped together, and "hoodledashers," long strings of empties towed in tandem. These caused great delays at the locks, where they must be broken up and sent through singly. So too the log booms, unwieldy rafts of timber being floated to sawmills, which had to be cast free, sluiced down, then regrouped into cribs below.

All of these created hazards to boatmen and headaches to lockkeeps, and a bitter enmity grew between them. Besides their houses at the locks the tenders kept stores, some very large, where rivermen could shop while they waited for clearance through the narrow passages, a captive market because of the distance in most places from the canal to the towns.

Then in the middle of construction Governor DeWitt Clinton committed a cardinal political sin. He did not watch his back. So much involved with orchestrating his ditch, he was finding less and less time for administration and did not stand for the office at the next election. To his shock the new governor cut his throat, removed him from the Canal Commission, and left him in limbo.

But by then the work was so far along, the impetus so strong, that his enemies did not dare try to stop it. Two years later Clinton corrected his mistake, ran for governor again, was elected by the overwhelming majority of forty

An early packet approaching a crossover. Courtesy Fort Hunter Canal Society.

A freighter going through Lock 30, Tribes Hill. Brown's store is on the right. Courtesy Fort Hunter Canal Society.

to one, and reinstated himself as head of the commission.

And at last the cliff hanging was over. The canal was finished, its full length opened on October 25 in 1825 with close to a five-hundred-mile-long celebration. Sallying forth from Erie Basin, the *Seneca Chief* packet led a boat parade that must have stretched from the Erie to the Hudson and on to New York Harbor. Carrying symbolic containers of water from around the world, laden with state and national dignitaries, DeWitt Clinton on the prow, the boat slid majestically past the first signal cannon, towed by a prize team that the champion driver, the hogee, on the canal did his best to control. It could not have been easy when the cannon boomed its announcement.

Like a noisy telegraph, the second gun to the east, placed within hearing distance of the first, sounded off. On down the long waterway they followed one another, rattling to Albany, then along the Hudson. Within eighty minutes New York City had the long-awaited word. Clinton was on his way.

At the legal speed of four miles an hour it was an awesome, triumphal procession. Without stops Albany could be reached under six days, but on this inaugural there were festivities all along the way. Buffalo had begun them. Then Lockport, Brockport, Rochester, Bushnel Basin, Palmyra, Lyons, the Montezuma Swamp, Weedsport, Cassirs Corners, which later became Syracuse, Oneida, Rome. And from Rome to Utica, Herkimer, Little Falls, Canajoharie, Alexander's Mills, Fonda's Ferry, Agusla Aqueduct, Cohoes, Waterford, where all freight exited the canal, and finally Troy and Albany. Only Schenectady played dog in the manger. The Durham Boats were built there, the town depended on that industry, and they saw it doomed in favor of the long barges that carried so much more. Schenectady held a mock funeral when the *Seneca Chief* hove to.

With more whiskey flowing than Erie water, it is doubtful that anyone aboard still had the energy to be aware when the lead packet stepped regally down the last sixteen locks from the Mohawk into the Hudson. Reaching New York at last, the grand finale was celebrated as the "Wedding of the Waters," when the symbolic water casks were emptied into the harbor to mingle with the Atlantic and presage the Empire State.

The Erie Canal gave credibility to the boast. In the years it had paid the indebtedness and it earned high profits until in 1882 the politicians blushed and discontinued the collection of tolls. The Erie was a free ride from then on.

She was a way of life, her "canawlers" a subculture unto themselves. Eyed askance as were Gypsies, they were preyed on by the landsmen, and the boaters paid back in kind. Particular targets were the lock tenders. The traffic rules were set by the commission, a leisurely four miles an hour that could be maintained by the mule and horse teams that towed the craft along the channel, but it was irksomely slow when compounded by jam-ups at the locks. Boats going downstream, west to east, had the right of way. The lockkeepers could speed a craft through or hinder it, sending it into a swirl of current where it could collide with another boat or against the buttress of the lock. Alternating boats with the loggers' cribs, timbers chained together in a rectangle that could navigate the locks, traffic could be indefinitely delayed for those toward whom the keepers held grudges. In retaliation ingenious ways were found to circumvent the payment of tolls. "Shunpiling," the boatmen called it.

The "boaters" season lasted about eight months, until the water froze, the canal was drained, and craft sat out the winter on the bottom. Boating families lived aboard in cabins, sent their children to school ashore, and paid no taxes, further disenchanting the propertied citizens. The single "trippers," who spent the summers on long hauls the full length of the canal, found it expedient when cold weather came to choose a town, go on a riotous drunk, and spend a comfortable winter in some warm jail at town or county expense. Herkimer solved that nuisance by moving its jail nine miles inland, a far piece for shanks' mare. The unmarried captain of a line boat or packet, whose tour was called a "trick," made do with a bunk in his "cuddy" quarters. Smaller craft owned and skippered by individuals with wives or cooks aboard flew such penants on lines strung above decks as trousers, skirts, long johns, bright and drab. And craft that passed each other in friendly manner in summer hailed across the water their best wishes with "Full freightings, Captain."

"Prog," was served on all boats; a sample

The Yankee Hill Lock 28 with its store on the right. Courtesy Fort Hunter Canal So-ciety.

1976 aerial view of Yankee Hill Lock 28, being restored by the New York State De-partment of Parks and Recreation. The Mohawk River, today's canal, is on the right. Courtesy Fort Hunter Canal Society.

Passengers enjoying the top deck of an 1825 packet boat on the Erie Canal. Courtesy Fort Hunter Canal Society.

Changing mule teams. Courtesy Fort Hunter Canal Society.

breakfast on a packet might be coffee, pork, pickled gherkins, "pritties," which were potatoes baked or boiled, eggs, fresh-made bread with butter and cheese from the Herkimer County dairies. For the less pretentious there was "black pork," cured similar to jerky, and "skimmagig," buttermilk.

The "roaring gidap" they called her. With the spring breakup the first out was the "fog gang," its duty to clean the canal of debris floating or sunk where it could snag bottoms, and for them the old "jigger boss," still sixteen half gills a day, became "fog jigger boss."

Ashore the runners were busy drumming up packet trade, and the "scalpers," or cargo agents, were out in force. Then the "foo-foos" swarmed in, foreigners heading west in search

ROCHESTER
AND
ALBANY.

Red Bird Line of Packets,
In connection with Rail Road from Niagara
Falls to Lockport.

1843.  **1843.**

12 hours ahead of the Lake Ontario Route!

The Cars leave the Falls every day at 2 o'clock, P. M. for
Lockport, where passengers will take one of the following new

Packet Boats 100 Feet Long.

THE EMPIRE!
Capt. D. H. Bromley,

THE ROCHESTER
Capt. J. H. Warren,

and arrive in Rochester the next morning at 6 o'clock, and can
take the 8 o'clock train of Cars or Packet Boats for Syracuse and
Albany, and arrive in Albany the same night.

☞ Passengers by this route will pass through a delightful country, and
will have an opportunity of viewing Queenston Heights, Brock's Monument,
the Tuscarora Indian Village, the combined Locks at Lockport, 3 hours at
Rochester, and pass through the delightful country from Rochester to Utica
by daylight.

N. B.---These two new Packets are 100 feet long, and are built
on an entire new plan, with

Ladies' & Gentlemen's Saloons,
and with Ventilators in the decks, and for room and accommoda
tions for sleeping they surpass any thing ever put on the Canal.

For Passage apply at Railroad and Packet Office, Niagara Falls.

September, 1843.
T. CLARK,
J. J. STATIA, } Agents

*A typical advertisement for canal transporta-
tion in the 1840s. Courtesy Fort Hunter Canal
Society.*

of new homes. Many of the Irish who had
built the "ditch" took up land along the banks
and new towns sprouted. Besides the import
and export cargoes there developed a vast
traffic in local produce and animals from the
fertile, productive valley itself.

In the boaters' watery isolation their jar-
gon multiplied and further separated them
from the shore folk. Canal scrip backed by the
commission was readily accepted, but "red
dog" notes, worthless or suspect bank notes,
were refused. "Rhino," cash, was fine and "fat
rhino" made you rich. The "big figure" was
three cents for grog and a night's lodging. A

tankard of ale, a "foamer," cost a "fip," about
six cents.

Of course there came the "owlers," the
smugglers' boats that poled through silently
by night while others were tied up against the
shore.

The "towpath news" spread word-of-
mouth information and gossip "spilled the
nosebag," sometimes "stretching the blanket"
in outright lies, much of it passed by those
who "hit the togs," traveling by shanks' mare
up the log roads.

The "long-eared robins," the mules, had
frequent spavines and hock disease, a constant
distress to the "hogees" and those who made
"walking passage" by driving them.

The land population swelled rapidly.
Schenectady, "Old Dorp," was the fastest
growing town on the canal, then Rochester,
the "Young Lion of the West." Syracuse exploded, mining the great salt deposit nearby.
Everywhere taverns and hostleries proliferated,
some still boasting an enduring fame.

Back on the canal it cost $10 to $15 a day
to operate the horse-drawn boats, but they
were in such demand that the profits were
staggering. They weren't all passenger or
freight craft and the life was not all work.
After the fog gang cleaned up in the spring
the best harbingers to the twenty or thirty
thousand people who made their homes on
the water and to the ports of call were the
thespians, the troupes of actresses, actors, musicians who played to avid audiences. The Erie
Book Boat took a traveling library up and
down. The *Kitty*, out of Utica, began as a circus boat and later converted to the *Good
News*, a gospel craft run by the Rescue Mission, which changed its berthing to Syracuse.
The *Rambler* of Rochester was a charter
packet that hauled fans to the football games
nine miles out of Utica.

The "canallers" sang and frolicked,
brawled and worked, and made their part of
history while old and new communities doubled, tripled, quadrupled, and the intervening
areas filled with a cornucopia of farms.

In 1825, even before the Erie opened, the
western states began their own canals. Ohio
began at Lake Erie and in two years linked
the water highway with thirty-eight miles of
Miami River canal to Portage Summit, later
called Akron, then dug on to Cincinnati. By
1836 Indiana had begun three others, from

An empty freighter pausing to graze its team. Courtesy Fort Hunter Canal Society.

Enlarging Phillips Lock, east of Amsterdam. Courtesy Fort Hunter Canal Society.

Building Lock 12, Tribes Hill, on the north side of the Mohawk, during the "canaliza-tion" of the river in the early 1900s. Courtesy Fort Hunter Canal Society.

Fort Wayne down the Maumes. They reached Toledo in 1843, joining the Miami-Erie at Defiance, thence on to Terre Haute and Evansville by 1849. Eighty miles across Ohio, 380 down and across Indiana.

But Clinton's Erie was the key, the main artery opening the west. At Buffalo, where goods were transferred to the lake ships, those using the Erie Basin increased 150 per cent in the first two years of operation. Freight rates between Buffalo and New York dropped from about $100 a ton overland to $10 by water and time was cut between Buffalo and Albany from fifteen days to six.

From its opening in 1825 until tolls were discontinued in 1882 the Erie had paid for its construction and operation, furnished funds for construction of several lateral canals, and also provided some revenue for general state government projects. Gross income had hit $121,461,872. After all costs had been paid she showed a profit of $42,599,717.

By 1835 traffic so choked the channel that enlargement began, a widening to seventy feet,

deepening to seven feet, and a lengthening of the locks to accommodate larger boats. The dredging curtailed the traffic flow and the need to shut down half the locks at every location while the other half worked on created havoc until 1862. It helped that the New York Central Railroad, paralleling the canal within sight of the boats, siphoned off much of the transport.

The railroad fought the canal improvement and for a while after the enlargement the Erie fell into neglect for a period. Then the burgeoning outpouring of products from the Middle West became more than the trains could handle and in spite of their competition the Erie's tonnage increased to 4,500,000 in 1889.

In 1905 a second expansion of the canal was begun, a revamping that ironically changed the route back nearer to DeWitt Clinton's first vision of capitalizing on the natural waterways by "canalizing" the Mohawk River itself. The new system, completed in 1918, would take barges three hundred feet

A high-speed motorized freighter used to ship perishables. Courtesy Fort Hunter Canal Society.

The Emita II, *a modern packet boat, moving westward through Lock 17 at Little Falls. When the lock was built in 1915 it was one of the highest lift locks in the world. Courtesy Kay Stevens.*

long, forty-two feet wide with a ten-foot draft, but while it was under construction traffic again slowed to a trickle.

As late as 1900 horses still pulled their loads up the towpaths, though they were being given up in favor of steam packets, and no towpath was built along the canalized river as the channel was too far from shore.

The year 1918 brought other major changes. The old land-cut canal with its towpath was abandoned and on the canalized route the old hand-operated devices on locks, gates, and dams gave way to electricity, and no low bridges spanned the river. The first huge oil barges came in the early 1920s and later in the same decade the diesels appeared. By the second half of the twentieth century 4,750,000 tons were being moved annually, about 70 per cent of it petroleum, over the course that had seen up to forty thousand pioneers head west in a year. As the cost of rail freighting rose, the barges came into their own again, and since the bankruptcy of the New York Central the tankers and water carriers of hard goods are on another upsurge of popularity.

The Erie is a long way from dead but the bones of her original construction can still be discovered. For a summer outing in your car turn off the New York Thruway at Fultonville, drive along the lovely Mohawk, cross the bridge, and watch the barges and pleasure boats glide underneath. Turn east on Route 5 to Fort Hunter and see the only two remain-

ing locks of the original Clinton Ditch in New York State, built there in 1822, and the locks and aqueduct of the 1841 improved era.

For further sightseeing drive west through the old village of Fonda to Little Falls, where the great three-foot square stone blocks of those locks jut from the fox grape tangle. Turn north toward Boonville along the Black River branch canal to see examples of the beautiful stone walls tight fitted together by the early masons. The whole north-central portion of the state was webbed by feeder canals and many reminders can be found of the great days when thousands made Erie water their home on the river that opened the West.

In recent years a cruise schedule has been initiated running the old *Rome Haul*. Eastbound, it begins near the west end of Oneida Lake, makes an overnight pause at Herkimer, another at Amsterdam, and winds up at Albany. The packet-type *Emita II*, sixty-four feet long, is a modern, comfortable version of the old passenger boats.

Take it for a nostalgia ride and somewhere along the canal you are sure to hear a soft echo sing over the water from the past:

> *Oh, the E-Ri-Eee is a-risin'*
> *And the gin is a-gettin' low.*
> *I scarcely think*
> *I'll get another drink*
> *'Til I get to Buffalo.*

8

The Great Lakes:
Gateway to the Heartland

BY T. V. OLSEN

Friar Louis Hennepin, the first white man to gaze on Niagara Falls, was one of seventeenth-century France's more intrepid adventurers. He was also, despite his priestly calling, a fanciful liar who claimed among other things to have traveled down the Mississippi River to its mouth. But he proved an accurate prophet when he wrote of the Great Lakes: "It were easy to build on the sides of these great Lakes an Infinite Number of considerable Towns which might have Communication one with another by Navigation for Five Hundred Leagues together, and by an inconceivable Commerce which would establish itself among them."

Father Hennepin penned these words in 1680. Sixty-five years earlier, Samuel de Champlain, Royal Geographer of France, had looked on the waters of Lake Huron, central waterway of the Great Lakes chain, and merely commented in his journal that blueberries and strawberries and squashes were plentiful along the shore. A few weeks later, with his retinue of Indian guides, Champlain "discovered" a second mighty body of water, Lake Ontario, and couldn't think of anything more epochal to record than his excitement at watching the savages hunt "stags and other animals" by chasing them into the water and leisurely finishing them off with spears.

Every age, every nation, has its visionaries and its matter-of-fact observers. James Monroe, making a tour of inspection through the "Northwest Territories" in 1785, saw dim prospects for the Great Lakes region. "A great part of the territory," he wrote, "is miserably poor, especially that near Lakes Michigan and Erie."

At the same time, a time when the young United States was confined to thirteen fed-erated states east of the Alleghenies, the vigorous vision of Thomas Jefferson was designing a confederation of western states that would embrace the Lakes' wilderness. These he assigned a curious mixture of names derived from native Indian and classical Greek sources —such as Sylvania, Michigania, Cheronesus, Assensipia, and Metropotania. The names and projected boundaries never materialized, but Jefferson's blueprint for a rich new territory he saw worthy of recognition as free commonwealth states, not mere colonial possessions, would prove to be sound.

The Great Lakes—feeders of America's heartland—made a bountiful reality of Jefferson's dream. They fired the imagination of poets as well as statesmen. Longfellow, who never saw his "Land of Sky Blue Water," captured its primal magnificence in *Hiawatha*—the beautiful, lonely reaches of forest and wide

Samuel de Champlain. Courtesy of the New-York Historical Society, New York City.

water, the profusion of wildlife, the romance of Indian cultures that relied on the bounty of its lakes and woods. Cultures that endured for thousands of years, changing little, changing the Lakes and their shorelands hardly at all.

Then came the white man.

In 1837, when the coronation procession of young Queen Victoria passed through the old streets of London, the Great Lakes country was still—despite a recent influx of settlers—almost totally a "howling wilderness" dotted with redmen's villages, white men's forts and trading posts. When the old queen's funeral cortege filed down the same London thoroughfares in 1901, the same American territory was thoroughly mined and logged off and tilled: tamed to vast rolling farmlands and teeming industrial centers more productive than Victoria's England at its height of empire.

No region on earth has been so transformed in so brief a time. The conversion from wilderness to civilization was inevitable, made so by the driving expansionist fever of nineteenth-century America, its fiercely innovative spirit, its passion for technology; by the Midwest's untouched resources of fertile prairie, staggering timber wealth, ranges of iron and copper ore; by a chain of Great Lakes that could accommodate an unlimited traffic between the East Coast and the nation's heartland. What at the beginning had been crude outposts of civilization—places called Duluth, Milwaukee, Chicago, Gary, Detroit, Toledo, Cleveland—were great cities by the turn of the century. Nourished by the bustling commerce of the Great Lakes, these places grew and thrived, while similar inland outposts merely changed to inland villages or vanished completely.

Weighed in the whole sweep of geological time, the Great Lakes are relatively young. They were gouged out by glaciers which advanced out of Canada during five separate epochs; glacial meltwater filled their basins. The last of these two-mile-deep ice sheets, the Wisconsin glacier, determined the present-day contours of the Lakes. It covered the area from 65,000 to 6500 B.C.

Within a thousand or so years after its retreat, men were using the Great Lakes for transportation. People of the Old Copper Age built villages along the south shore of Lake Superior; they mined copper on the Keweenaw Peninsula at the west end of upper Michigan. This first known use of metal by North American Indians began about 4000 B.C. Copper artifacts found along the shores of Lake Huron indicate an extensive trade carried on by water. The Indians threaded between islands and along rugged shorelines by dugout and birch-bark canoe; they fished the waters, trapped and hunted the forested shores.

Early French explorers seeking a fabled "Northwest Passage" to China used the same primitive mode of travel. Between 1618 and 1632 Etienne Brulé, one of Champlain's youthful protégés, performed the amazing feat of single-handedly (with various Indian companions) exploring, mapping, and describing the entire region from Lake Ontario to the west end of Lake Superior. After the explorers—Jean Nicolet, Radisson and Grosseilliers, Marquette and Joliet—came the *voyageurs* and *coureurs de bois* (free trappers).

The Great Lakes and the rivers that fed into them or drained out of them rang with the lusty songs of old Normandy, sung by the French-Canadian canoemen to time their paddle strokes as their great *canot du nords* (north canoes) swiftly plied the waterways, bringing supplies to the lake posts at Green Bay, Grand Portage, Sault Ste. Marie, and Michilimackinac, bearing rich cargoes of fur back to Montreal and Quebec on the St. Lawrence River.

In 1679 came the tall-masted sails of a true ship.

Rene Robert Cavalier, Sieur de la Salle, was the son of a modestly wealthy merchant, but a feudal aristocrat and imperialist by disposition. Most audacious and ambitious of all the French trader-explorers, he dreamed of establishing a string of forts and posts along the Great Lakes that would solidify a French trade empire from the St. Lawrence to the Mississippi Valley.

La Salle's plan included the building of a large cargo vessel with deep holds that could accommodate immense stores of supplies and tradable goods. It would have to be built above the Niagara River, which connected lakes Ontario and Erie, a river shallow and rapids-broken by all accounts. Previous explorers had commuted between these lakes by Indian trails.

At his base camp of Fort Frontenac at the foot of Lake Ontario, La Salle assembled a large contingent of skilled shipwrights, carpenters, and blacksmiths and placed them under joint command of the adventurer and Recollect Friar Louis Hennepin and La Motte, a La Salle lieutenant.

In late fall of 1678 the party crossed Lake Ontario in a three-ton sailing craft to the mouth of the Niagara and worked slowly upriver, often portaging their ton or so of equipment. Vague reports hadn't prepared the Frenchmen for the great Niagara escarpment and its thundering falls, whose height Father Hennepin typically overestimated as five hundred feet.

Hennepin and La Motte selected a site at Cayuga Creek above the Falls, where they were joined by La Salle. Here they laid their keel and set to work on the ship's hull while Seneca Indians gathered at the spot to watch in awe and apprehension. They had reason to be apprehensive.

The completed *Griffin* was sixty feet long with a raised quarterdeck and an anchor that had required four men "well stimulated with brandy" to carry around the Falls. The vessel weighed between forty-five and sixty tons (Hennepin); five cannon bristled from her portholes. When she was afloat, the crew bared heads and sang a *Te Deum*, while the Senecas—badly rattled by a salute of the cannons—were soothed with a cask of brandy.

On August 17, 1679, the *Griffin* set sail across Lake Erie, making good time till she reached Lake Huron on August 23. Here she nearly foundered in one of the sudden squalls that would plague Great Lakes mariners forever after. She passed safely through the Strait of Mackinac into Lake Michigan and dropped anchor at Green Bay in early September. La Salle's agents, sent from Fort Frontenac the previous year, were waiting with great quantities of furs bartered from the Indians.

Mindful of his impatient creditors, La Salle decided to dispatch the *Griffin* back to Niagara with a holdful of furs while he remained behind to explore the Wisconsin wilds. On September 18 the *Griffin* spread sail for her return journey, and was never seen again. Probably she went down in a storm that lashed the Strait of Mackinac next day. No clue to her fate, no sign of her wreckage or cargo, no survivor or corpse of her crew, ever turned up.

It was more than a century before another ship of the *Griffin*'s size raised sail on the Great Lakes.

Scaling down their ambitions somewhat, the French traders developed an efficient craft for heavy hauling of furs. Propelled by four long oars, rigged with a square sail, the *bateau* came into wide use for transporting of goods between the St. Lawrence and Niagara, between Niagara and Michilimackinac and Detroit. Ten-ton sloops appeared on Lake Ontario, then Lake Erie, to assist the growing traffic. Detroit became a key shipbuilding port.

The Seven Years' War (1756–63) brought New World conflict between France and England to the Great Lakes. The British opened a shipyard at their beachhead of Oswego on Lake Ontario, and in August 1755 the first English ship to touch the Lakes slid down the ways. She was a forty-three-foot sloop christened the *Oswego*; a warship armed with twelve cannon, she was swift and maneuverable. With the completion of five sister ships by the following year, British sea power came to inland America.

The fleet fared badly in its one brush with the enemy. On June 27, 1757, the first salvo between warships was exchanged on the Lakes. Finding himself outgunned, Captain Broadley, commander of the English vessels, retreated. On August 14, Marquis de Montcalm of Quebec fame launched a surprise attack on Oswego with a fleet of small paddle boats. Again outgunned, this time by French shore batteries, Broadley retreated.

Biding their time, the British altered their strategy without abandoning its premise: dominion of the Great Lakes would wrest North America from French control. In 1758 and '59 they seized the French garrisons at Fort Frontenac and Niagara, using brigades of whaleboats, *bateaux*, and canoes rather than warships. Quebec fell on September 13, 1759, and Montreal the following year. Major Robert Rogers and his famous Rangers sealed British supremacy over the western Lakes by journeying from post to post, showing the terms of capitulation signed at Montreal to French commanders at Detroit, Mackinac, Sault Ste. Marie, St. Joseph, and Green Bay.

English traders reaped the rich harvests of the Great Lakes fur trade for over a half century till the War of 1812 put an end to British influence along the south shores. During that period the only naval action waged on

America's inland waters was in 1763–64, when British ships broke the siege of Detroit by Chief Pontiac's Ottawa braves. No major engagement of the American Revolution was fought on the Lakes. The 1782 Peace Conference of Paris fixed the present border that divides four of the Great Lakes between the United States and Canada.

America's second war with England began with great confidence among U.S. war hawks that Canada would be highly vulnerable to attack, Great Britain's military resources then being tied up in the conflict with Napoleon. That assurance was dashed early in the war of 1812 as one post after another in Michigan and Wisconsin fell to the British forces. It was a decisive clash on the Great Lakes that not only restored the "Old Northwest" to American control for good, but also gave the U. S. Navy one of its classic victories and U.S. schoolbooks one of their classic slogans.

In the fall of 1812, President Madison sent a twenty-year-old naval lieutenant named Oliver Hazard Perry to command American operations on the Lakes. The British, having occupied Detroit, already had the nucleus of a fleet; the Americans had to build their entire fleet from timber along Erie's forested shore.

On September 10, 1813, at the west end of Lake Erie near Put-in-Bay, Perry's vessels engaged the British squadron under command of Captain Robert H. Barclay, a one-armed veteran of Trafalgar. Though he had eight ships to Barclay's six, Perry's fifty-four guns were outnumbered by the British armament, which included cannon of superior range.

Those cannon were inflicting severe damage on the smaller American vessels when Perry's flagship, the *Lawrence,* closed with the *Detroit,* Barclay's flagship. For twenty minutes the two ships hammered broadsides at one another. Perry had stationed some sharpshooters armed with Kentucky rifles in the rigging of his ships, from which they sniped at British commanders. Not very "cricket" behavior by English standards, but very effective. Within an hour most of the chief British officers were killed or wounded.

When the *Lawrence* became disabled, Perry lowered his colors, but not in surrender. Under enemy fire he transferred himself and his flag to the *Niagara,* his second largest vessel. This was commanded by Lieutenant Jesse D. Elliot, who had shown scant taste for close fighting.

Colors aloft once more, Perry executed a bold maneuver, running the *Niagara* into the heart of the British line, putting three enemy ships on his port, three to starboard. While he raked the foe with broadsides, the other American ships closed from the flanks. The tide of battle turned when a chance shift of wind entangled the rigging of the two biggest British ships, in effect disabling them. After three hours and the loss of forty British seamen, thirty Americans, and a hundred wounded on each side, Barclay struck his colors.

In abandoning his flagship, Perry had denied the motto emblazoned on his own standard—James Lawrence's famous dying words "Don't give up the ship"—but made up for it by composing one equally memorable in his victory dispatch to General William Henry Harrison: "*We have met the enemy and they are ours*—two ships, two brigs, one schooner and one sloop."

With hostilities terminated by the signing of the Treaty of Ghent on Christmas Eve, 1814, American development of the western Lakes began in earnest. Settlers thronged into the future Midwest. Farms began to stipple the virgin prairie. But in the upper forests of the Lakes region, commerce continued to center around the increasingly lucrative fur trade.

The shrewd and ruthless John Jacob Astor organized his American Fur Company into a monopoly that absorbed or wiped out all rivals large and small. From the company's base of operations at Mackinac Island, brigades of Astor agents paddled everywhere across the western Lakes, up and down branching waterways. In 1817 alone Astor outfitted and sent out 240 boats laden with trade goods, each manned by two traders and six hands apiece. In September 1827 he sold in a single day "200,000 muskrats at Public Sale and 350,000 at Private Sale." When the trade began to decline in the 1830s, John Jacob, now a multimillionaire, quietly sold out his interests.

The age of steam came to the Great Lakes in August 1818.

Walk-in-the-Water, a sidewheeler 135 feet long and thirty-five feet in the beam, was built by the Lake Erie Steamboat Company of Buffalo and launched at Black Rock. Equipped with two fifteen-foot paddle wheels,

Oliver Perry leaving his ship. Painting by William H. Powell. New York Public Library Collection.

she could carry passengers from Buffalo to Detroit in a day and a half. Fare was $15 cabin or $7 steerage. *Walk-in-the-Water* was an imposing craft, but like other early steamboats she was constructed for service on rivers, not for the rough water and battering storms of the Lakes. For three years, however, she enjoyed both navigational and financial success sailing back and forth on Lake Erie with loads of passengers and barreled cargo.

One late afternoon of October 30, 1821, *Walk-in-the-Water* set out from Buffalo with a full contingent of passengers. The weather turned foul; the steamer strained against powerful headwinds. Heavy waves pounded the timbers and seams began to spring. Rather than risk his ship further in a maelstrom of storm and contrary wind, Captain Jedediah Rogers put about and headed back for Buffalo.

As night closed down, the captain lost his bearings. Water was pouring into the hull; he started up the pumps and dropped anchor to wait for daylight, desperately hoping his frail craft wouldn't break up before then. But as more seams opened and the pumps could no longer cope with the situation, Rogers decided on what seemed a lesser evil: to cut the steamer loose from her three anchors and let her run ashore.

Twelve miles from Buffalo, *Walk-in-the-Water* grounded on a sandbar well offshore and keeled onto her side. Crewmen fought their way to high ground with a hawser which they lashed to a tree, making a lifeline whereby the passengers could be worked ashore in a rowboat. All were saved.

The craft was a total wreck except for her engine, which was salvaged and installed in a

Walk-in-the-Water, *the first steamboat on the Great Lakes, opposite Detroit, August 1820. New York Public Library Collection.*

new vessel, the *Superior.* This steamer and the *Henry Clay,* a companion ship commissioned in 1824, provided passenger service between Buffalo and Detroit for over a decade.

Many of the passengers were "emigrants," bent on trying their fortunes in the western lands. Travel routes west, apart from the Great Lakes and the Ohio River, were then limited to a few roads that were seldom more than narrow rutted trails across prairie and woodland; they were bisected by rivers, creeks, and swamps which made overland travel both difficult and hazardous. Transportation by water, where available, was much preferred. After 1820, with all easily available land along the Ohio claimed by settlers, emigrant travel on the Great Lakes increased dramatically.

The whole nation hailed the opening of the Erie Canal in 1825. With the Hudson River and Lake Erie connected to provide an all-water route west, rapid development of the Lakes states and territories was assured. In 1833 sixty thousand people passed through Buffalo, the key stopover point between canal traffic and lake traffic, going west. The number increased to eighty thousand the following year and picked up every successive year except for the "panic" years of 1838 and '39.

The Black Hawk War of 1832 ended the era of the red man east of the Mississippi; it cleared the way for settlement of northern Illinois and southern Wisconsin. Topsail schooners laden to capacity with prospective settlers and their freight of wagons, plows, and household goods set sail from Buffalo for the ports of the western Lakes. Cabins were crowded, the holds filled, the decks piled high.

Nearly a thousand sailing ships and 990

City of Detroit in the 1830s. Courtesy of the New-York Historical Society, New York City.

steamers dropped anchor at Cleveland in 1836. Thousands of emigrants got off the boats at Sandusky. On a single day in October 1838, 285 wagons drove into that lake port from Ohio's rich wheatlands and unloaded produce destined for the eastern cities. In 1835, 225 sailing ships arrived at the sandbar that blocked the mouth of the Chicago River. They disgorged hundreds of emigrants who were brought ashore by rowboats, their goods ferried in by rafts. Three years before, Chicago had been a raw frontier post of 150 people; by 1838 it was a bustling community of eight thousand.

All this was a bare prelude to what lay ahead.

Most of the Lakes harbors were very shallow. *Walk-in-the-Water* had to anchor far out at Cleveland; the harbor at Kenosha, Wisconsin, was too shallow for entry; larger vessels couldn't cross the sandbar at Chicago. Early canals, also, were shy on depth: four and a half to six feet deep, later increased to eight or ten feet. So boats built and rigged for Great Lakes

transport had to be designed with specific conditions of weather, winds, harbor, and cargo in mind.

Designers and builders burned the midnight oil in shipyard offices poring over captains' reports on keels, hulls, and wind drifts; they worked constantly on plans for improving existing models. Would a particular vessel have to negotiate the canals? Would it unload its cargo offshore or at one of the wharves under construction at Cleveland, Detroit, Chicago? What was the maximum payload it could handle, the minimum crew necessary to operate it?

Most of the boats were built by or for individual owners in the yards at Sackets Harbor, Oswego, Buffalo, Cleveland, Sandusky, Detroit, Saginaw, Manitowoc, Milwaukee, Chicago, and scores of smaller towns. For a quarter century before and a quarter century after the Civil War, sailing ships had their peak era on the Great Lakes.

Forests of masts and webs of rigging towered above every wharf and negotiable harbor.

Pungent smells of tar and sawdust overhung the waterfronts; hammers and saws and adzes made a bedlam of racket. Each vessel was tailored to its prospective owner-captain and he belonged to a finicky race: picky about his pet whims of design and their translation into wood, cable, and canvas.

In 1852 William Bates, a shipbuilder at Manitowoc, Wisconsin, came up with a simple yet ingenious device that revolutionized Great Lakes shipping. In the keels of his vessels he boxed a stout timber that was weighted at the stern end and swiveled on a pin at the bow end. When a Bates-designed ship passed into a canal or shallow harbor, the timber fin, or centerboard, could be raised; in deeper water it could be lowered as a stabilizer.

Every kind of sailing ship had its day in the Lakes trade. The "canallers," a familiar sight on Lakes Ontario and Erie, were squat and square and flat-bottomed, designed for lock travel. The three-masted square-rigged British frigates made ideal warships because several of their twelve to sixteen individual sheets of canvas could take a shell hit without crippling the vessel's maneuverability. But small commercial shipowners couldn't afford the large crews necessary to man all that sail power, though frigates did make serviceable cargo ships under steady winds. More favored were the two-masted brigs or brigantines, square-sailed at the foremast, fore-'n'-aft rigged at the main. Built in all sizes from a hundred to five thousand tons, they were capable of speeds up to thirteen knots.

Ultimately, as the channels of harbors, rivers, and canals were deepened, the bulky square-riggers gave way to the sleek, graceful fore-'n'-aft schooners, two-, three-, and four-masted. These required smaller crews and their rigs could be swung clear of the hatches, making it easier to load and unload cargoes.

Most men of their crews were from "down below," as Lakesmen put it: salt-water tars from the Atlantic—Americans, Englishmen, Germans, Scandinavians—attracted by the prospect of high wages and short voyages. Their fare was plain: salt beef, salt pork, hard bread, beans, and potatoes, with a half pint of whiskey per day and a month's allotment of twelve shillings to buy "extras" from the ship's stores.

Life aboard a Lakes craft may have seemed princely to such men, but they endured brutally harrowing conditions all the same. Some were swept overboard and lost in storms, others crushed in falls from rigging to pitching decks. Some ran amuck and killed their captains, their mates, or themselves. They played as hard as they worked, raising all kinds of hell ashore; boardwalks of every Lakes port thumped to their rolling sea gaits.

In the late 1830s young Douglas Houghton, Michigan's first state geologist, beached his canoe along the shores of the Keweenaw Peninsula and struck inland with his specimen sack. He made a find that would turn the Keweenaw's rugged wilds into a mining-boom region. Now hailed as "the father of U.S. copper mining," Houghton didn't live to enjoy the acclaim of his discovery. A few years later, as he was paddling his canoe around a rocky jut of land, a wintry squall overturned the craft. His body wasn't found till next spring.

Houghton's reports brought a swarm of speculators into the country. They came by bateau and mackinaw boat, for there were no roads into the region. In the spring of 1843 the schooner *Swallow* broke through shell ice at Copper Harbor to disgorge the first gang of miners on Keweenaw shores. The *Algonquin* and the *Astor* quickly followed.

Men from many walks of life—farmers, sailors, mechanics, livery hands, clerks, storekeepers—tramped ashore bearing picks and shovels, rucksacks of salt pork and dry beans. Hardly any had previous mining experience; their methods were haphazard. They scoured the peninsula without plan or pattern, mistakenly digging or blasting at sites where they found bits of "float" copper borne from their lodes by ancient glaciers.

Claim jumpers were everywhere; so were resentful Indians. To keep order of sorts, the War Department sent two companies of infantry to Copper Harbor. The soldiers built a barracks and stockade and named it Fort Wilkens after the Secretary of War. Then they settled down to grimly await an uprising by the local Chippewas. The latter, puzzled by developments, concluded that the stockade had been built to protect the soldiers from drunken miners.

By 1845 prospectors with mining know-how were arriving at Keweenaw; eastern capitalists organized companies and sent in geologists. The Pittsburgh and Boston Mining

Company set up operations at Cliff Mine, the world's first commercial mine to extract native copper as its only product. Over the next thirty-five years, the operation produced 38,000,000 pounds of copper and repaid its investors twenty times over. The Minnesota Mine in Ontonagon County and the Quincy Mine on the Pewabic lode also paid off handsomely.

A still greater boost to Lakes commerce was forecast in 1844.

As surveyor William Burt was running a section line near Teal Lake in the rough country below Lake Superior, his compass needle veered wildly. Burt sent his chainmen to look for the cause. They found a rusty purple outcrop: first of the great finds of iron ore in the Superior region.

Nature produces copper in a pure state; iron is found as a ferrous compound. Blast-furnace temperatures are required to separate and purify iron; its value per pound is less than copper. With the nation still in its industrial infancy, decades passed before the region containing three fourths of America's iron ore could start to realize its potential.

In 1847 Philo M. Everett, a storekeeper with no mining experience, opened a pit mine in the Marquette Range near Negaunee, Michigan, where he mixed and smelted the first iron ore in the Superior district. Financially his venture provided a failure, and so did other early operations.

Full-scale mining in the Gogebic Range, extending eighty miles across Wisconsin and Michigan and discovered in 1849 by Charles Whittlesy, didn't commence till 1880. George Stuntz mapped the rich Vermilion Range of the Duluth area in 1852, but extraction of ore didn't begin until thirty-five years later. The Menominee Range of upper Michigan, found by John Longyear at the time of Stuntz's discovery, didn't take center stage from the Marquette Range till the seventies. The most fabulous iron range of all, the Mesabi, was finally opened by the Merritt brothers in 1892, many years after they discovered its earth-locked riches.

The great ore freighters that would become a permanent part of the Lake Superior scene did not appear till well after 1855, the year that the Soo Canal opened at Sault Ste. Marie, permitting large-scale traffic between Lakes Superior and Huron. Before that time, ore-carrying ships were small vessels launched on Superior waters after being portaged on rollers through the streets of Sault Ste. Marie. Still unmarked by lighthouses or channel buoys, the world's greatest and cruelest lake presented bitter dangers for a light craft.

All fifteen vessels that crossed the Soo Portage were battered to extinction on Lake Superior. The schooner *Merchant* went down in July 1847 with its mixed cargo and crowded passenger list. The *Manhattan* was sunk in a collision. The steamer *Monticello* was beached after being half wrecked in a violent gale.

Most typical, perhaps, was the fate of the broad-beamed sidewheeler *Julia Palmer*, caught in a snowstorm between Copper Harbor and the Soo. After her fuel gave out, the crew burned the furniture and wooden fittings. When these were consumed, the steamer drifted for fourteen days out of sight of land. Her hull sprang a leak; passengers bailed day and night to keep her afloat. Finally she ran ashore at Whitefish Bay, too weakened by her ordeal for further heavy service.

By 1850 the clamor for a canal at Sault Ste. Marie was loud enough to reach the halls of Congress, but it met powerful opposition. Daniel Webster shook his leonine head and bellowed that he'd "never vote a penny to bring the rocky, bleak, inhospitable shores of California one step nearer Boston."

At the time eastern capitalists saw the proposed canal as a threat to their interests; they changed their tune as more eastern money was invested in the Superior ore regions. In 1852 Congress authorized a four-foot-wide canal strip across the Soo Portage.

Meantime, that same summer, an agent for the E. T. Fairbanks Company named Charles T. Harvey arrived at Sault Ste. Marie. Harvey's firm manufactured scales; an enterprising young man whose job was selling scales, he had a quick eye for the problems of moving weighty objects. Harvey sized up the situation, then composed a letter to his bosses urging them to put some financial muscle behind a canal project.

The company directors agreed, authorized Harvey to handle the matter, and warned him to keep costs down.

Early in 1853 Harvey sold the Michigan legislature on his plan for a canal with a lock 350 feet long by seventy feet wide, eleven and a half feet deep over the sills. Harvey himself was appointed special agent for the state with the job of selling 750,000 acres of land that had been allocated to Michigan by the federal government for the purpose of financing canal construction. When contractors offered bids for the job, the E. T. Fairbanks Company won with a bid of $1 million.

Charles Harvey was placed in charge of the Saint Mary's Falls Ship Canal Company, a Fairbanks subsidiary. Losing no time, he went to Detroit and hired five hundred men from the ranks of westward-bound immigrants. He chartered the steamship *Illinois* and loaded it with horses, mules, food, and equipment. As yet he had no inkling of the difficulties he'd encounter.

The steamer reached the Soo on June 1,

1853; the crew quickly threw up a bunkhouse and cookshack. As a detailed survey of the canal route was laid out, Harvey was chagrined to find the cut would have to be a foot deeper than anticipated.

By early fall he was already fighting time. The work went slowly. Tons of dirt and rock had to be wrestled loose by hand and carted away by wheelbarrow and wagon. More workers were needed. Harvey sent agents to New York, Cleveland, Detroit; they rounded up another five hundred men. Winter was coming on and Harvey felt the squeeze of desperation.

"More men," he told his agents. "Get me more men."

By first snowfall he had a crew of sixteen

Rail portage between Lake Superior and Lake Huron in the early 1850s, prior to the building of the Soo Canal. New York Public Library Collection.

hundred working on the cut. The weather was savage—turning the earth flinty, filling the ditch with snow, freezing men's hands. Supplies ran short; the men went on strike. Harvey retaliated by cutting off all rations. They went back to work.

Thanks to seasonable conditions, construction forged ahead steadily through spring, summer, and fall of 1854. Harvey was riding high in confidence as the second winter closed down. He sent engineers to study possibilities for the final-stage passage that would connect with Lake Superior.

They returned with a report that stunned him. An offshore reef of solid rock blocked the route. Removing it would take months of work and, they estimated, about a quarter million dollars.

Harvey wrote his company and requested $250,000. They sent him $30,000.

He was heartsick. Was the whole project doomed? Then he had a brainstorm: an idea as radical as it was doubtful. His engineers listened and shook their heads; it would never work, they told him. However, he had no choice but to try.

Harvey worked through the winter to implement his plan: a giant gravity punch that would be raised and lowered by a steam engine. If the reef could be reduced to rubble, a dredge could finish the job. The tip of the punch was forged from a four-inch steel bolt which got so hot it burned down the blacksmith shop. A massive oak beam backed by a three-ton weight was affixed for a shaft.

When spring came, Harvey rafted his steam engine and punch close to the reef barrier. The oak shaft broke in half at the first blow. The punch was lost in ten feet of water. Doggedly, Harvey retrieved the punch, fashioned a heavier shaft, and tried again.

At first the repeated poundings of the punch only sent stone chips flying. Then larger chunks broke off. It took weeks of laborious beating and dredging to trough out the last-stage channel.

The Soo Canal was completed and dedicated on June 18, 1855, a full six weeks ahead of schedule. On August 14 the brig *Columbia* passed through the new locks, carrying a hundred tons of red iron ore from the Marquette Range to the Cleveland-Cliffs Iron Company smelters at Cleveland.

At last huge-scale transport between the ore beds of the west and the coal and limestone beds of the east was possible. As America's steel industry boomed at Pittsburgh and Youngstown, Cleveland and Toledo, so did the nation's rampant growth. Thousands on thousands of tons of ore poured into the white-hot mouths of furnaces, producing guns and cannons and cannon balls for the Union troops, rails and engines for the railroads, machinery for ships and farms and sawmills. Andrew Carnegie's empire fattened. With the perfection of the Bessemer steel-making process, the Carnegie profits soared till they reached $40 million a year by 1900.

Shipyards along the Lakes boiled with activity. Always the cry was for greater capacity, more speed, improved efficiency in loading and unloading. Sailing ships with their cumbersome masts and sailing gear began to vanish from the Lakes, their wooden hulls structurally inadequate for the age of steel. In 1844 two small iron steamers—the 133-ton *Surveyor* and the 583-ton *Michigan*, built at Buffalo and Erie respectively—were launched for the purpose of the U. S. Government's coastal survey. By the 1880s four great carriers capable of bearing two thousand tons of ore apiece were operating on the Lakes. This was the famous "iron fleet": *Iron Duke, Iron King, Iron Age,* and *Iron Cliff.*

The big freighters ran into troubles of their own. Like their smaller predecessors, many foundered in the fierce Lakes storms. They became weighted with ice during late-season runs. They dragged keel in shallow channels; they scraped bottom at places like the St. Clair flats, ripping loose their underplating. Structural strengths improved as the carriers grew longer and wider. By 1892 the biggest measured 330 feet with freight capacities of nearly 3,000 tons. The 454-foot *Malietea,* launched in 1897, could carry 7,500 tons in her hold. She was still active during World War II, long after her carrying capacity had been superseded by twentieth-century ships. No record for size of vessel has ever held for long on the Great Lakes.

The logging era of the Lakes country was wild and colorful, fiercely rapacious, and relatively short-lived. The story of nineteenth-century logging was the same everywhere in the middle states: a pioneer sawmill set up in the woods by a driving stream quickly became the nucleus of a logging boom town which rarely

The Great Lakes: Gateway to the Heartland

An early lock on the Sault Ste. Marie Canal. New York Public Library Collection.

survived its boom days. Nowhere was the cycle of boom-and-bust more evident than along the shores of the western Great Lakes.

Immigrants from a Europe that carefully husbanded its timber resources were dazed as they viewed the shorelines of Wisconsin and Michigan from the decks of west-bound steamers. From every lake port the deafening din of sawmills roared across the water. Tall dunes of yellow sawdust grew along the shores. Great booms of pine logs confined by chains jammed the harbors; immense rafts of lumber were towed by tugboat from the sawmill towns to the railhead ports. From the port towns, steamers conveyed loads of supplies up rivers to feed the camps.

After the Civil War, the surge of Western settlement created a demand for lumber that reached its peak during the 1880s. By 1900 the pinelands of the upper Midwest were stripped of their bounty. It was the most

profligate rape of a natural resource in all of human history. Thousands of acres were not even logged; they were simply burned and cleared to make room for farms. The lumber moguls had bought up choice tracts of timber at the federal government's price of $1.25 an acre; now they contrived to unload those stumped-off lands at a profit. Not realizing the poor-yield quality of the acid pine soil, settlers flocked in to buy up the denuded acres and sow crops.

Many were Yankees from the eastern seaboard, but now there were others as well: immigrants who hailed from every port in Europe. During the second half of the nineteenth century, hundreds of them crowded the wharves of Buffalo and boarded sailing ships and steamers for passage through the Great Lakes.

First to come were the men who wrested ore from the bowels of the copper and iron

The enlarged Sault Ste. Marie Canal about 1938. New York Public Library Collection.

The great ore ships that carried iron from the Mesabi Range, circa 1930. New York Public Library Collection.

The City of Erie *transported many westward-bound immigrants at the turn of the century. New York Public Library Collection.*

Late-season problems—heavy ice and the threat of being stranded in the frozen lake waters. New York Public Library Collection.

ranges: the "cousin jacks," miners from Cornwall accustomed to living half their lives underground, along with Irishmen, Scandinavians, Germans, and Italians. Men from the forests of Scandinavia, Norwegians and Swedes and Finns, predominated in the logging camps. Strong and hardy men all, whatever their nationalities, for the weak died quickly under the brutal conditions of the frontier camps.

When the big trees were gone, the loggers cleared the stumplands and took up farming. They were joined by friends and relatives from abroad, who brought their families and often took up trades they had followed in the old

countries. In both rural and urban areas they banded together according to nationalities, thus preserving their native languages and folkways for generations in the new land.

Hungarians and Czechs concentrated in Cleveland, Poles and Italians in Detroit, Hollanders in western Michigan, Norwegians in north-central Wisconsin. A fifth of the entire population of Norway and Sweden came to the New World. By 1900 fully 225,900 people in Minnesota were Swedish immigrants and their American-born children.

Of all the immigrants from northern Europe who settled the Great Lakes region, the Germans were the most numerous and influential. Their proportion of gifted and educated people was exceptionally high, many of them liberal thinkers who had renounced the stiff religious and political doctrines, the expanding militarism, of nineteenth-century Germany. They settled in Sandusky on Lake Erie and spread down the Miami-Erie Canal toward Cincinnati. They literally transformed Milwaukee into a German city, complete with huge breweries, singing and debating societies, German newspapers, and a true German sense of *gemuetlichkeit* that prevailed until World War I.

Whole lines of "immigrant boats," wood-burning steamers whose decks were piled with household goods, dropped anchor at Detroit, Milwaukee, and Chicago. Multitudes of new-comers poured onto the pre-emption lands of the Midwest prairies, swiftly converting wild grasslands to fields of wheat and corn and barley. The golden flood was funneled into Lake Michigan ports. By the 1850s Chicago was the greatest grain-shipping port in the world, shipping out over 50 million bushels of wheat a year.

Some who followed their high hopes to America never reached their destinations.

On the night of August 20, 1852, running in dense fog off Long Point on Lake Erie, the new propeller-driven *Ogdenburg* collided with the stately *Atlantic*. The *Ogdenburg*'s prow smashed the liner's port side forward of her paddle box; Erie waters rushed in. The *Atlantic*'s five hundred passengers, including two hundred Norwegian immigrants in the steerage, swarmed up through flooding passages to the deck. They threw tables, benches, chairs, anything that would float, overboard and leaped in after them. The *Ogdenburg* rescued 250 people; the rest perished in the fog-bound waters.

Maritime disasters on the Great Lakes have claimed the lives of thousands. On June 17, 1850, the steamer *G. P. Griffith* was bound from Buffalo to Chicago with a load of immigrants. The all-wood vessel caught fire on Lake Erie and burned to the water, with a loss of 285 lives; 297 passengers died on the night of September 8, 1860, when the side-wheeler *Lady Elgin* was rammed and cut nearly in half by a loaded lumber schooner ten miles off Winnetka, Illinois. The worst disaster in Lakes history occurred in Chicago Harbor on the placid morning of July 24, 1915. The steamer *Eastland* was loading passengers for an excursion to Michigan City when she heeled sideways and overturned in twenty-one feet of water. Of the 2,500 persons crowded

The *Lady Elgin at her Chicago wharf, 1860, the day before she was rammed and sunk. New York Public Library Collection.*

onto her decks, 835 were drowned. Most of them had been trapped on the lower decks.

During their recorded history, the Great Lakes have been a graveyard for more than six thousand sizable vessels. Even a giant ore carrier of today may fall victim to Lake Superior at its raging worst. On the stormy night of November 10, 1975, the 729-foot *Edmund Fitzgerald*, once the "monarch of the Great Lakes," sank in 650 feet of water off Whitefish Bay, leaving no trace of its twenty-nine-man crew.

The great lumber rafts are long vanished from the Lakes; copper mining has declined to a trickle. The former dense lodes of iron ore are exhausted, but surface mining of low-grade taconite ores by modern flotation and screening processes continues, and so does a brisk lake freighting of ore to the smelting ports. All the Great Lakes are being revitalized by chemical treatment, which is restoring the commercial fisheries, though pollution remains a serious problem.

The opening of the St. Lawrence Seaway in 1959 has provided a steady increase in the shipping of such bulk cargo as iron ore, coal, fuel oil, wheat, corn, and barley. Hundreds of ships of many nations pass up and down the Seaway each year. Travelers can embark directly from Chicago, Detroit, Cleveland, and Buffalo for ports throughout the world.

The Great Lakes of today continue to carry "their share of the freight."

9

The Missouri and
the Yellowstone

BY REX BUNDY AND
EDITH THOMPSON HALL

At the border of North Dakota and Montana, the Missouri River, nicknamed "The Big Muddy," divides into two branches—the upper Missouri and the Yellowstone rivers. Both offshoots were traveled by the early trappers and traders, who dreamed that one day the Missouri and its tributaries would become a vast water highway. This dream was to become a reality in the early and mid-1800s.

Survival on the mighty Missouri-Yellowstone waterway was no mean feat. Nautical pioneers had to face violent storms, raging winds, and beating hail, crushing ice, treacherous rapids and jagged rocks and hostile Indians. One day the waters might swell to an awesome fifteen miles in width, only to become a narrow, shallow channel a few days later. Many men made great fortunes navigating the rivers; many others lost their boats and their lives.

The first boats of the white man to traverse the mighty river were the frail birchbark canoes of the early explorers and fur traders. These travelers quickly discovered that the Missouri was different from other rivers they knew in North America. Its bed was studded with hidden snags and sawyers, submerged rocks and white water that made travel by birchbark canoe a hazardous adventure.

The Indian tribes indigenous to the Missouri River had a solution for those early explorers and fur traders in the form of dugout canoes, called pirogues. These pirogues were made by either gouging out, or burning out, the inside of a log into a thin wooden shell one inch thick on the sides, and from two to three inches thick on the bottom. Naturally, all the pirogues varied according to the whims of their makers—some had a small keel, while

others were flat-bottomed. Some were square-sterned and slightly undercut, but all had either a rounded or semirounded bow. Most builders of this type of boat left bulkheads at intervals, which strengthened the boat considerably and also provided compartments for the stowage of cargo.

One unique cargo carried by the compartmentalized pirogues was bear oil. This substance does not solidify unless exposed to cold, and also remains sweet much longer than does lard or other animal fat. To make the most of these advantages, two or three men would paddle upriver and kill as many bears as they could find, render out the oil, pour it into the pirogue, lash a tanned hide over it, and return to a ready market in St. Louis. Bear were plentiful in the early days along the Missouri.

Pirogues were normally made from walnut trees, and in pioneer times there were enormous specimens along the lower Missouri. Some measured six feet in diameter and forty feet to the first limb. The length of the pirogue was limited, therefore, only by the weight of the finished boat and by the number of men and quantity of goods it was to carry. Though heavy and awkward to handle, it was practically unsinkable. The sturdy bottom allowed it to hit snags and run up on gravel bars with a certain amount of immunity. It did not, however, carry enough cargo to satisfy the fur traders, so often two were fastened together with poles or planks. This increased the stability of the craft and also increased the cargo capacity. This led to a further improvement. The six- to ten-foot space between the two hulls was decked over and provided storage space for hides and trade goods.

As the volume of the fur trade grew, the

Mackinaw boats and flatboats on the Missouri, 1820–40. Courtesy National Park Service.

demand for larger craft led to the development of the Mackinaw, a flat-bottomed boat of shallow draft, built of hand-sawed planks cut from the abundant trees that grew along the river's edge. Twenty or thirty feet long, with a beam of eight to twelve feet, a sharp prow, and a square stern with a rudder, they were great cargo carriers for traveling downriver, as they could skip over most obstacles. Their great fault was that they could not buck the strong upriver currents on the return trip. This drawback did not daunt the rivermen who considered the Mackinaws one-way boats which, upon arrival at their destinations, could be sold for the planks of which they were constructed. This ingenious offspring of the Missouri carried an enormous amount of downriver cargo even after the advent of the steamboat.

Manuel Liza, an ex-seaman, was the first to really navigate the waters of the Missouri and the Yellowstone. He was not content with the crude craft then in use and wanted a boat with a keel, a deck, a cabin, and a sail, plus a hawser for cordelling (towing) the boat

Manuel Liza. Courtesy Missouri Historical Society.

Keelboat with sail. From the painting by Karl Bodmer. Courtesy Nebraska State Historical Society.

upriver by man power. He had one built to his specifications and, on its maiden voyage, proved its efficiency by averaging eighteen miles a day, fully loaded, against the Missouri's powerful current.

As a result of Liza's performance, many seventy- and eighty-foot keelboats with sails appeared on the Missouri. Keelboats became the principal mode of river transportation on the upper Missouri until the arrival of the steamboats, and even then they were still used on the smaller tributaries.

Steamboats reached St. Louis, Missouri Territory, one decade after they were proven a feasible method of water transportation in the East: Robert Fulton had demonstrated his *Clermont* on the Hudson River on August 17, 1807, and the first steamboat reached St. Louis on August 2, 1817, when the *Zebulon M. Pike* steamed up the Mississippi River and tied up at this already famous fur-trading post.

Immediately, the question arose of whether or not a steamboat could navigate the turbulent waters of the Missouri River. The tales told by the keelboatmen of their mighty struggles to overcome the upper Missouri seemed to preclude any steamboat travel on that wild portion of the river. Their stories of the terrible currents encountered, especially those of the *embrasadas*—formations consisting of countless buffalo carcasses, trees, brush, mud, sand, huge blocks of ice and rocks, all piled by the force of the river's current into huge wing dams, with a tailrace so swift and violent that no steamboat would ever be powerful enough to move against them—made it seem foolhardy to put a thin-skinned steamboat on its waters. A successful voyage, according to the keelboatmen, would be as impossible to accomplish as harnessing the wind or saddling a hummingbird in full flight.

Colonel Elias Rector was determined to find out how much truth there was to these tales. In 1819 he organized a steamboat company, bought a steamboat named *Independence*, loaded her at St. Louis, and set off up the river. The *Missouri Intelligencer* of May 28, 1819, reported the event—the safe voyage of the first steamboat up the Missouri to Franklin with passengers, and a cargo that consisted of flour, whiskey, sugar, etc. To add to its laurels, the *Independence* chugged on up

Colonel Elias Rector. Courtesy Missouri Historical Society.

the river past Franklin to Chariton. Both towns held a joint celebration and over twenty-three toasts were made. From the flow of liquor at the party, the *Independence* could have returned to St. Louis without the benefit of the Missouri's waters.

On June 21, 1819, Major Stephen H. Long's Yellowstone Expedition left St. Louis. This was a military operation for the purpose of making scientific observations and establishing Army forts along the upper Missouri, especially at the mouth of the Yellowstone River. Included in this operation were four steamboats, the *Thomas Jefferson, R. M. Johnson, Expedition,* and the *Western Engineer.*

The *Thomas Jefferson* hit a snag at the mouth of the Osage River and sank, thereby gaining the dubious honor of being the first steamboat wrecked on the Missouri River.

The *R. M. Johnson* and the *Expedition* proved totally unfit for travel on the river and it was only through the herculean efforts of the soldiers, dispatched earlier via keelboats, that the boats were able to make it as far upriver as they did. They finally reached the mouth of the Kansas River where they wintered, returning to St. Louis in the spring.

The *Western Engineer,* however, had been built expressly for this expedition, and incorporated into her construction were two of the features later considered essential to steamboat travel on the Missouri, especially on the upper and mountain portions of that river. First, she was a sternwheeler. This enabled her to run up on hidden sandbars, sawyers, and snags without smashing her paddle wheel. Second, she drew only nineteen inches of water when empty.

The *Western Engineer* was built to impress the Indian tribes on the Missouri River and there is no doubt that she did just that, according to a firsthand description published in the St. Louis *Enquirer* and dated June 25, 1819:

> The bow of the vessel exhibits the form of a huge serpent, black and scaly, rising out of the water from under the boat, his head as high as the deck, darted forward, his open mouth vomiting smoke and apparently carrying the boat on his back. From under the boat, at its stern, issues a stream of foaming water, dashing violently along. All the machinery is hid [sic]. Three small brass field pieces, mounted on wheel carriages, stand on the deck. The boat is ascending the rapid stream at the rate of three miles an hour. Neither wind nor human hands are seen to help her, and to the eye of ignorance, the illusion is complete that a monster of the deep carries her on his back, smoking with fatigue, and lashing the waves with violent exertion.

The *Western Engineer* made it upriver as far as Manuel Liza's fur post, the newly established Fort Missouri, nine miles from Council Bluffs, where she went into winter quarters. The following spring she returned to St. Louis. The expedition was a fiasco in a military sense, but it provided additional proof that steamboats could navigate the lower Missouri up to that imaginary line drawn by the keelboatmen at the mouth of the Platte River, which, to them, separated the lower and upper Missouri waters.

The decades following the government's abortive expedition were the heyday of the keelboats, but the increasing demands of commerce, including those of the fur trade as well as those arising from the expansion of settlements, caused many men to enter the steam-

The Western Engineer. *Courtesy Nebraska Historical Society.*

The steamboat Yellowstone. *Courtesy Nebraska Historical Society.*

boat business. Some Mississippi River steamboats were available, and more were in the stages of construction. Since it had not been determined, as yet, that Mississippi steamboats were totally unfit for this new water highway, many were put into service. They were used exclusively on the lower stretches of the river to pick up loads from the Mackinaw boats and the fur-trading posts they could reach. They also hauled Indian annuities and supplies to the nearer Army posts.

In 1830, Pierre Chouteau, of the American Fur Company, had the steamboat *Yellowstone* built. She was the first steamboat to be constructed exclusively for the upper Missouri River waters. A sidewheeler with one boiler and one engine, she had a direct drive which necessitated shipping one wheel when forced to turn sharply. Her over-all length was 130 feet, with a beam of nineteen feet, and she drew six feet of water, a great handicap on the changeable river she was built to navigate. She was a twin decker, having a lower (main) deck and a cabin (boiler) deck. Her engine was subject to habitual breakdowns and the crew was forced to propel her upstream by using poles during those periods of enforced overhaul.

She made her first appearance on the Missouri River on April 15, 1831, when she left St. Louis for the mouth of the Yellowstone River. She did not reach her destination, but only succeeded in reaching Fort Tecumseh, now Pierre, South Dakota, at the mouth of the Bad (Teton) River. There she discharged her cargo, took on a full load of buffalo robes, furs, and ten thousand pounds of buffalo tongues—a great delicacy—and immediately left for St. Louis to avoid being caught by low water.

In 1832 the *Yellowstone* made the round trip from St. Louis to Fort Union just above the confluence of the Yellowstone and Missouri rivers, opening the upper Missouri waters to steamboats.

One of her passengers on this historic trip was George Catlin, who left a heritage of oil paintings of the authentic dress and dances of the Indian tribes of the upper Missouri region, plus various portraits of important Indians. His most important contribution, perhaps, was his writings on Indian life of the upper Missouri.

In 1833 the *Yellowstone* again made the round trip to Fort Union and on this trip carried another distinguished passenger, Prince Maximilian of Wied. Accompanying him was the artist Karl Bodmer, who left many paintings of the Missouri River region. Bodmer also made a further trip to Fort MacKenzie, located six miles above the mouth of the Marias River, via keelboat, and was the first artist to sketch the Missouri River's mountain waters. This same year the American Fur Company put a better boat, the *Assiniboine*, into service. Unfortunately, she had a short life. Also a sidewheeler with a single engine and boiler, she was destroyed by fire on June 1, 1835, at the head of what is now known as Sibley Island in present-day North Dakota.

With the loss of the *Assiniboine*, the American Fur Company leased other boats to carry their supplies to Fort Union. The *Yellowstone*, their own boat, was the only one that made the round trip in 1836, but in 1837 she was joined by the *Clara* and the *St. Peter's*. The latter boat was accused of carrying the smallpox epidemic, causing many deaths among the Mandan, Aricaree, Assiniboine, Gros Ventre, Crow, and the tribes of the Blackfoot Confederacy—Piegans, Bloods, and Sarsi.

In 1838 the *Antelope*, leased by the American Fur Company, made a round trip to Fort Union, but in 1839 she fell short of the fort by four hundred miles. It was then realized that she drew far too much water for the upper Missouri, except at flood stage. She was sent to a boatyard to be remodeled for a more shallow draft. However, steamboat builders still clung to the idea that two paddle wheels were better than one, and the *Antelope* was not changed from a sidewheeler to a sternwheeler even though she was the forerunner of the light-draft mountain steamboats.

The following two decades of Missouri River steamboating were a period of trial and error on the part of the steamboat builders. It was not until the middle 1850s that certain safety features were added, such as water- and steam-pressure gauges on the boilers. Prior to that time, the engineer had guessed at the amount of water in the boiler, although he did have what were called water cocks, small brass faucets inserted into the boiler that could be used to determine the height of the water. Without the steam gauges, though, the engineer was entirely in the dark as to the pressure being generated. Some engineers made a wrong estimate and blew themselves and their boats out of existence. It is remarkable that more of the crude, early-day steamboats were not destroyed in this manner.

Engineers also faced the additional hazard of mud collecting in a steamboat's boiler. All Missouri River steamboats used its waters to generate steam, and as the Big Muddy was well named—some went so far as to describe the liquid called water as "too thick to drink and too thin to plow"—mud accumulated during a day's run. Most Missouri River steamboats were tied up at night, due to the dangers of the numerous snags, sawyers, and sandbars. During this enforced layover the fires were drawn and some luckless roustabout would crawl into the boiler and shovel out the steaming mud. Even after boilermakers devised a method of blowing the mud from the boilers while under way, the dirt still caused considerable damage by working its way into the engine, causing rapid wear on valves and pistons. As a result of the many hazards of Missouri River steamboating, most steamboats carried enough material to completely rebuild their working parts.

During the decades between 1839 and 1859, one man rose head and shoulders above all others in the operation and construction of the forerunners of the shallow-draft mountain boats. That man was Captain Joseph La Barge. He is credited with many of the innovations that improved the steamboats for use on the upper Missouri. Each year he would devise some new method of overcoming certain problems and would then incorporate it into steamboats he had built for himself. He also became the foremost Missouri River pilot of the time and trained his brothers, Charles and John, although neither reached his pinnacle of fame.

To the La Barge brothers goes the credit for establishing the head of navigation on the Missouri River. In 1859, Captain John La Barge, in command of the *Chippewa*, reached a point three miles below the mouth of the Marias River, a spot called Brule Bottoms. The following year, 1860, three steamboats, the *Chippewa*, the *Key West*, and the *Spread Eagle*, traveled together to Fort Union. The *Spread Eagle* was a far larger boat than the other two and, upon arrival at Fort Union, her cargo was transferred to the two smaller boats,

Captain Joseph La Barge. Courtesy State Historical Society of Missouri.

which then proceeded upriver. Both arrived at Fort Benton on July 2, thereby establishing it as the head of navigation on the wild and stormy Missouri. According to the unpublished journals of C. P. Hubbard, a passenger on the *Key West*, the *Chippewa* was tied to the bank when the *Key West* arrived.

Prior to the arrival of the steamboats, Fort Benton was a small fur-trading post established by the American Fur Company in 1847, under the direction of Alexander Culbertson, for direct trade with the tribes of the Blackfoot Confederacy. Although Fort Benton was merely a straggling log-cabin hamlet sitting on the open prairie with rutted wagon tracks for streets, it tapped an enormous fur region whose peltries had previously been transported to civilization by keel- and Mackinaw boats.

The establishment of Fort Benton as the head of navigation on the Missouri was to take much longer than might have been anticipated when the *Key West* and *Chippewa* arrived in 1860. The following year, no steamboat got closer than Cow Island. The unfortunate *Chippewa* might have made it but for the accident that blew her up on May 19, just a few miles below the mouth of the Poplar River.

This accident was caused by thirst—and not for Missouri River water. A roustabout went into the small hold with a candle to tap a keg of whiskey for his own enjoyment. When he appeared on deck, drunk and yelling "*Fire!*" the boat immediately ran ashore so that everyone could debark. It was then hurriedly cast adrift because the hold not only held whiskey, but also carried a considerable cargo of gunpowder which, when it exploded, shattered the *Chippewa* into splinters. A newspaper of the day carried the story of the accident, and also mentioned that the careless deckhand was "severely pummelled [sic]" by the angry passengers.

The advent of the Civil War was a great deterrent to trade on the upper and mountain waters of the Missouri River. Many of the men who worked those waters had either gone to war or were awaiting the inevitable call to service. When a flotilla of eighty-two steamboats from St. Louis answered the call to move General Grant's army from Fort Donelson in 1862, it included not only Missouri steamboats, but many upper and mountain steamboats as well. As a result, only four steamboats left St. Louis for Fort Benton that year, while in 1863 only three, the *Shreveport*, the *Alone*, and the *Nellie Rogers*, were dispatched to the mountains. None of the boats reached Fort Benton. The *Shreveport* made it as far as Cow Island, but the other two made it only to the mouth of the Milk River.

Cow Island, as well as many other sites on the mountain waters of the Missouri above Fort Union, had been in use for a number of years as dumping sites for cargo from steamboats unable to proceed upriver. From these spots, lighter cargo was transferred to keelboats or to fast four- to six-mile teams for delivery to Fort Benton. Heavier and bulky freight was transported by ox teams, called "bull-trains."

In 1863 an event occurred that changed the picture entirely with regard to the river

The *Chippewa, about two years before she exploded. Courtesy Montana Historical Society, Helena.*

traffic on the upper and mountain waters of the Missouri. In February, Sidney Edgerton, later to become the first territorial governor of Montana Territory, left Bannack, Idaho Territory, carrying five pounds of gold nuggets and twenty pounds of gold dust sewn in the lining of his buffalo-robe overcoat. He went straight to Washington, D.C., and displayed this gold to President Abraham Lincoln personally. He also gave the President a fair summary of the extent of the gold fields in operation, plus an estimate of prospective operations. Time proved his estimate far short of actual production, but the Union benefited greatly from Idaho and Montana gold.

The year 1866 was a banner year for steamboats on the mountain waters of the Missouri. The Civil War had ended and many of the steamboats that had carried Union troops and supplies on the shallow rivers of the South during that epic struggle were once more in operation on the mountain waters of the Missouri. No fewer than twenty-nine boats unloaded cargo at the levee in Fort Benton. There were actually thirty-two shipments unloaded because the *Deer Lodge* made two round trips from St. Louis, arriving at Fort Benton on May 18, and again on July 13. The *Luella* delivered three loads, one from St. Louis, one from Fort Union, and one from Pablos Rapids. The feat of the *Deer Lodge* was considered remarkable by the Mississippi River pilots, as they called the Missouri a "rainwater creek" above Fort Union.

The year 1866 also saw the first arrival of Captain Grant Marsh at Fort Benton. He was destined to become the best-known captain on the entire upper Missouri watershed. Although Captain Marsh admitted that on his first trip out of St. Louis he had felt his way upriver from Fort Union to Fort Benton, he and his boat, the *Luella*, made two extra trips to Fort Benton that year.

In 1865 the American Fur Company sold all their holdings to a new firm, Smith, Hubbel & Hawley. The new owners decided to abandon Fort Union and move their business to Fort Benton. Captain Marsh and his boat, the *Luella*, were selected to make the move.

Fort Union had been the greatest of the Indian trading posts within the boundaries of the United States. For years the most powerful tribes of the Northwest Plains region had traveled there to trade. To Fort Union from all over the vast watershed of the upper Missouri had come the factors of the remote fur-trading posts, and the *coureur de bois*. Here, too, had visited some of the world's most famous scien-

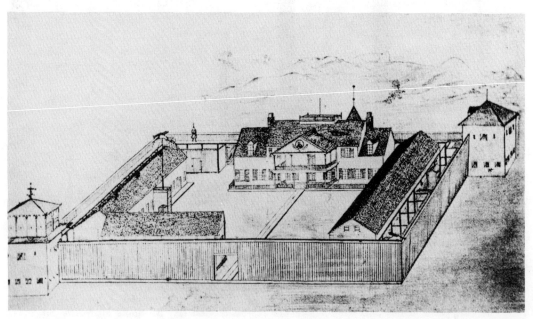

Fort Union in 1864. Courtesy Montana Historical Society, Helena.

Captain Grant Marsh. Courtesy State Historical Society of Missouri.

tists and explorers. When Fort Union passed away, there passed with it the last vestige of the fur trade as an independent commercial institution.

The *Luella's* third load that season was taken on at Pablos Rapids, where she picked up the passengers of the *Marion*, who had been stranded when the rapidly falling river had left their ship aground. Captain Marsh purchased the *Marion's* machinery, which he took back to Fort Benton and sold.

By the time this was accomplished, it was late in August and the *Luella* was the only boat left at Fort Benton. No captain had ever before dared to stay so late in the season, but Captain Marsh was confident in his ability to get out of the upper river safely. He advertised in the Helena papers that the *Luella* would leave for St. Louis the first week in September, and then went on a hunting trip with friends in the Highwood Mountains to show his unconcern. His judgment turned out to be correct.

The profits to be made for a season's work

by a steamboat on the mountain waters of the Missouri proved a veritable bonanza. When the *Luella* left Fort Benton on September 2, 1866, she carried 230 miners and $1,250,000 in gold—the most valuable cargo ever carried down the Missouri River. From this one season's work, the *Luella* showed a net profit of $24,000. Ten mountain boats are on record as having made a profit of $40,000 or over on just one trip from St. Louis to Fort Benton. In 1867 the *Ida Stockdale* made a net profit of $42,594—twice her original construction price—so everyone wanted to become a part and parcel of this new Eldorado. The huge profits to be made transporting supplies and people to the gold fields sounded even more attractive than the gold mining itself.

The fact that steamboats could, and did, make a profit in one season that more than recouped the entire construction cost of a new boat encouraged new transportation companies to be organized. The Civil War had hampered the building of steamboats compatible with the vagaries of the mountain water of the Missouri, so many of the deep-hulled crafts from the lower Missouri and the Mississippi were put into service.

Even though the new companies did not expect their deep-hulled steamboats to cope with the waters of the upper Missouri, they dispatched the deep-hulled lower-river boats fully laden and gambled on their survival. Their captains damned the risks and set off for Fort Benton. If the boats survived, they'd take them back again.

The poor performance record of these deep-hulled steamboats in the mountain trade proved beyond doubt the necessity of the shallow-draft craft then coming into use. The steamboat builders had finally discovered they could not change the Missouri to fit their boats, so they were forced to build boats to fit the Missouri.

Steam-driven capstans had long been in use on the steamboats of the Missouri River, and all the mountain boats were also equipped with a pair of large spars to be used when the boat ran aground on a sandbar or other obstruction. When needed, the spars were raised and set in the river bottom with their tops inclined at a slight angle to the stern. The top ends of these spars were rigged with a heavy tackle block over which a hawser was passed. One end of this hawser was fastened to the guards of the steamboat and the other end wound around the capstan. As the capstan revolved, the paddle wheel of the boat pushed forward and in this manner the boat was lifted and moved ahead at the same time. Then the spars were reset farther ahead and the operation repeated until the boat was literally lifted over the obstruction. From its resemblance to a grasshopper when the spars were in place, and from the way the boat moved forward in a series of "hops," this operation became known as "grasshoppering."

Along with the development of the shallow-draft mountain boats, various tall tales evolved concerning them. One favorite was about the pilot that chased the river back and forth trying to find enough water to float his boat. He finally gave up in disgust and "grasshoppered" five miles across country, catching the Missouri by surprise. Another told of the steamboat that was plowing along in the dark, to avoid Indians, when its pilot suddenly realized that the river didn't sound right. He stepped out of the pilothouse to investigate and found himself on a boat ten miles up a dry coulee, churning along on a heavy dew.

One of the most serious problems of Missouri River steamboating was the scarcity of fuel in a usable form. This was especially true on the upper Missouri and the mountain waters. Wood was the only fuel used, and the average steamboat consumed about twenty-five cords of hardwood—oak, maple, ash, elm, hickory—thirty cords of the softer woods—cedar, pine, and cottonwood—every twenty-four hours.

In the early days of steamboating, the wood was cut by the crew as needed, and the boat depended on chance accumulations of driftwood, called "rack heaps," that piled up on the river's banks, sandbars, and islands during high water. Dry standing timber on the riverbanks was also used for fuel, but Indian harassment sometimes made the cutting and accumulation of this fuel extremely dangerous. These two sources were soon exhausted as steamboat traffic increased in volume, and many of the steamboats began stripping the dry wood from the buildings of the numerous abandoned trading posts that had been constructed on the river's bank. The quick consumption of this last easily accessible fuel supply accounts for the fact that although the sites of many, if not all, of the early fur-trading posts are known, there is no trace remaining of their buildings.

With the disappearance of easily available dry wood, it became necessary to cut a great many green cottonwood logs for fuel, and these burned with scarcely enough heat to keep up steam. This fact, and the attendant dangers and delays in acquiring fuel, led to the establishment of wood yards at convenient spots along the river. These were usually founded by the steamboat owners. Along the lower stretches of the Missouri, this system of fuel supply worked well, but above Fort Union the establishment of wood yards was impractical, due to the harassment by Indians. As a result, there came into being an intrepid breed of men called "woodhawks." These men cut steamboat fuel with axes and one- and two-man saws, forming billets that were easily handled by one man to facilitate loading on the steamboats. Larger logs were split into more manageable chunks. The woodhawks established their yards at heavily wooded "points" extending into the Missouri River. They stacked their goods by hand at a spot on the riverbank where the depth of water enabled the steamboat to tie directly to the bank.

Woodhawking was not an avocation for the faint-hearted or the timid, and many men gambled their lives against the attractive prices paid for cordwood as fuel for the steamboats. Two woodhawks who became well known above Fort Union were Francis X. Biedler and John "Liver-eatin'" Johnston. They soon were the subjects of many tales, including one concerning the celebration of the captain's birthday on the steamboat *Nile* in 1869. That boat had stopped at their wood yard and purchased their wood. The two men were invited on board to share in the entertainment and, in honor of the occasion, the crew of the boat served ice cream. Biedler and Johnston, never having encountered ice cream before, were startled by its extreme coldness on such a hot day. Biedler would not admit his ignorance, but Johnston was more forward and asked in a startled whisper, "X, where in hell does this stuff come from?"

"Shut up, you damned fool," growled Biedler, swallowing a spoonful, "it comes outta cans."

The life of a woodhawk, however, was not all ice cream and cake, since he was isolated hundreds of miles from settlements and far beyond the protection of the Army. In fact, the woodhawks had to rely solely on themselves for protection. Many of these rugged individuals teamed up with others of their ilk, but there were some who preferred to depend entirely on their own initiative.

Many steamboat captains had eyed the mouth of the Yellowstone River on their trips to Fort Benton and speculated on the possibilities of putting a steamboat on its waters; however, shallow water and numerous sandbars seemed to discourage any such activity. Nevertheless, in 1864, the Army commandeered the *Chippewa Falls*, along with other steamboats including the *Island City* and the *Alone*, to carry supplies for General Sully's expedition, a venture dedicated to the harassment of the Sioux after their uprising in Minnesota.

A few bands of Sioux had crossed the Missouri River into the "breaks," a rough, desolate region later described as "hell froze over," seemingly headed for the Yellowstone River region. Sully's orders were to persecute all Sioux encountered, while at the same time exploring the possibility of establishing an Army fort on the Yellowstone River. The three steamboats sailing up the Missouri were ordered to attempt to navigate the Yellowstone, if possible, and to rendezvous with Sully on the river.

The *Island City* struck a snag in the Missouri and sank directly opposite the point where Fort Buford was later erected. Corn for Sully's horses, barreled pork for his troops, and the material to build the first Army post on the Yellowstone were lost. This loss of material and supplies canceled the Army's first attempt to establish a military post on the Yellowstone River.

The *Chippewa Falls* and the *Alone* had proceeded upriver to Fort Union, where the *Chippewa Falls* unloaded most of her cargo and then steamed forty miles up the Yellowstone, proving navigation of that stream to be feasible. She then returned to Fort Union, picked up the supplies she had unloaded, and with the *Alone* traveled up the Yellowstone to a point above the present site of Glendive, Montana, searching for Sully and his troops. They finally made contact with Sully at a spot just below Glendive.

Even though steamboating was now proven practicable on the Yellowstone River,

it did not advance as rapidly as it did on the Missouri above the confluence of the tributaries. This was due to the fact that the Yellowstone Valley was very sparsely settled by white men, and was inhabited by hostile Indians. Many of these tribes considered the Yellowstone region their personal hunting grounds. This was especially true of the Crow, Assiniboine, Gros Ventre, Piegans of the Blackfoot Confederacy, and many of the various tribes of the Sioux Nation. Although each Indian tribe considered the others its hereditary enemies, most of them considered the white man their deadliest common enemy.

Due to the above reasons there was a gap of eight years between the advent of the first two steamboats on the Yellowstone and the arrival of others. When more boats did come, they were once again under the auspices of the United States Government.

Railroads were thrusting their way farther and farther westward, and surveys were being made. Because of the Indian trouble, these surveys had to be accompanied by Army troops. In 1872, General David S. Stanley was in command of the first survey's escort in the Yellowstone Valley. He was accompanied by Lieutenant Colonel George A. Custer, in command of portions of the 7th Cavalry. The expedition was, in turn, accompanied by the steamboats *Far West*, *Key West*, and *Peninah*. A supply base, named Stanley's Stockade, was established at the mouth of Glendive Creek, and here the *Far West* and the *Peninah* unloaded their cargoes, at which time they were discharged from government service. The *Key West* was retained under the command of Captain Grant Marsh.

On August 17, 1872, the newly built *Josephine* arrived on the scene. She was a true "mountain boat," built to specifications ideal for steamboat service on both the mountain waters of the Missouri and on the Yellowstone. She was built at Pittsburg and was equipped with two boilers and two engines with a steam pressure of 160 pounds per square inch. She was, naturally, a sternwheeler, and was rated at 214 tons—183 feet long with a beam of thirty-one feet, she drew less than four feet of water fully loaded and was the first of the mountain steamboats to be equipped with twin capstans.

The *Josephine*, under the command of Captain Grant Marsh, established the head of

The steamboat Far West. *Courtesy State Historical Society of Missouri.*

navigation on the Yellowstone River on June 3, 1875, when she tied up overnight to a large cottonwood tree, known for years after as "The Josephine Tree." The tree was 483 miles above the mouth of the Yellowstone River, slightly south of present-day Billings, Montana, the extreme high of steamboat navigation on that river.

While on this same exploration trip for the Army, the *Josephine* steamed twelve miles up the Big Horn River, unaware that one year later another steamboat captained by the same man would travel that same river on an errand of mercy.

Many people are aware that the *Far West* carried the wounded of the ill-fated campaign that resulted in the Battle of the Little Big Horn and the annihilation of Lieutenant Colonel George A. Custer and 266 officers and men of the 7th Cavalry on June 25, 1876. Few, however, know that the *Far West* set a record on this trip that was never equalled on the upper portion of the Missouri River drainage.

Most of Reno's and Benteen's wounded needed medical attention that was not available anywhere other than at Bismarck, Dakota Territory, and after the news of the battle was brought to Captain Marsh at the mouth of the Big Horn River he took the *Far West* up that river to the mouth of the Little Big Horn River, fifteen miles from the battle site. From that spot the *Far West* traveled down the Big Horn River and into the Yellowstone, down the Yellowstone into the Missouri, and on to Bismarck, a total mileage of 710 miles in fifty-four hours—an average speed of thirteen and one seventh miles per hour.

During the period of Indian trouble that resulted from the Battle of the Little Big Horn, commercial steamboating grew on the Yellowstone, thanks to the establishment of military posts including Fort Keogh and Fort Custer. Most of the steamboats traveling the Yellowstone were under contract to the Army, but they also carried what little trade was transacted by the sparsely settled region. After the settlement of the Indian question, the population of the Yellowstone Valley increased very rapidly and the steamboats did not have to rely on government contracts. Towns and villages sprang up along the Yellowstone and each became a potential market for shipping.

Eleven months after the Battle of the Little Big Horn, Thomas McGirl and Oscar Hoskins built a combination stage station and trading post on the banks of the Yellowstone River athwart the Bozeman, Montana Territory-Bismarck, Dakota Territory, stage line. This spot, named Huntley, became the head of navigation on the Yellowstone and remained the head of navigation as long as steamboats rode the Yellowstone's waters.

The practice of leasing, or commandeering, steamboats by the Army was a bonanza for the steamboat owners in most cases, since the government paid $300–$350 for each day that the boats were in use. This practice was more prevalent on the Yellowstone than on the mountain waters of the Missouri. On the Missouri, most, if not all, of the Army supplies were carried at the regular cargo rates in force for civilians, except when supplies accumulated to such an extent that it was cheaper to lease the entire boat.

The last mass leasing by the Army in the upper Missouri drainage involved the steamboats used to transport the Sioux and Cheyenne who had eventually surrendered after the Custer debacle. The Indians who had capitulated at Fort Keogh, near Miles City, Montana, were transported to the Standing Rock Reservation by the *Eclipse, General Terry, Josephine, Black Hills,* and the *F. Y. Batchelor.* The Indians collected at Fort Buford were shipped on the *Helena, Star of the West,* and the *Far West.*

In the later years of steamboating, one pioneer woman, the wife of steamboat captain Charles P. Woolfolk, became the only female pilot to navigate the mountain waters of the Missouri and the shallow, sneaky waters of the Yellowstone. A nineteen-year-old bride in 1881, she had boarded her husband's boat, the *General Meade,* at Sioux City, Iowa, to join him on his trip upriver. The *General Meade* was bound for Fort Benton carrying supplies for traders and Army troops stationed along the river.

Mrs. Woolfolk was the only passenger on board, and during the long journey both her husband and the pilot, T. J. Anderson, took the greatest delight in teaching her to handle the huge wheel and ring the signal bells. Upon arriving at Fort Benton, Captain Woolfolk and Anderson went ashore to arrange delivery of the remaining cargo. They soon discovered, however, that the cargo was loaded backward, and it became necessary to move the boat to another berth on the levee. The engineer asked Mrs. Woolfolk if she could do it. Mrs. Woolfolk met the challenge by putting into practice what she had learned on the upriver journey. She moved the steamboat like an old hand, and from then on handled the wheel and signals at every opportunity on various boats, not only on the Missouri, but on the Yellowstone as well. She was one of the last pilots on that river.

The oddest powered craft to travel the waters of the Missouri-Yellowstone was the *Baby Mine.* She had no commercial value, being merely a cockleshell, and was powered by a long-distance swimmer named Paul Boynton. He towed her downriver, while swimming on his back, from Glendive, Montana, on the Yellowstone to St. Louis, Missouri, on the Missouri River and used a double-bladed oar to increase his speed. Indians who saw him propelling himself through the water named him "Beaver-With-Two-Tails."

The railroads, always the economic enemy of the steamboats on the waterways of the United States, had rapidly extended to points on the Missouri River. In 1859 the Hannibal and St. Joseph Railroad reached St. Joseph, Missouri. The Sioux City and Pacific reached Sioux City, Iowa, in 1868. In 1870 the Illinois Central reached the same place and Sioux City became, and remained for a long time, one of the most important ports on the Missouri River.

In 1872 the Northern Pacific reached Bismarck, Dakota Territory, and a new river port was established, taking considerable business from the river towns on the lower Missouri River. In 1880 the Utah Northern laid tracks into Montana from Ogden and attracted a large share of the trade that had previously been hauled in steamboats. In 1883 the Northern Pacific was pushing into the upper Missouri region and soon controlled most of the business that originated between Bismarck and Fort Benton. The arrival of the Great Northern in Helena in 1887 was the final blow.

Upper Missouri River steamboating did not die abruptly, however, because well into the twentieth century steamboats were still hauling grain from Washburn, North Dakota, to ports downriver. World War I caused a recurrence of steamboating on the upper Missouri, but this was a flash in the pan compared with the halcyon days of steamboating.

The last steamboat to tie up to the levee at Fort Benton was the *Mandan*. When she went downriver in 1921, the era of steamboating on the mountain waters of the Missouri and the shallow waters of the Yellowstone came to an end.

Diesel boats now push barges laden with oil, coal, etc., from St. Louis upriver to various river towns, but through traffic is stopped by the numerous dams built to tame and control the wildest river in the United States. There are, of course, still occasional excursion steamboats which recall the days of Captains Joseph La Barge and Grant Marsh.

10

The Red River of the North

BY REX BUNDY

Water transportation on the Red River of the North had no genesis until the arrival of the steamboat. Unlike other waterways that contributed to the settlement of the West, the Red did not carry the canoes and pirogues of the early explorers and the fur traders or the flatboats of the settlers. The very nature of the river's course and the surrounding terrain made it much easier, and faster, to travel with a limited load on the surface of the adjoining rolling prairies. Woodlands created no obstacles as the only trees and shrubs were those in the immediate vicinity of the rivers and creeks. Then, too, there was an international hindrance, a monopolistic situation which no other waterway had to contend with in the United States. And this monopoly had been in effect for over a century prior to the formation of the United States.

In 1670, Charles II of England granted the Adventurers of London Trading into Hudson's Bay, now known as the Hudson's Bay Company, a monopoly on *all* trade in that vast, remote region that embraced the complete drainage of all waterways into Hudson's Bay. In the heartland of that enormous, remote region lay the valley of the Red River of the North, approximately 125 miles east of the precise geographical center of the North American continent. In this huge area controlled by the Hudson's Bay Company, settlers were forbidden with the exception of those men who had served their time as employees of the company and in this way became "free" men.

It was not until 1811 that enough pressure from the crown was brought to bear on the Hudson's Bay Company to force them to honor the stipulation in their charter that they establish agricultural settlements. And to retain their control, the company granted one of its stockholders, James Douglas, the Fifth Earl of Selkirk, 116,000 square miles of land in the heartland of the North American continent and named this grant the District of Assiniboia. The complete valley of the Red River of the North was included within this grant.

Selkirk gathered his first settlers from the Highlands of Scotland and from Ireland. Later he recruited settlers from the Hebrides, Switzerland, and Lower Canada. The first of these settlers arrived in 1812, having spent the winter at York Factory on Hudson's Bay. They established Fort Douglas, later renamed Fort Garry by the Hudson's Bay Company, which is now the city of Winnipeg, Manitoba, at the confluence of the Assiniboine River and the Red. This became the center of the Selkirk colony far beyond the American agricultural frontier and created a future market for American goods.

Many factors controlled the era of the steamboat on the Red River. One was the War of 1812, which presaged the establishment of the international boundary line. Another was the establishment of the international boundary line. Another was the establishment of the Forty-ninth parallel as the boundary between Canadian and United States possessions extending from the Lake of the Woods to the Rocky Mountains in 1823. Yet another was the Treaty of Traverse de Sioux in 1851, when the Sioux ceded the lands east of the Red River between Lake Traverse and the Buffalo River in Minnesota Territory to the United States. Even before the treaty was ratified, there was an influx of settlers into the Indian country. These settlers took up claims along the east bank of the Red and began building cabins and laying out townsites. This small-scale boom gave the country

St. Paul, Minnesota, in 1853. Courtesy of the New-York Historical Society, New York City.

considerable advertising even though the profit from the scanty fur trade and small lumber industry was practically nil.

The most important reason for the advent of the steamboat was the Hudson's Bay Company's change in policy in 1857. After nearly two centuries of dictatorship over the northern portion of the North American continent, Sir George Simpson, director of the Hudson's Bay Company in North America, arranged with the United States Treasury Department to bring Canadian-bound goods of English origin through the little settlement of St. Paul, Minnesota Territory, in bond.

The reason for picking St. Paul as a distributing point for the bonded goods was the fact that these goods would be within five hundred miles of their destination and would have traveled by the cheapest method of transportation of that time—water. This move eliminated the long delay, high cost of transportation, and the uncertainty of receiving goods from England via the old water route used exclusively by the Hudson's Bay Company. At the time the Hudson's Bay Company

was granted their charter in North America, Lower Canada was held by France, who controlled the northern waterway access into the interior of the continent—the St. Lawrence River and the Great Lakes. So the company was forced to establish a far-north water route via Hudson's Bay and up the Hayes River into Lake Winnipeg. The fact that Hudson's Bay was ice-locked nearly year-long not only limited the amount of supplies the company could bring in, but also added to the uncertainty of any ship making port at York Factory on Hudson's Bay in any given year.

The St. Paul merchants were delighted when the first trial shipment of goods in bond was made by the Hudson's Bay Company in the summer of 1858. At the time this shipment was made, Minnesota had achieved statehood, having been admitted to the Union on May 11, 1858. Federal funding was shut off with the loss of territorial status and all the Minnesota citizens were concerned.

These goods in bond originated in England for the express use of the Hudson's Bay Company and the settlers of the Selkirk settlement. They were heavily wrapped and sealed with lead seals and were not for dissemination within the United States as they entered the country duty-free, but the St. Paul merchants immediately saw the possibilities involved in supplying a vast enterprise, the Hudson's Bay Company, whose estimated exports, at that time, were $1,800,000 annually and whose imports were estimated at $1,000,000. The freight charges on the imports and exports would be a financial bonanza. This windfall, coming in the midst of a depression, led to frantic scurrying to establish transportation facilities other than the slow Red River cart caravans.

For years goods had been hauled between St. Paul and the small settlement of Pembina, located on the west bank of the Red River exactly where the Forty-ninth Parallel crossed the Red, by the unique, ingenious Red River carts. These carts were built without the use of iron in any form. They were made entirely of wood and lashed together with rawhide. Their two wheels were originally made by sawing a four-inch slab from a huge cottonwood. Later, when artisans became plentiful in the Selkirk settlement, these wheels were made like a regular wagon wheel with one exception: they were dished outward to allow the heavy gumbo mud of the Red River Valley to fall from between the spokes in wet weather. They were pulled by one animal, preferably an ox, and could carry a load estimated at a thousand pounds. Naturally they were slow and the nature of their drivers, the Red River métis, was also a handicap to a speedy journey as they might decide to go on a hunt instead of delivering their freight loads.

The Red River carts could travel three trails. The earliest led up the Red from Pembina to Lake Traverse and over the height of land and down the Minnesota River to Traverse de Sioux. Here the goods were loaded on barges or steamboats for river shipment to Mendota, Minnesota. This became known as Kittson's Trail and it could follow the west or east side of the Red but always stayed within twenty miles distance to facilitate the fording of the Red's tributaries. The great disadvantage of this trail was the fact that low water might make the Minnesota River unnavigable between Traverse de Sioux and Mendota.

Another trail, known as the Sauk Valley, or Plains, Trail, was established from St. Paul

to Pembina because St. Paul had far better facilities for steamboats from the south than had Mendota. This high, dry trail led north along the east bank of the Mississippi to Sauk Rapids and St. Cloud. Cart trains following this trail forded the river at St. Cloud and then traveled up the Sauk Valley to the northwest. Using this route, they could either cross the Bois des Sioux River to join Kittson's Trail west of the Red, which was easier traveling, or go down the east side of the Red to Pembina. (This eastside trail is now the route of U.S. Highway 52.)

Another route, the Woods Trail, went up the Mississippi to Crow Wing and from there to Detroit Lakes. From here it could join the other trails near Moorhead, Minnesota. One portion of this trail was cut through eighty miles of forest by eight men in 12 days in the winter of 1844. This trail later provided the route for the Northern Pacific railroad and U.S. Highway 10.

In 1851 steamboats began operating between the Falls of St. Anthony (St. Paul) and St. Cloud. So the Red River carts could now be accommodated at St. Cloud, and this route, the Sauk Valley, or Plains, Trail, became the most traveled and later was used by the stage and freight lines linking the Mississippi and the Red River steamboats.

In the fall of 1858, Ramsey Crooks, New York agent for the Hudson's Bay Company, contacted Russell Blakely of the St. Paul firm of Blakely and Burbank in regard to a firm to act as the Mississippi country agent for the company. Naturally, Blakely recommended his own firm, but with a slight change in name from Blakely and Burbank to J. C. & H. C. Burbank and Company. Sir George Simpson acted on Crooks' recommendation and the appointment assured the fact that nearly all the goods shipped into western Canada, as well as goods being shipped out, would be channeled through St. Paul, Minnesota.

In the winter of 1858–59, Sir George Simpson notified his new agents he was shipping 150 tons of goods in bond through the United States via the Mississippi River. He also mentioned that he hoped water transportation could be arranged as he was well aware of the length of time it took a caravan of Red River carts to traverse the distance between St. Paul and Pembina, and then in floating the goods downriver to Fort Garry.

The St. Paul merchants were not lacking

Russell D. Blakely. Courtesy Manitoba Archives.

involved, demanded a $2,000 bonus to move his boat to the Red. The St. Paul merchants, acting as a sort of Chamber of Commerce, accepted his demand and a contract was signed, supposedly, to that effect. At least there are various references to the fact that Northrup posted a bond to put an operational steamboat on the Red River.

Anson Northrup went to work immediately. The upper works of the *North Star* were demolished and the machinery dismantled. Lumber for the new hull was cut at the Chapman Mill on the Gull River. Everything needed was assembled on the Leaf River, a tributary of the Crow Wing, and the entire party left the Leaf on February 21, 1859, bound for the Red.

The party consisted of thirty-two men and the motive power to haul the sleds loaded with machinery and lumber consisted of thirteen yokes of oxen and seventeen teams of horses. The men hoped to make the 140-mile trip to the town site of Lafayette, opposite the mouth of the Cheyenne River, by March 20. However, the trip proved more arduous than expected due to cold weather and snow, and the party did not reach the Red until April 1. Forty-nine days later, at 10:45 A.M. on May 19, the first steamboat rode the waters of the Red River of the North.

The little steamboat was ninety feet long with a beam of twenty-two feet and drew fourteen inches of water when empty, and like all the steamboats that followed her on the Red, she was a sternwheeler. She was christened with appropriate ceremony on the day of her launching and Northrup wanted to name her the *Pioneer*. His crew demurred and insisted she be called the *Anson Northrup*.

Considerable work was still to be done on the upper structure of the little steamer and it was not until May 25 that she attempted her first journey. On that date she left Lafayette headed upstream for Fort Abercrombie, where she arrived on May 29. It was Northrup's intent to return downriver the next day, but the post commander offered enough lumber to complete the steamboat's unfinished upper cabin. While this work was in progress the news spread of the steamboat's arrival and the merchants of Breckenridge, Minnesota, convinced Captain Northrup he should make the short journey to their waterfront and load freight for Fort Garry that had arrived at Breckenridge via the Mississippi and the Min-

in initiative and had anticipated the hopes for water transportation. In October of 1858 they sent Russell Blakely and John R. Irvine to make a survey of the Red as to the possibilities of steamboats on that river. On their return to St. Paul, Blakely told the merchants the stream was navigable about seven months of the year. This, of course, to depend on a shifting head of navigation because the upper reaches of the river could be used only in the spring and early summer. On the strength of Blakely's statement, the St. Paul merchants offered a bonus of $1,000 to the first person to operate a steamboat on the Red River.

Anson Northrup had a beat-up little steamboat, the *North Star*, that he had been running on the Crow Wing River carrying supplies to lumber camps. The boiler and the machinery of this little steamer had originally been installed in the *Governor Ramsey*, the first steamboat built above the Falls of St. Anthony in 1850. This made the machinery secondhand, at best; however, the boiler was thirdhand, having been originally used in a locomotive engine and no record is available as to its age.

Northrup, after contemplating the work

Anson Northrup. Courtesy Minnesota Historical Society.

nesota rivers. From the head of navigation on the Minnesota, the freight had been hauled to Breckenridge by Red River carts.

The first freight carried by steamboat on the Red River of the North left Breckenridge, Minnesota, aboard the *Anson Northrup* on the fifth of June, 1859, bound for Fort Garry (Winnipeg). The steamer was at Pembina on the eighth of June and arrived at Fort Garry on the tenth. She was received with a noisy and exuberant welcome by the Fort Garry citizens and the officials of the Hudson's Bay Company. Then to add to her laurels as the first steamboat on the Red, the little steamer made an excursion trip downriver to Lake Winnipeg, thus becoming the first steamboat on that body of water.

On June 15, the *Anson Northrup* began the first upstream trip on the Red River carrying freight and seventeen passengers. However, this upstream journey took considerably longer than the downriver run and the steamer did not arrive at Fort Abercrombie until June 23. This was due to bucking the current, the sad disrepair of the boiler, and the necessity of mooring each night, plus taking off running time to cut wood for fuel. And evidently this return trip was not to Captain Northrup's liking because upon arrival at Fort Abercrombie he left the steamer in charge of a carpenter named Claghorn and departed for St. Paul along with the steamer's passengers.

Russell Blakely was at Fort Abercrombie at the time and he chided Northrup for leaving the steamer. Northrup told him, in no uncertain terms, that if he wanted to operate the steamer he could buy it and run it himself. So, for a few weeks, it could be said the steamer was abandoned, although during this time it was used to ferry Red River carts across the Red.

J. C. Burbank and Company bought the *Anson Northrup* for a reported $8,000 in July 1859. The company hired Captain Edwin Bell to take charge of the steamboat. In the meantime, Georgetown, Minnesota, on the Buffalo River, a few miles upstream from its junction with the Red, was designated the head of navigation. The Red between that point and Breckenridge had become very shallow by this time and would get more so during the hot months of August and September.

The same organization, J. C. Burbank and Company, had also established a stage and freight line to connect St. Paul with the Red. Their original plan was to use Breckenridge as a head of navigation but low water changed their point of contact to Georgetown. And immediately after purchasing the *Anson Northrup*, they had dispatched a wagon train of freight to the Red but it became bogged down in a rainstorm. This was just as well as the wagon train's destination was Breckenridge. Russell Blakely contacted the wagon train and diverted it to Georgetown.

In the meantime, the new crew of the *Anson Northrup* had taken the steamboat downriver to Georgetown. Here they were kept busy making repairs on the boiler while waiting for the arrival of the wagon train of freight. Upon the arrival of the freight, the little steamer made a second trip to Fort Garry. But by this time the river had fallen considerably and, arriving at Goose Rapids, Captain Bell found fast water, huge boulders protruding from the surface of the stream, and a large gravel bar at the foot of the rapids. As he could not negotiate the rapids loaded, Bell was forced to unload all the freight and have it hauled around the rapids by teams brought down from Georgetown. He got rid of the boulders by digging huge holes downstream and rolling them into the holes. The gravel bar was surmounted by building a brush dam to obtain a head of water sufficient to float the *Anson Northrup* across. All this took consid-

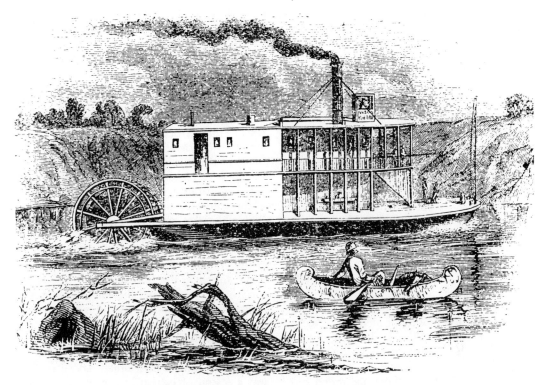

The S.S. Anson Northrup. *Courtesy Manitoba Archives.*

erable time and when the steamer arrived at Fort Garry the season was far advanced, and the water so low it was decided to lay the steamer up for the season. She was taken to Indian River and winterized. The crew returned to St. Paul via the regular Red River cart caravan and thus ended the first steamboat transportation season on the Red River of the North.

During the winter of 1859–60, J. C. Burbank, on the advice of Captain Bell, made a complete inspection of the steamer. He found they had bought a lemon as well as a steamboat. The hull was new but built of green pine lumber and leaked like a colander. The machinery was old and worn, the boiler had a cracked head, the flues leaked, and the stay bolts were weeping. However, they had her repaired as well as possible that winter for the upriver run in the spring. Measurements were also taken for a new head for the boiler and sent East with the stipulation that the new head be delivered to Georgetown, Minnesota, by early spring.

In the spring of 1860 the *Anson Northrup*

was taken upstream to Georgetown, where she was refurbished and completely repaired. Not only that, she was rechristened the *Pioneer* and under that name had the river to herself until 1862, when the *International*, the most famous of all Red River steamboats, was put in service.

This second boat on the Red was also secondhand. In June of 1859, Captain John B. Davis started up the Minnesota River in the steamboat *Freighter* with the avowed intentions of taking her through Big Stone Lake, Lake Traverse, the Bois de Sioux River, and into the Red. The water was high enough, but he started too late. The boat grounded, and was abandoned a few miles before she reached Big Stone Lake.

Had Captain Davis started his journey sooner it is entirely possible it would have been completed although there is no water connection between the Minnesota River and Lake Traverse except in times of flood. When in flood the entire country, at that time, was one huge lake and the *Freighter* could have steamed into the Red without trouble. Also, there is no place in the world that can compare to this one short stretch of land, probably only a mile or so in length, between the two waterways. It is the only obstruction for a through water route from the Gulf of Mexico to Hudson's Bay. A short canal at this point would have enabled the Atlantic Ocean to connect itself in an endless merry-go-round.

However, Captain Davis did not make it and the boiler and machinery of the *Freighter* were sold to the Burbank Company. They hauled them to Georgetown, where the company built the *International*.

On May 20, 1862, the *International* made her maiden voyage—one that did not get off to a very good start. She soon ran into brush and trees and tore off her smokestacks, requiring a delay of four hours. This may have been caused by her size, which was considerably larger than the *Pioneer*. The *International* was 136 feet long with a beam of twenty-five feet and drew four feet of water loaded.

The *International* was destined to be queen of the Red River water transportation for a period of nine years. She also set a record that was never beaten, making one round trip

from Moorhead, Minnesota, to Winnipeg, Manitoba, in five days and eighteen hours.

In 1862 two steamboats were in service on the Red although that winter this was reduced to one when the *Pioneer* rolled over and sank at her winter quarters near Fort Garry. She was never put back into service.

This same year saw the beginnings of the Indian troubles that would plague water transportation on the Red for a number of years. Many of the tribes that roamed the Red River Valley were bickering among themselves and not averse to lifting the hair of any convenient white man. Due to the unsettled times, J. C. Burbank and Company, although they controlled the only steamboat on the Red, found they had little or no cargo with the exception of the Hudson's Bay Company's supplies. As a result, they sold the *International* to the Hudson's Bay Company and the company immediately put Norman W. Kittson in command.

In 1863, even though the Indian trouble was seemingly under control, the different tribes of the Red River Valley were still having difficulties with each other. Added to this was a season of extremely low water, and by

The International, *once the "queen of the Red River," at old Fort Garry. Courtesy Manitoba Archives.*

The Selkirk. *Courtesy Manitoba Archives.*

the last of June the *International* was moored under the guns of Fort Abercrombie for the remainder of that year.

The onslaught of the Civil War caused practically a standstill of Red River transportation. Few settlers were moving into the region, and those that were there were being called into the armed service of the North. The frontier receded to the more heavily settled regions. Scarcely any trade was conducted through the United States by the Hudson's Bay Company, as they had reverted, during the war years, to their centuries-old water route—Hudson's Bay-Hayes River-Lake Winnipeg.

In 1864 the *International* departed from Fort Abercrombie on April 19—backward. The steamer was too large to complete a turn in that portion of the river and was forced to travel downstream with her stern leading her until arriving at the mouth of the Wild Rice River, where enough room was available for her to complete the maneuver. Even with such an early start on the season of 1864, the *International* made only one trip that year and

spent most of the time at Fort Abercrombie, where she was laid up for the winter the latter part of July.

"Stagnation" is the only word to describe water transportation on the Red for the following six years. The *International* made occasional trips when a paying cargo could be collected. And it was not until 1870 that the Red's water transportation took an upswing that resulted in a fantastic boom lasting less than a decade.

The vital year for water transportation on the Red was 1870. That year the province of Manitoba was established and the two-century monopoly of the Hudson's Bay Company was broken completely, as far as the question of settlement was concerned. It also ushered in the first competition for freight on the Red when James J. Hill, manager of Hill, Griggs and Company, authorized the building of the *Selkirk* at McCauleyville, Minnesota, just across the Red from Fort Abercrombie.

The *Selkirk*, the third steamboat to make its appearance on the Red, was somewhat smaller than its only competitor, the *Interna-*

tional. She was twenty-six feet shorter and two feet narrower in beam and drew a foot less water. However, it was this steamboat that brought the entanglements of higher finance, shady practices of politicians, and the ruthlessness of empire builders to the water transportation on the Red.

The *Selkirk* made her maiden voyage from McCauleyville, Minnesota, on April 12, 1871, with 115 passengers and 125 tons of freight scheduled for Fort Garry and intermediate points. She continued to make trips all during the season of 1871 and for a time was the only steamboat allowed to carry goods in bond for the Canadian settlements and the Hudson's Bay Company even though the Hudson's Bay Company owned the other boat on the river. This was due to the machinations of James J. Hill when he convinced the United States Treasury Department that goods in bond should only be carried on a bonded boat of American registry—the *Selkirk* was the only boat on the Red that qualified!

The Hudson's Bay Company retaliated by transferring the ownership of the *International* to Norman W. Kittson, an American citizen. Kittson got busy and by June of 1871 the *International* became a bonded boat and was put into the general trade. Then began the real steamboating on the Red River of the North.

The winter of 1871–72, Kittson, backed by the Hudson's Bay Company, built the *Dakota* at Breckenridge, Minnesota. This made three bonded boats in service. The competition became very brisk, accompanied by price cutting, until a merger was worked out whereby the three boats were transferred to the ownership of the newly created Red River Transportation Company and competition ceased.

In the summer of 1872 the Northern Pacific Railroad was completed as far as Moorhead, Minnesota, and the St. Paul & Pacific as far as Breckenridge, Minnesota. With two railroads in contact with the Red, trade with Manitoba increased so rapidly that numerous other steamboats were being built, or in the stages of being built. And in 1873 the first, and only, propeller-driven commercial boat appeared on the Red, the *Maggie*. She was a tugboat and was not built for use on the American portion of the Red. She was transported to Moorhead by the railroad and launched on the river and proceeded downstream to Winnipeg.

The year 1873 also saw the genesis of the boom in steamboat construction. The *Cheyenne* was built at Grand Forks, Dakota Territory, and taken for debts by the Red River Transportation Company. That winter a Canadian, Captain McLain, built a boat at Breckenridge named the *Alpha*, but due to legal difficulties was forced to sell her to the

The Alpha. *Courtesy Manitoba Archives.*

The Manitoba, *one of the elite steamboats in service on the Red River of the North.*
Courtesy Manitoba Archives.

expanding Red River Transportation Company, which now controlled all the steamboats on the Red.

Once again the settlers of Manitoba were faced with a monopoly. This did not set well with the merchants of Winnipeg or the businessmen located in Moorhead and St. Paul. As a result, the Merchants International Steamboat Company was formed. This company had two steamboats framed on the Ohio River and shipped to Moorhead by rail where they were fabricated in the winter of 1874–75. The two boats were named the *Manitoba* and the *Minnesota.* They were identical in size, both being 135 feet long, thirty-one and a half feet in beam, and displaced 4.9 feet of water when loaded. Both steamers were put in general serv-

ice in the spring of 1875 and, to become bonded, their registry and management were held by the Americans in the company. However, this was a short-lived line due to price cutting and the fact that the management was not familiar with the ins and outs of river transportation. It was not long before the company was forced, by debts, to turn both steamers over to the Red River Transportation Line. The competition they created, however, caused considerable ill feelings, and when a collision occurred on June 5, 1875, between the *International* and the *Manitoba,* in which the *Manitoba* sank, some sources described the incident as deliberate on the part of the Red River Transportation Company. But this accident occurred in shallow water and the *Mani-*

toba was soon raised and placed in service again.

Not too many accidents were recorded on the Red, although nine drownings were attributed to steamboats between the years 1875 and 1878. Although the cry "Man overboard" was heard frequently, the very nature of the river in its upper reaches was such that fatalities were not often indicated. One such happening occurred when a man with his head in clouds of whiskey vapors attempted to waltz across the deck of a steamer with a rolled umbrella as a partner. He took up too much space on one of his swooping glides and waltzed off into the river. Aid was immediately given and the unfortunate terpsichorean was pulled from the river by one of the "roosters," as the deckhands were called. Damages sustained amounted to ruined clothes, one plug hat, one umbrella, and one shoe, plus the extinguishing of a beautiful glow.

From 1875 until the winter of 1877–78, no other steamboats were built, but in the winter of 1877–78, the *J. L. Grandin* was built at Fargo, Dakota Territory. She was 125 feet long with a beam of thirty-two feet and drew four feet of water when loaded. Used mostly to haul wheat and produce from the huge Grandin Farms, she was also put in general service to Winnipeg during the growing season. Two years later, in 1880, the *Pluck* was built at Moorhead. She was ninety-five feet long with a beam of sixteen feet and drew three and a half feet of water. Two years later, in 1882, the *H. W. Alsop* was constructed at Moorhead. She was 125 feet in length with a beam of twenty-four feet and drew three feet of water.

Steamboat building ceased at this time and it was not until 1890 that the *Fram* was rebuilt at East Grand Forks. Prior to that time the *Fram* had been used on the Red Lake River above Crookston, Minnesota. She was also one of the smallest of the Red River steamers, having a hull length of seventy-one and a half feet with a nineteen-foot beam and drew three and a half feet. No other steamboats were built for service on the Red until the *Grand Forks* was built at Grand Forks, North Dakota, in 1895. Her hull was 123 feet long with a beam of twenty-six and a half feet and drew four feet of water. The machinery and boiler of the *H. W. Alsop* were installed in this boat and she was the last steamboat built on the Red River for commercial purposes.

During the early flurry of steamboat construction, three other boats were built at Moorhead: the *William Robinson*, a small propeller steamer; the *Marquette*, a fair-sized boat; and the *Northwest*, reputed to have been the largest of all the Red River steamboats. These three were used in service around the city of Winnipeg and on the Assiniboine River.

One other steamer deserves mention in the history of the water transportation on the Red and that is the *Baby*. Perhaps the first, and only, recreational steamer to be built for those waters in 1877 by Mr. De Camp of Moorhead, she had a hull length of twenty-one feet with a beam of six feet and was driven by a propeller wheel twenty-two inches in diameter and could run at twelve miles per hour.

The steamboat era on the Red covered a span of fifty years, and of those fifty years, only six could be designated as real steamboating. However, those six crowded years wrote an important and colorful chapter into the history of Minnesota, North Dakota, and the tiny Selkirk settlement that eventually became the province of Manitoba. To Minnesotans the trade that flourished with the steamboat era became a solid foundation for the welfare of the state. To the settlers of the Red River Valley it was the pioneer's prayer for relatively cheap, swift, and regular service in communicating with the outside world. It was a bridge, flimsy at times, to the expanding frontier and marked the end of virtual isolation.

By 1878 the clang of the railroader's spike mauls was ringing the knell of steamboat transportation. Like many other waterways, the Red was no different in expediting the demise of its own value to the region it served. Cargo after cargo of steel rails traveled down the river. Then came the history-making trip of the Selkirk, which ended at St. Boniface on October 8, 1878. On that trip the *Selkirk* carried the first locomotive into Manitoba, the "Countess of Dufferin."

From then on there was a steady decline in steamboat travel on the Red. It did not disappear abruptly as there were too many established farms along the river that, as yet, had no connection with the railroads so cargo and freight were still available. However, the

The Grand Forks, *the last of the large steamers on the Red River of the North. Once a proud cargo carrier and later an excursion steamer. Courtesy Manitoba Archives.*

far-seeing men of the Red River Transportation Company had made arrangements to sell all their steamboats to a Manitoba concern, the Winnipeg and Western Transportation Company, and in that same year, 1878, the *Cheyenne* and the *Alpha* were sold. In the spring of 1879 the *Manitoba*, the *International*, and the *Minnesota* also became their property and the once proud fleet of the Red River Transportation Company disintegrated.

So the dispersal, as well as the beginning, of the Red River steamers was unlike that of other waterways. Not many of them rotted at their moorings. The *Alpha, Cheyenne, Manitoba*, and the *International* all operated on the Saskatchewan, Assiniboine, and lower Red River under British registry. The *Minnesota*, renamed the *City of Winnipeg*, sank while crossing Lake Winnipeg on her way to the Saskatchewan River. But the railroad once more caught up with the other four and they were dismantled. Their boilers and machinery

found further use on the Yukon River steamboats.

Wrecks, and other means of destruction, caused the demise of some Red River steamers. The *Dakota* burned in midstream near Pembina, North Dakota. The *Selkirk* was swept from her moorings at Grand Forks, Dakota Territory, in 1884, carried downstream, and wrecked on a bridge pier. The *J. L. Grandin* broke her moorings twice, once in 1882, when she floated down the Red and into the Elm River and was retrieved unharmed, but in the flood of 1897 she once again broke loose, and when the water receded she was left stranded high and dry and served as a reminder of the great days of river travel. Another steamboat, the *Grand Forks*, made a gala tourist excursion in June 1909, but shortly after that voyage she met with an accident and sank. She was the last of the large boats on the Red and with her sinking the curtain dropped on an era.

11

Steamboats on Texas Rivers

BY ELMER KELTON

April 12, 1836. The last defenders of the Alamo had been dead a month and six days. After long weeks of struggling in cold rain and deep mud, weakened by sickness and internal strife, Sam Houston's ragged little army of Texian volunteers stood on the banks of the swollen Brazos River and looked across.

Behind them, killing and burning everything in its path, plodded the victorious army of General Don Antonio Lopez de Santa Anna y Perez de Lebron, known in history simply as Santa Anna. An insufferable egoist, bitterly cruel, Santa Anna had laid waste the rebellious Mexican state of Zacatecas before crossing the Rio Grande to slaughter his way across Texas by the Alamo and Goliad. He had announced his intention to do the same to Sam Houston's men if ever the retreating Houston would stand and face him. Houston kept waiting for what he considered the proper place. Groce's plantation on the banks of the Brazos was certainly not it.

Confrontation at this point might have become necessary, and Houston might very well have lost had his troops been unable to cross the river. Fortunately the steamboat *Yellow Stone* was loading cotton bales along the Brazos River to try to carry them out ahead of the Mexican Army. The *Yellow Stone* was one of the newest arrivals in a small but growing fleet of commercial craft working the lower reaches of the principal Texas rivers: the Brazos, the Colorado, the Sabine, the Red.

She had been built in 1831 for use in John Jacob Astor's fur trade among the Indians along the upper Missouri and the Yellowstone rivers. For three years she had steamed those northern rivers in summer and the Mississippi in winter before changing ownership. In December 1835 she had transported forty-seven volunteers, the Mobile Grays, down to Texas to join the war against Santa Anna. She was a deep-draft vessel with a 130-foot keel and single engine. She was considered of high class in the Texas trade because she sported two stacks.

Sam Houston commandeered her with full approval of Captain John E. Ross to carry his men safely across the river. Ross placed cotton bales along her decks to protect both his boat and the soldiers aboard her from enemy fire. He made the transfer without undue difficulty. Afterward, however, he got the *Yellow Stone* away just in time. Advance elements of the Mexican Army tried to capture or sink her as she made her smoky way downriver, carrying civilian refugees and running for safer waters. Near Richmond, Mexican soldiers on the riverbank tried to rope her two proud smokestacks as she steamed by. Dodging, she nearly went aground.

Houston's army, growing again, moved on down toward Harrisburg, in later times destined to be swallowed up by the burgeoning city of Houston. Santa Anna, afraid the Texian Army would flee to the neutrality of Louisiana before he could catch them, set out in a rush with a striking force, letting the main body of his army straggle along behind. Even though he might conquer all of Texas, the victory would be hollow to him if he could not take Sam Houston with it.

On the afternoon of April 21, with Buffalo Bayou to their backs, the San Jacinto River to their left, and twelve hundred Mexican soldiers sunning themselves in camp on the open prairie ahead of them, the Texians advanced. They caught the general and most of his men at siesta. Eighteen minutes later Santa Anna's power was destroyed, and Texas was free.

Texas had other official business for the *Yellow Stone*. On May 4 she transported the president and other officials of the new Texas Republic to the San Jacinto battleground. On May 5 Houston boarded her with his humbled, fearful prisoner Santa Anna. He had saved the general from lynching at the hands of bitter Texians, not out of pity, but because of a hardheaded realization that dead men cannot sign treaties. He intended to see Santa Anna give Texas her independence for once and for all. The *Yellow Stone* carried the two generals down to Galveston to board an ocean-going ship for New Orleans.

Late that year the *Yellow Stone* had a final and sad duty to perform for Texas. On December 28 she carried the casket and the funeral cortege of the Father of Texas, Stephen F. Austin, down to his burial place at Peach Point.

Twenty years later, Sam Houston was still trying to get the Texas government to pay Captain Ross's widow the old claim for the *Yellow Stone*'s services in a time that changed history.

Basically, despite valuable service rendered by the *Yellow Stone* and several hundred other river-trade vessels like her during the 1800s, Texas was never vitally dependent upon river transportation. The majority of traffic crossed the rivers; it did not move upon them. Towns grew along the rivers because of the water supply for drinking, for livestock needs, for irrigation and industry, but not for water transportation. Commercial boat traffic was confined to the eastern part of the state and to less than a dozen rivers. Farther west, rivers were too shallow; many ran but little in the dry time of the year. Even the brownish Brazos and its reddish sister the Colorado often dropped to such a low state during summer months that steamboats caught upriver had to be tied off to the bank until fall rains floated them out.

In one recorded instance such a boat's crew, grounded after exploring too far up a narrow tributary, planted and harvested a crop of cotton while waiting for the fall freshets to liberate their vessel from the mud.

Not even Texas' original Indian tribes had much of a water culture except a few in the piney woods country of deep East Texas, paddling swift pirogues along the Sabine and the Neches-Angelina. To those Indians out on the Edwards Plateau, the Cross Timbers, the Trans-Pecos, and the high plains, a river was meant to catch fish in, to drink from, or to water the horses. It was a good place to hunt game. But it was, sometimes, a fearsome thing to cross. To ride upon it was unthinkable.

By and large, this attitude was shared by the white settlers who eventually displaced these Indians.

The first Europeans to attempt to navigate a Texas river were, naturally enough, the Spanish. In the autumn of 1519, four Spanish ships were outbound from Jamaica, their mission to find a passageway for the Orient. Under command of Captain Alonso Alvarez de Pineda, they sailed up to the muddy mouth of the Rio Grande. His ships were in need of repair, and to him this bay seemed a good place for it, even if the palm-lined waterway which stretched westward out of sight was not the open door to the silks and spices of China. He dropped anchor. While some of the men careened the ships, scraped barnacles and caulked the hulls, others accompanied Pineda afoot upriver, exploring the many Indian mud and reed towns clustered near the bank. For a distance of eighteen to twenty miles they traveled, trading, making friends. The Indians seemed peaceably inclined to these strange bearded creatures from another world. Pineda convinced himself that this river which he named Rio de las Palmas—for its tall palm trees—would never lead him to Cathay. When the ships were ready to sail, he was too.

But the following year three more wooden ships came from Jamaica, these under the command of Diego de Camargo. They did not drop anchor in the bay. Instead, they sailed upriver about twenty miles, their bobbing masts reaching taller than the palms. Again, they traded, but unlike Pineda's men they did not make friends; they made enemies. A shore party came under fierce attack, and in the desperate fight to get back to the river the Spaniards lost eighteen of their 150 or so men and all seven of their cavalry horses. One of the three ships grounded and had to be abandoned. The other two fled downriver, pursued by angry Indians, harassed by flights of arrows flung from the shore.

Once into the Gulf they began a painful voyage down to Veracruz, losing one of the ships along the way. The remaining ship, in bad condition, sank in Veracruz Harbor a few days after its arrival.

During the next three centuries the Spanish slowly colonized Mexico, and the Indian settlements which Pineda and Camargo had found along the Rio de las Palmas turned gradually to Mexican villages. But river traffic amounted to little. Goods were unloaded from ships at the mouth of the Rio Grande and hauled upriver by mule, cart, or wagon. The biggest vessel which plied the brown waters was an occasional ferry. The river was an obstacle, not a highway.

Not until Americans intruded upon the scene was this to be changed. In June of 1829 a Connecticut Yankee, former roommate of steamboat inventor Robert Fulton, arrived at the mouth of the stream which by then was widely known as the Bravo. He was Henry Austin, cousin of the Texas colonizer Stephen F. Austin, who had brought the first legal American settlers into Mexican Texas. Henry Austin owned a sidewheeler named the *Ariel*, capable of traveling at seven knots and carrying a hundred thousand pounds of freight. It was his hope that he could earn a grant of land in return for establishing commercial navigation upon the Rio Bravo.

The *Ariel* was a shock to the natives. Her ear-piercing whistle was like nothing they had ever heard. The wood smoke which billowed from her single black stack sometimes lay across the riverbank like a stifling blanket. And Austin himself was a difficult man to get to know. Whether the trouble was his own, or that of the Mexicans, or more probably simply an inevitable clash of cultures, the fact is that he speedily came to dislike the Mexicans as much as they disliked his steamboat. He explored upriver some three hundred water miles as far as the mouth of the Salado, but he found the Bravo too shallow for him from that point west. He contented himself to making the run between Matamoros and the town of Camargo.

Austin tried vainly to build up a profitable trade. During the fall of 1829, when he should have been having his best run of business, much of his crew was sick and the boat remained tied up. Next spring Austin himself was too sick to navigate the sluggish, shallow, difficult Rio Grande.

That summer, cursing the Mexicans, he steamed the *Ariel* out of the Rio Grande forever and took her up the coast to the mouth of the Brazos River. He worked his way past the treacherous Brazos bar and went up as far as Brazoria. The settlers along the Brazos were mainly Americans, his own kind. The land also was considerably richer than that along the Rio Grande, at least in his view. Finally he was about to make his fortune.

But that fall when he attempted to leave the river with a cargo of goods, he ran aground on the shallow bar that was always to plague boat captains on the Brazos. He managed to free the *Ariel*, but her hull was leaking. He put in at Harrisburg December 29, thoroughly disheartened, and took passage on a ship for New Orleans. He left behind him his dream of wealth in Texas. The *Ariel* gradually rotted and finally sank in the mud of Buffalo Bayou.

This pattern of initial failure was to be repeated on many Texas rivers. It is a grim irony of history that the pathfinders usually open the way for others but find only defeat for themselves.

Not a great deal more was done on the Rio Grande until the Mexican War. In 1846, in pursuit of the American victory, General Zachary Taylor built Fort Brown on the Texas side of the river opposite Mexican Matamoros, by then already a thriving city. Taylor wanted to establish permanent communications with another American outpost far upriver at the Presidio del Norte. He ordered several light-draft steamboats out of the yards at Pittsburgh, Pennsylvania, mounted cannons upon them, and started them patrolling up and down the river from Fort Brown. They were the *Corvette*, the *Whitesville*, the *Colonel Cross*, and the *Major Brown*.

The *Major Brown*, drawing only two feet of water, was dispatched upriver in October of that year to attempt ascent all the way to the outpost. Captain Mark Sterling took a ship's crew plus nineteen privates and a noncommissioned officer. The trip went fairly easily as far as notorious Mier, where a Texian force had been defeated and captured at Christmas, 1842, in an ill-planned attempt to avenge a Mexican invasion that had reached all the way to San Antonio. From Mier onward, the *Major Brown* kept grounding on the shoals. She managed to reach Laredo, some six hundred miles by water from the mouth of the river, but there she was tied up because the

The Steamboat Ceres. *Courtesy of the New-York Historical Society, New York City.*

flow had slackened too much to allow her to return downstream. While Sterling waited with most of his men, guarding the boat against damage by hundreds of curious Mexicans who traveled great distances to see it, Dr. A. Rackliffe and a party of three went by horseback another hundred miles to the presidio.

As a result of this exploration, river traffic became common in later years as far as Laredo. Beyond there, it was never practical.

Out of that Rio Grande traffic was built some of South Texas' early fortunes. Charles Stillman, an American merchant in Mexican Matamoros, built a ferry between the Mexican city and the growing settlement around Fort Brown. When the government steamboats were offered for sale as war surplus, he bought several. They were ill suited to the Rio Grande's special problems. Most, in time, wound up rotting, grounded by some mischance. Stillman formed a partnership with two young men who had captained steamboats for the government during the war and had stayed on afterward to work for themselves.

One was a shrewd Quaker named Mifflin Kenedy. The other was a brash Irishman, Richard King, who had run away from a New York apprenticeship at age eleven and had made his own way ever since on the sea and on southern rivers. King was sure he knew what kind of boat was needed for this treacherous river that marked the boundary between two vastly differing countries. He designed the boats, and Stillman paid for them. Out of this partnership came the nucleus of the King fortune that built the huge King Ranch, and some of the impetus for the blossoming of Brownsville and Corpus Christi as major shipping and receiving points in the Gulf Coast trade.

The first boat captains to try a river usually paid a high price for intrepidity. In the winter of 1838, two years after Texas had won her freedom from Mexico, the *Ceres* made her way into Sabine Pass and headed up the Sabine River, searching for cargo to carry out. She reached the settlement of Belgrade before wrecking herself on a submerged log.

Steamboat Cayuga. *Painting by James Bard. Courtesy of the New-York Historical Society, New York City.*

In the spring of 1840, Captain Peter D. Stockholm set out to do better in the *Washington*. He reached Fullerton's Landing just south of Sabinetown but had to tie up because of a drop in the river's flow. There the *Washington* still sat the following January, when a sudden rise in the river wrenched her loose from her moorings and smashed her against the bank. Nothing was salvaged except the steam engine.

It was two years later before Captain Stockholm tried again, this time in the *Scioto Belle*. Luck, and probably a wealth of experience, rode with him on this trip. He made it all the way to East Hamilton in Shelby County and returned safely to Sabine Pass with a load of cotton. He set the stage for a successful and rapidly expanded trade on that river, culminated eventually by the advent of big steamers of the *Uncle Ben* class, which could carry a thousand bales of cotton or more.

The Brazos was the first Texas river to support steamboat operations of real size. Jared Groce, one of Austin's first American settlers, built a large plantation on the Brazos and constructed Texas' first cotton gin in 1825. He built a barge to float the first bales

down to the Gulf and meet ocean-going ships. There was not at that time, or for many years afterward, anything more than a local trader market for cotton in Texas. It had to be shipped out raw for processing in the East or in Europe.

Henry Austin's ill-fated attempt with the *Ariel* in 1830 was a portent of hard times to come for other steamboatmen. The *Old Washington* managed to go upstream to Washington-on-the-Brazos, later to be the site of the signing of Texas' declaration of independence, before wrecking on a sandbar. But two years later another Brazos River steamboat, the *Sabine*, successfully ran a Mexican blockade at Velasco, the river's mouth, in one of the several skirmishes that preceded the revolution. The *Cayuga* entered the Brazos River trade in 1835, just before the war began. She ferried civilian refugees from Harrisburg to safer haven in Anahuac just ahead of Santa Anna's invading army. Soon afterward she was pressed into service by President David G. Burnet and his cabinet officers as temporary floating capital of the Republic of Texas until she could set them on solid ground at Columbia.

Twenty years and more after the *Ariel's*

misadventure, the Brazos bar was still a major obstacle. William Hendley of Galveston wrote this in a letter to S. Gildersleeve of Portland, Connecticut, February 23, 1851:

"Since I last rote you the Brazos Bar has been playing the duce with Steam Boats & Sail Vessels the Steamer General Hamen which was owned amoung us here (our selves ⅛) got on the Bar last Sunday and threw over bord about 10000 dollars worth of her cargo and damageed the ballanc which was about as mutch more she finally got in to the River with her loss of her Rudder and leaking badly. . . .

"The Lone Star in attempting to gow in about the same tim got over the Bar and came to Anchor the Current & Drift running out strong. She parted both Shains and went to sea again after beating on the Bar and along down the beach some two or three miles finally got to Sea after throwing over board her deck load the wind being N.E. and a thick fog and in attempting to get into the river some two or three days after went on the South point where she now lies partly filled with sand and water and all her Cargo more or less damagd but I thing she will she will be got of and her Star will shine a spell longer as she is to well built to be laid on the Beach to dry yet."

Like the Brazos, the Colorado (not to be confused with the mighty Colorado of the Far West) had a fearsome natural obstacle, a series of "rafts," driftwood, and other debris built up over the ages—just a few miles above the point where it emptied into Matagorda Bay. William C. McKinstry in 1839 surveyed the river all the way from the republic's new capital at Austin down to the mouth. Settlers dismissed him as a dreamer. In his report, which he printed privately the following year with mile-by-mile descriptions of the river's varying widths, depths, and bends, he stated, "On my trip down the river I met with very little encouragement from many of the citizens residing on the Colorado, the general impression being so strong that the river could never be made navigable for steam-boats, that before I had proceeded halfway . . . I found it advisable not to trouble the people with my 'visionary expedition.'"

He predicted that the Colorado would prove navigable by steamboats for more than six months of the year, a forecast which eventually proved true.

The heaviest river commerce in Texas came to be on the Red, after the clearing of its great raft. But other rivers enjoyed their own shares of trade. Especially in the earlier years, steamboats which sought commerce along the unpredictable Texas streams tended to be castoffs from bigger rivers farther east, particularly the highly competitive Mississippi, where only the most efficient boats could remain commercially successful for long. When a boat had outlived its usefulness there it was often dispatched to smaller western rivers to work out whatever life it might still have left.

The boat mortality rate was high in Texas. The enemies were not Indians, for steamboats tended to ply rivers only in those regions well "tamed" and settled down for farming and commerce. The hazards were sudden drops in the water level or sudden rises from unseen rains upriver, causing angry brown waters to tear boats from their moorings or break them to pieces with huge twisting trees ripped out by their roots. Unseen snags lay hidden just beneath the surface of the water, waiting to rip the belly out of a boat. Long "deck-raker" limbs reached far out from shore, strong enough sometimes to demolish a pilothouse or rip off a smokestack.

The river commerce figured heavily in Texas' rather limited physical contact with the Civil War. The state contributed tens of thousands of men to the war and lost most of its wealth to it. But the land itself was only lightly touched by combat. That little came mostly because of Union efforts to stop the river traffic that was helping keep the Confederacy financially alive.

The Union blockade of southern ports was designed to cut the Confederacy off from foreign markets for its produce, particularly cotton, and to stop the importation of munitions and supplies for which this produce was sold. Although daring blockade runners managed to elude the Union gunships to a degree, the blockade was in the major sense successful.

One of its problem spots was the mouth of the Rio Grande. Cut off from other shipping ports early in the war, the Confederacy soon found an outlet in Matamoros, Mexico. Great wagon trains of baled cotton began raising dust from East Texas down across the old Spanish Camino Real to San Antonio and on south to the Rio Grande at Brownsville. From there or from Matamoros on the opposite side it was sent by steamboats and lighters to be loaded onto foreign ships lying at anchor at Boca Chica on the mouth of the river. Union warships were helpless to interfere with foreign vessels. They could not even tamper with the Texas-owned lighters which flew the Mexican flag. Here the Confederacy had a wide-open market for its sale goods and a wide-open door for receiving European munitions.

It was decided in Washington that the only solution was to take Brownsville and set up a Union blockade along the Rio Grande. A Gulf storm arrived simultaneously with the invading force of almost seven thousand men on twenty-six transports at Boca Chica, November 1, 1863. Seasick and weary, the major part of the force was three days getting ashore in the pounding surf. The men were in little condition to fight.

However, the Texas contingent at Brownsville was in the incompetent hands of one Hamilton Bee, put there by higher command which wanted him as far away as possible, and the mouth of the Rio Grande had seemed the last place to expect trouble. Bee panicked at wild rumors, dumped his siege guns into the river, set huge stores of Confederate cotton afire, and retreated in haste. The fire spread to store buildings and dwellings. While a terror-stricken Brownsville populace fled across the river to sanctuary in Mexico, much of their town burned behind them.

Union General Nathaniel P. Banks marched into blackened Brownsville November 6 and placed it under martial law. Some of the townspeople came back to live under Union occupation; many remained in Mexico, refugees. Rio Grande steamboats were pressed into federal service. Soon they were carrying troops upriver, stopping—they thought—the great cotton trains.

But the Union capture of the lower river proved to be only a nuisance, not a fatal wound, to the Texas cotton men. The wagon trains were diverted far upriver to Laredo, out of reach of the Yankee steamboats and horseback patrols. There they crossed over, then proceeded downriver in the neutral safety of

The sternwheeler White Water *worked on the Brazos River from 1880–95, principally hauling cotton. Courtesy John Douglas Smith.*

the Mexican side, sometimes jeering at the Union soldiers who were constrained by international law from doing anything except whistle back.

The following year, Colonel Santos Benavides, leading Texas-Mexican volunteers in service of the Confederacy, defeated Union troops that had ventured as far inland as Laredo. Then another Texas patriot, the venerable Rip Ford, ran the Union troops out of Brownsville in a brilliant use of deception and guerrilla tactics. Though he had an inferior force that never numbered more than twelve hundred men, he euchred the Yankees out to a stand on the Gulf shore. There they remained neutralized through the rest of the war, helplessly watching the full-scale resumption of the Rio Grande cotton trade.

Even more disastrous to the Union side was the battle of Sabine Pass, a monument to the pure brass of a young Irish saloonkeeper named Dick Dowling. This invasion, two months before the one on the Rio Grande, was meant to stop all traffic on the Sabine and Neches rivers and to drive a Union wedge between Texas and Louisiana. It was also designed to capture forty thousand bales of cotton, mostly brought down from inland to the Gulf by steamboats.

The only thing that stood in the way of the Union invaders was a small mud fort guarding Sabine Pass. On this fateful day, September 8, 1863, it was manned by the twenty-five-year-old Dowling and forty-two men, mostly dock-wallopers, section hands, and bar-keepers. All but two were Irish, considered renegades and outcasts, left there because no regular Confederate units wanted them. A mud fort, the superiors said, was a fit place for such a motley lot of bad apples.

Up to Sabine Pass sailed twenty-one Union warships, carrying an invading force of nearly eight thousand men. The invasion was to be led into the narrow straits by four gunboats: the *Clifton*, the *Arizona*, the *Sachem*, and the *Granite City*. These would make short work of the little fort, and the invasion could begin in earnest from seven transports that would follow close behind, backed up by other ships waiting out in the Gulf. It is significant, perhaps, that this was a joint army-navy operation, each branch carping against the other. Moreover, none of the naval officers were regulars. Another significant point is that the Union officers dreaded that the superior Con-

federate warship *Alabama* might show up in the middle of the operation and play havoc with them. In any case, the invasion began with much confusion and many lost signals.

Meanwhile, the Irishmen were at the fort less because of their fighting ability than because the commander saw them as laborers; their principal job was to repair and build it up, not defend it. They had six cannons, four of them condemned and discarded by a military ordnance board before the war had begun. While they waited to see what the Union ships were going to do, they dragged up logs and set them in place to make it appear their armament was fearsome. Another point in their favor was that they had done some target practice. They had stuck poles in the straits at various points and had the range on every one of them.

At 6:30 A.M. on invasion morning, the *Clifton* fired twenty-six shells at the fort. The Irishmen kept still. It was a good thing for Dowling's men that their fort was of mud and sand, for the Union shells sank into the morass without doing much damage. Had it been of conventional stone and mortar, it would have been blown to pieces.

A Union landing party set out in rowboats but bogged down in deep mud and abandoned the attempt. A Texas "cotton-clad" steamboat arrived from upriver and stood by to do what it could to lend the Irishmen a hand. This was the *Uncle Ben*, which before the war had plied the Sabine all the way up eight hundred miles by water to Belzora and at times came downriver with a thousand bales. Now she was in Confederate service, with cotton bales strategically placed for protection against Union guns.

The Union commanders were contemptuous both of the mud fort and the little steamboat. The *Sachem* and the *Arizona* were to steam up the Louisiana side to divert the fort's cannon fire. Then the *Clifton* was to rush down on the Texas side with its nine-inch guns blazing before the defenders could change the direction of their cannons. The *Granite City* was to follow and protect the landing of ground troops. Then the transports would cough up their men to wade ashore, and the plum would quickly be in Union hands.

The ships began to move, blasting at the fort. The Irishmen ashore held their fire. For a while it appeared this was going to be uncontested victory. Suddenly the *Sachem* came abreast of some strange poles stuck up on the Louisiana shore. All hell broke loose. The fifth Texas shot put a hole completely through the *Sachem*'s hull. From then on it seemed that every shot struck home. The boat went aground.

The *Clifton* came rushing up to do its appointed job. The Texans hastily redirected some of their cannons. Dowling aimed for the ships wheelhouse and hit it. Under full power when the shell struck, the *Clifton* careened out of control and went aground in a salt marsh, sideways and totally vulnerable just three hundred yards from the Texas guns. Before the commander could get his own guns back into action, a Texas shell blew out the boiler and sent crewmen and soldiers jumping over the side to escape the scalding steam.

The unexpected disaster to the *Sachem* and the *Clifton* caused panic on the other boats. The *Arizona* ran aground. Commanders of other vessels turned around and rushed for the safety of the open Gulf. The *Arizona* managed to extricate itself from the mud and started a hasty retreat, only to go aground a second time. Some of the boats that had not even been in the battle had trouble getting out across the bar. The *Crescent* and the *Laurel Hill* threw several hundred horses and mules overboard to lighten their loads. The halters were tied to the animals' forefeet; every one of them drowned.

The *Clifton*, what was left of it, wanted to give up. Dick Dowling dared not let the Yankees know how small his force really was. He walked out alone to accept the surrender. The cotton-clad *Uncle Ben* moved in to secure the *Sachem* on the other side of the channel. Not until hours later, when almost five hundred prisoners from the *Clifton* and the *Sachem* were safely put away, did the blushing Dowling let the astonished Henry Dane of the *Clifton* know that he had done all this mischief with forty-two men, six guns, and several pine logs.

Because of Dowling's victory, the Union never again seriously threatened the Sabine and its river traffic.

The golden years for the Texas riverboat trade came for perhaps two decades after the

A belle of the Brazos River, the sternwheeler Hiawatha *settled on a huge live oak stump in 1895 and was allowed to sink into the Brazos River mud. Courtesy John Douglas Smith.*

The Alice Blair was brought to Texas' Brazos River from the Mississippi and carried passengers from Columbia to Velasco in 1892. Courtesy John Douglas Smith.

Civil War, until the gradually expanding railroad system offered cheaper and faster transportation.

Through all the decades of the steamboat trade, Texas vessels tended to be utilitarian. Like the farmer's rail fence, they were "poor for looks but hell for stout." As a group they lacked the style, polish, and luxury of the more famous steamboats that worked the Mississippi. Passengers roughed it like the crew and sometimes fell in to help if the boat ran aground or was stopped by a snag or a deck-raking limb.

There was danger, too, for the cotton, which was bread and butter to the steamboat-man, was highly flammable. Once a bale of cotton caught fire, it usually burned until every scrap was gone. Often it took the rest of the cargo with it, and the boat as well. A notable tragedy—one of Texas' worst—was the burning of the river steamer *Mittie Stephens* on Caddo Lake, February 11, 1869. Fire broke out just before midnight. The captain brought the boat to shore, but the fire was on the prow and cut off most of the hundred or so passengers. Unable to reach the dock, many leaped from the stern into the water. Some swam to shore in the darkness; others drowned. Many more, particularly women and children, clung helplessly to the boat as it gradually burned down to the water line, and they eventually either drowned or suffocated. Death loss was recorded as about sixty; no one ever knew for sure.

A scattered few luxury boats would have done the Mississippi proud, particularly in the latter part of the steamboat era between the Civil War and the final decade of the nineteenth century. One of these was the *Neches Belle*, whose eventual fate was symbolic of a fading way of life. She was described by those who remembered her in later years as a "glorious" boat, able to carry a complement of passengers in fine style at the same time that she carried a thousand bales of cotton on the Sabine and the Neches-Angelina rivers.

Other great boats died in wild moments of glory, burning spectacularly or smashing themselves to pieces on a bar. The *Neches Belle* died a slow death from the cancer of litigation, a victim of legal snarls and slow courts. She made her last run about 1898 with a load of bridge timbers from Orange to Logansport.

Ironically, these were for the Houston East and West Railroad, which was helping bring down the curtain for the *Neches Belle* and all her proud sisters.

At Logansport she was moored because of a lawsuit. The suit dragged on for years, until the untended boat rotted and finally sank. She still lies at the bottom today, what is left of her, a sodden hulk that still shows in the brown mud when hot, dry summer causes the river to fall.

Her steam whistle was salvaged. For many years it sounded starting and quitting time for workers at nearby Patoutville, Louisiana, in a factory producing sugar—to be shipped out by rail.

12

The Argonauts:
Around the Horn

BY PAUL BAILEY

The dramatic announcement of the discovery of gold in California in the winter of 1848 set a world in motion. It made 1849 the year when ten thousand wagons rolled west, when America's rivers became arteries to funnel the gold seekers toward the new El Dorado, when ships of America and the world drove themselves across two oceans like eager flocks of homing waterfowl. Along the Atlantic seaboard and, less feverishly, in ports world-wide, good hulls and ancient ones that could be caulked to seaworthiness again were set to the wind with all the canvas their masts and spars could bear. The voyage to the fabled gold fields was a matter worthy of solemn, decisive choice. To make it, the traveler usually bought an all-or-nothing one-way passage.

John Goodman, an authority on the traffic of the forty-niners by sea, estimates that at least a thousand vessels were engaged in the journey to California in that one epochal year. No less than seven hundred of them took departure from American seaports.

The Year of the Argonauts was, of course, 1849—though the time of the phrenetic epic tapered out to years beyond the climactic one. And even the term "argonaut" becomes loosely applied to most anyone with gold fever who gambled on his own ability to reach California's mines by any power—ship, wagon, muleback, or afoot. The real and true argonauts in their sea assault on the promised land found no women of Lemnos at the end of their voyage; no deliverance from the Harpies, nor any encounter with the clashing rocks of Symplegades. Few of them actually found gold. But all of them encountered perverse adventures enough to titillate generations yet unborn.

The year 1849 definitely stands as dramatic peak to the sea trails west. Still it would be an unfair beggaring of history to assign to the eager gold rushee all merit and all acclaim. Ships were prowling the west coast of North America centuries before the California gold rush—their own restless and inquisitive Jasons clutching at their own particular vision of the golden fleece.

Jim Gibbs, in his *Disaster Log of Ships*, reminds us of the Spanish maritime contact with the west coast of North America in the ancient hulks of treasure galleons already known and located along California's sea trails. Gibbs mentions about 3,500 feet off the beach of southern California's community of Oceanside lies what is reputed to be Cortez' treasure ship *Trinidad*. With her, in sand and silt in which she is partially buried, lies a fantastic treasure in gold and artifacts stolen out of early Mexico. The *Trinidad* is supposed to have been built in Acapulco around 1540 to carry Francisco de Ulloa, Cortez' lieutenant, back to Spain with a cargo of New World loot. Ulloa, in a bold attempt to find the seven lost cities of Cibola, detoured north. The ship was lost. He and his crew perished.

There were many other tales of wrecked Spanish treasure ships, with enough loot already recovered by divers to give credence to at least some of the claims. Certainly the sea trails west were rather heavily trafficked long before the argonauts of vintage '49. By 1579 Sir Walter Raleigh and his ship *Golden Hind* had not only penetrated the Golden Gate, but had circuited and posted San Francisco Bay as a British possession. Between 1792 and 1794 Captain George Vancouver, seeking the fabled Northwest Passage, made repeated fleet visits to the Pacific Northwest—naming bays and points down the Alaskan coast to the Puget

Sound inlets and the Columbia River headlands.

But even this had been superseded by Russian penetration as far south as California, and by the probing and possessive expedition —in 1792—of Captain Robert Gray and his ship *Columbia*, under sponsorship of a group of Boston merchants. Gray not only marked the principal bays of the Pacific Coast, aided Vancouver in his British geographic reconnoitering, but penetrated the mighty river which carries the name of his little Boston ship.

In 1811, John Jacob Astor, in a carefully planned attempt to gain American monopoly of the lucrative Pacific fur trade, dispatched the vessel *Tonquin* around the Horn to the Pacific side of the continent. She was burdened with a full cargo of every conceivable necessity to the venture. This early and adventurous odyssey culminated in the penetration of the Columbia River from its mouth, and the establishment of the American trading post of Astoria in Oregon.

Preceding, by two years, the traumatic announcement that California's stream beds and gravel banks were laced with free gold came another shattering event—America's war with Mexico—a war in which the entire Pacific West was wrested from Mexico by the United States. This tragic event would spell doom to the agrarian Spanish-speaking population of the American Southwest, and bring on such an overwhelming invasion of strident and possessive Anglos as to forever alter the face of the land and its ethos.

In 1846—as part of the military effort against Mexico—the United States Government dispatched the ship *Loochoo*, bearing a regiment of New York volunteers under command of Colonel Jonathan D. Stevenson. Most of these men, as with other soldiers after hostilities, remained to share in the gold rush.

Also astride this twin-edged drama; the ship *Brooklyn* arrived in San Francisco Bay on July 31, 1846. Aboard were the first Anglo-Saxon colonists under the new flag—238 Latter-day Saints, led by Samuel Brannan. The enterprising Brannan, besides being leader of this contingent of Mormon colonists, was a publisher. Aboard the *Brooklyn* was the printing plant of his New York newspaper, which, when set up at Yerba Buena (the village destined to become San Francisco), would be-

come the *California Star*. Not only was Brannan destined to rise with the gold rush to become California's first millionaire, but he would be the very man who carried the first samples of gold from the American River.

The *Brooklyn*, a 450-ton square-rigger, rebuilt to house the Mormon colonists, had cleared New York Harbor February 4, 1846—the very day the first Mormon contingents, under leadership of Brigham Young, had crossed the Mississippi into Iowa, following the Illinois expulsion of its Mormon population. Brannan's company of Saints was expected to meet and greet Brigham Young's pioneers—on the safe and serene side of the North American continent.

When the *Brooklyn* sailed into San Francisco Bay, "Captain Montgomery was there with the *Portsmouth* sloop of war, and we were landed under her guns. We expected to fight . . . [but] we landed, and there was no one to lift a stick or a stone against us. Our praises to God for the deliverance He had wrought out for us, and our joy to once more set our feet on terra firma, after being six months on the sea . . ." Once California was secured from the Mexicans, the resourceful Mormon colonists transformed Yerba Buena into the beginnings of lively and fabulous San Francisco.

They were to set stage for the human flood so soon to come. Theirs would be the Anglo faces to greet the lonely, wearied men who would enter the Golden Gate from the sea. Their leader, Samuel Brannan, would emerge as propitious cog in the wheel of history. The *Brooklyn* Saints, and the members of the Mormon Battalion serving in the Mexican War, would be first in California's gold fields. Brannan, the publisher, would be destiny's choice to make California's gold the rallying cry to the world.

First news of the discovery of gold in California was received in the East with incredulity and skepticism. Not until fall and winter, 1848, did New York newspapers begin copying Brannan's, Beale's, and Loeser's San Francisco announcements. Only when ships began arriving with California gold dust and bullion, and President Polk's declaration finally gave official confirmation that the rumors indeed had sound basis in fact, did doubt speedily change to conviction.

The year 1849 dawned with the nation

Hard on the heels of the American annexation of California, the ship Brooklyn *brought the first new colonists to the port of Yerba Buena. Courtesy the DeYoung Museum, San Francisco.*

out of its head with gold fever. Homes and farms were mortgaged and sacrificed. Men quit their jobs, businessmen closed their offices and stores, physicians abandoned their practices, and even clergymen, like untold thousands of less divinely motivated citizens, began searching for ways and means to get to California. The farmers and townsmen living inland planned their journey overland. Those in maritime cities of the eastern seaboard began seeking ocean-borne transportation.

As the fever gripped men, they became as animals with the running fits. Before the epochal year of 1849 ground to its end, California would be engulfed with a tidal wave of hysterical, grasping humanity. "Since the migration of the Children of Israel, there was never such an exodus out of all lands as was seen in the year 1849" wrote Henry Hiram Ellis, who, in January of that mad year, sailed

out of Boston on the *North Bend.* "Ships from every port in the world poured their living flood upon the golden shore."

Of the first thousands who went by sea, many were lucky enough to buy deck space as passengers on any outgoing tub headed for Pacific waters. Others willingly signed on as able seamen at a fraction of the wage scale, or for free. But "do it yourself" travel became increasingly minimal, once the movement toward formation of companies took its unprecedented hold upon the migrating gold seekers. Where and how the corporate form of travel first emerged is obscure. But very quickly it became the general and accepted pattern to follow if one hoped to enter San Francisco Bay by sail or steam—or for that matter to do the journey overland.

An association would be formed of gentlemen eager for the California venture. President, vice president, secretary, treasurer, and board of directors would be elected or chosen. Plans would be made for the long trip. Mode of travel—whether by sea or overland— decided upon. The number and quality of recruits invited to fill out the company roll would be officially set. Then by invitation, personal solicitation, or by advertisement, other like-minded gentlemen were brought into the circle. The companies were invariably socialistic in base and concept. Liberty, Equality, and Fraternity seems constantly to have been their motto—every man to pay the same dues and assessments; receive the same treatment; share equally in the profits.

Theoretically it was all for one, and one for all, but, in the case of sea travel, it did not always work out so fraternalistically. Once aboard ship, the limited stateroom and cabin facilities usually went to the officers and direc-

tors, with other corporate brothers left to share deck space and steerage. Price for shares and inclusion in a company varied according to what sort of package deal was planned and offered. Every effort, however, was made to recruit badly needed mechanics, artisans, physicians, and plain shovelmen by selling them half shares, lending money to the less affluent, entry on promissory note—all indebtedness to be repaid out of profits from the gold they would gather once they reached the promised land.

These mining companies were recruited under grand titles, usually remindful of the premise for which they were organized. Sometimes they bore the names of the communities where originated, or were given pugnacious or patriotic designations. Of the hundreds of companies formed, many went to California with duplicate or near duplicate titles. Many

The Old Harvard Company, composed primarily of Harvard University alumni; purchased the three-masted Duxbury in 1849 for their journey to the gold fields.

times companies were named after the vessels the groups had chartered or purchased.

The bylaws of these bravely put-together mining groups read with virtuous sameness. Ardent spirits and drunkenness were forbidden. Profanity, gambling, and obstreperous conduct were subject to heavy fines. Repeated infractions of the laws of personal conduct subjected the offender to expulsion from the company, and forfeiture of his share. The number of members in each circle depended on the mode of travel west, the affluence of its collective membership, and, in the case of sea travel, on the ship accommodations.

The co-operatives were born in a fog of misunderstanding and misconception. And, popular and idealistic as they were, they inevitably perished and fell apart once California was reached. Initially the socialistic idea seemed to possess every advantage. The idea of a group of young townsmen, known to one another from boyhood, banding together for mutual gain and mutual protection seemed entirely logical and workable. There was brotherhood in the event of illness, accident, or financial distress. California was not only physically hazardous, but probably a dangerous place in which to live unless the group closed ranks for protection and defense. As equal partner in a socialistic union, one's share of the earnings would not be lost through illness or accident, nor would one's heirs be deprived in case of death.

Since most of the companies were conceived with the idea of trading in goods and merchandise in addition to mining gold for profit, many of the co-operatives purchased, and jointly owned, the vessels upon which they embarked for the great adventure. Provisions would be scarce and expensive in California, so full cargoes of food, implements, clothes, and trade goods not only secured the well-being of every member, but provided a surplus which hopefully could be sold at profit to miners less fortunate. Many company vessels carried lumber, house frames, and steamboats out of New England. These, at least in the first wave of immigration, proved readily salable. The patented machines, designed to separate gold from gravel by inventors who had never seen a placer mine, and which many a ship carried in quantity, found resting place with other useless knick-knacks on the mountainous dumps of San Francisco.

It was thought that the enlistment of mechanics and artisans would provide needed backup security. While the miners separated the gold from the California stream beds, their brothers would be practicing their trades and professions in the towns and cities, with profit from all phases flowing into the common pot. The ship itself could be profitably worked up and down the now busy Pacific Coast, and, if need be, could be sold.

Bitter fact is that the socialistic theory which seemed so sound and workable in New York, Massachusetts, and Maine, quickly fell apart when put to the test. Some of the brothers in the confederation proved to be lazy and refused to do their share of the common toil; others became ill; some speedily succumbed to the cholera, dysentery, and smallpox endemic in the gold fields; some, in spite of the high-sounding temperance clauses, chose dissipation and gambling in preference to pick and pan on the rivers and streams.

Most of the companies disbanded within two or three weeks after arrival. Their vessels —which were to make them money in coastal voyages, or were to serve as floating trade emporiums, or homes for the boys while they recuperated from work trips to the mines— proved an equal loss. What the travelers had not realized was that once arrived, any vessel would have extreme difficulty in shipping another crew to work her, that trade was an impossibility with the ancient, square-rigged, slow sailers which the companies had brought around the Horn. Most of the first crop of the forty-niner fleet were peddled off for a fraction of their cost, ended up as store or prison ships, or were abandoned to the mudbanks.

The dream of tying their floating home to a San Francisco wharf, as haven of rest or a store in trade, was soon shattered by the realization that only far-out anchorage was possible due to abysmal congestion; that the cost of lightering passengers or goods from ship to shore was ruinously expensive. Some of the first companies made profits on the cargo. But every arriving vessel seemed obsessed with the same idea. Trade goods were piled on the flats and beaches, with no San Francisco buildings to house them, and no one interested in buying or even stealing them. When it cost more to lighter cargo ashore than it did to haul it around the Horn, even wanted and needful items were abandoned or sold at a loss.

Reaching the door to the gold fields, both passengers and crews took off for the hills and the ships they left behind turned San Francisco's harbor into a "graveyard of ships." Courtesy U. S. National Museum.

Octavius Howe, in his *Argonauts of '49*, tells of one company starting from scratch, and sailing out their home-built *California Packet*, skippered by Captain George Kimball, of Frankfort, Maine. Without capital or credit, Kimball enlisted a company. Financial exigency made necessary the building of their own vessel. Choosing the seacoast village of Cutler, Maine, as site, Kimball went alone into the Maine woods and began cutting out the timbers. Slowly the company formed as neighbors and acquaintances engaged themselves in the venture. Meat and provisions were contributed by farmers who joined the group. The audacity of the undertaking brought in artisans and experienced joiners and shipwrights. Instead of wages for labor or services, shares were issued in denominations of $100.

While other vessels and other groups took off for California during that phrenetic year of 1849, the little Maine co-operative labored doggedly at their project. At last, on November 29, 1849, *The California Packet* was launched in Maine waters. As a do-it-yourself job she had fair dimensions: 144 feet long, thirty feet beam, and fifteen and a half-feet draft.

Her company of one hundred was indeed novel to the lore of the argonauts, in that it included twelve married and sixteen unmarried women and fifteen children. The remainder, of course, were young males to mine the gold. Everyone, including the crew, was a shareholder. *The California Packet* luckily picked up cargo worth $15,000 at Boston, and made fast and safe voyage around the Horn. What happened to her $15,000 cargo in San Francisco, and especially what happened to her female complement, vanished in the historical stew which was the gold rush.

While the companies were organizing, making shipping preparation, and going through military drill in their new and distinctive uniforms, many windjammers cleared port with passenger complements free of and unattached to any co-operatives, and with cargoes of equipment and trade goods aimed at fortuitous first arrival in San Francisco Bay. The bark *J. W. Coffin*, Captain Martin, sailed from Boston December 7, 1848, closely followed in the first days of 1849 by the *Sattillo*, Captain Rich, and the *Carib*, Captain Webb.

From the same port in mid-January sailed the ship *Edward Everett*, carrying one of Massachusetts' first, and certainly one of its best-planned, companies. Early in December of 1848 a number of like-minded young adventurers had met in an office on Exchange Street in Boston and had created the Boston & California Joint Stock Mining & Trading Company, with Henry Smith as captain and president. The membership, limited to 150, was soon filled. Included were eight whaling captains, a geologist, a mineralogist, four doctors. Its fifteen professional men included medical and divinity students out of Harvard. As backbone to its working force it carried seventy-six "mechanics." A trained clergyman, as company chaplain, would make certain the gold seekers were kept mindful of the Lord's word, the temperance pledge, and keep tally of the penalties for gambling and profanity.

The *Edward Everett*, purchased in total out of company funds from Benjamin Bangs, Boston shipper, was a stout ship of seven hundred tons, built at Medford only five years before. In her construction, Mr. Bangs had insisted on every modern innovation, including the installation of lightning rods—certainly a rarity of the day. She boasted six lifeboats, and on deck were two cannons "to repel pirates."

While the *Everett* was being readied for the great adventure, the now fully blossomed company moved their headquarters to Boston's Hanover House. When not drilling in military tactics on the common, the frequent meetings at the Hanover were taken up in instruction on mineralogy and geology by their own preceptors and in technical planning for the four- or five-month voyage. Aboard ship, everything was carefully detailed. The entire area between decks was reserved for ship's officers, company officers, and members. Along each side of the ship—from sail room aft to chain lockers forward—were three tiers of berths. Company physicians, as a "board of health," made certain one room was equipped as a dispensary, and provisioned with drugs, medical and surgical supplies, and twenty-five gallons of ardent spirits.

The *Edward Everett*, besides being provisioned for two years, carried a complete steamboat, four steam engines, and frames for two houses, which when erected in San Francisco would become one of the city's earliest hotels, aptly named Hanover House. Picks, spades, wheelbarrows, and other mining essentials were stowed in the hold—doubtlessly including some of New England's ingenious mechanical gold separators. Twenty able seamen were enlisted, men willing to work the ship to California with no other consideration than their passage—ten of this prize crew had previously served as mates on other vessels.

The *Edward Everett* sailed January 13, 1849. For the first two weeks she hit weather and rough seas, and a good portion of the company was sick. Latter half of the first month found them becalmed, and the men belatedly got their society organized with a deck band of fiddles and banjos. There were plenty of lectures and study circles, led by the experts aboard, and no lack of divine custody with chaplain and Harvard divinity students on hand. A newspaper, *The Barometer*, was issued Saturdays, with William H. Thomes and other ex-journalists editing. And the men lived well on their ample supply of provisions.

On March 29 the *Everett* passed through the Straits of LeMaire, and by April 5 had doubled Cape Horn in a bitter cold and stormy passage. Her able seamen brought her into Valparaiso on April 29. After more than three months at sea, the four days spent in this Chilean seaport were like heavenly reprieve from monotony and confinement. Ashore there were donkey rides, cockfights, a bullring, and a dozen divertissements that appealed to lonely men. If this were not enough, there were the colorful narrow streets, pink-tinted houses, and girls who lifted face veils seductively to the traveler.

Remainder of the voyage was one of steady headway. On July 6 the *Edward Everett* passed smartly through the Golden Gate, and finally dropped anchor in San Francisco Bay—174 days for the journey.

As with other vessels before them, they found the harbor glutted, with no hopes of

The Edward Everett *sailed into San Francisco Bay on July 6, 1849, carrying one of the best-organized companies of argonauts, the Boston & California Joint Stock Mining & Trading Company. Courtesy the Spalding Collection, Boston.*

dockage. Ship and company were moved over to the new port of Benicia, and the *Everett* was moored to a mudbank, in charge of William Thomes. While the "mechanics" lowered and launched the little steamboat, and partially unloaded supposedly useful equipment, the company miners, including the able seamen who had completed their obligation, prepared to move out. Their planned destination was Mokelumne Hill, where they had been told wealth awaited them. Militarily uniformed, armed to the teeth, with three six-mule teams pulling the wagons loaded with baggage, they took up the march—probably one of the more novel sights in a strange land.

After a week's labor on the Mokelumne gravel banks, the company, born in such high resolve, was dissolved. Reality of muscular labor, deprivation, illness, and uncertain return bore no semblance to the dream that had propelled these young hopefuls into the great adventure. The ship and the steamboat were sold at genuine loss. Provisions, trade goods, and equipment were abandoned.

The brave young men vanished into the California ferment. Some of them made a little panning gold, others became shopkeepers and mechanics to San Francisco and Sacramento, a few of the more enterprising members set up the house frames into San Francisco's Hanover House. Some even welcomed the chance to help sail the good ship *Edward Everett* back to Boston under new ownership.

In the early months of 1849, company after company, and vessel after vessel, fled the ports of Baltimore, Philadelphia, New York, and Boston. Howe states that the ship *Leonore*, a staunch and fast sailer, bearing the enthusiastic and hopeful New England Mining & Trading Company, cleared Boston two weeks behind the *Edward Everett*, made a stormy passage around the Horn, and arrived at San Francisco far ahead of that vessel. Her captain and company president, H. H. Green, brought her through in record time for square-rigged ships—149 days.

The *Leonore* likewise was amply provisioned, loaded for trade, and also carried a steamboat to be assembled in California. Her cargo of happy hopefuls had brought aboard everything to make the voyage carefree and pleasant. They had dancing and singing groups, and a banjo and fiddle aggregation they called the "Sacramento Minstrels." But after a good run of four days down the Atlantic the *Leonore* ran into gales constant and severe enough to put most of the passengers to bed with retching *mal de mer*. Once the weather straightened out, however, they cleanly rounded the Horn, to make first landfall at Talcahuana, Chile.

Like most of the Yankees hellbent for California, the Chilean loose life of cockfights, bullfights, and dark-eyed women proved almost overwhelming in appeal after seemingly endless weeks at sea. "We have bought a lot of the wine of the country for twenty-five cents a gallon, and the best cordials. You bet we live high!"

The Pacific run from Talcahuana to San Francisco was made fast and safely, and the *Leonore* sailed through the Golden Gate July 5—breaking all speed records for an American full-rigged ship. They had overtaken and passed every vessel sighted on the Pacific— including the brig *Charlotte*, out of Newburyport, and the *Oxford* and *Mary Wilder* from the home port of Boston. It was exhilarating to know that the only American vessels to outsail them from New England were the clippers *Grey Eagle* (139 days from Philadelphia) and the *Greyhound* (from Baltimore in the amazing time of 112 days). At that time the *Edward Everett* was still wallowing at sea.

As one of the fortunate early arrivals, the *Leonore*'s company enjoyed the rare opportunity of selling off ship and cargo at a profit. The steamboat they had brought out, for use on the rivers, at a cost of only $1,700, brought an immediate offer of $30,000. The company, however, clutching in their collective minds an exaggerated vision of instant wealth, turned down some of the offers, or postponed too long other chances for lucrative trade. Result

was that when the steamer was finally sold, time and demand had trimmed down her net worth. The stout, fast-sailing *Leonore* ended her career as one of the harbor's storeships.

Company members lugged off the *Leonore* eighty-three muskets, a case of swords, and a salamander safe as necessary adjuncts to their coming life at the mines. The safe would be receptacle for the gold they expected to haul back to San Francisco. There is no record that it was ever custodian to any company gold dust. On July 14 seventy members of the New England & California Mining Association went up the Sacramento River in boats, arriving August 5 in the settlement of Vernon. From there, in a summer heat of 120 degrees, they started overland. They arrived in the gold fields so stricken with chills, fever, and dysentery that none of their men could work for two weeks. Some found a little gold—never enough to compensate for the labor and misery of extracting it from the sand and gravel. Another gloriously conceived mining co-operative had foundered on a gravel bar.

For those who chose the long sea route it was a repetitious parade of sails and hulls down the long and stormy Atlantic trough, around the cold and gale-swept outer tip of South America, the shorter and more treacherous Straits of LeMaire, or that real short cut —the Straits of Magellan—so narrow and perilous that only small vessels with fore and aft rigging were nimble enough to negotiate its unpredictable storms and currents. Whichever way, the battered vessels reassembled in Chilean ports, took fresh stock and fresh courage, and the parade of sails resumed for the long Pacific run up to California.

It is difficult to make accurate count of the companies that were formed, not only in America, but world-wide, for this parade to the promised land. Any ancient hull—be she whaleship, dull-sailing merchantman, or packet —found ready sale to the travel groups everywhere springing up. It meant reprieve and final voyage for many a senile and barnacled old tub. In selling off these ancients-of-days the shipyards of New England were soon cleared for hull-laying of the new and coming clipper ships—dainty, beautiful, fast-sailing vessels, born out of the cumulative experience of the long haul, and destined to make America the maritime wonder of the world.

The great seaports of New York, Phila-

Fair sailing up the Pacific to the gold rush fields after the perilous journey around the gale-swept tip of South America. From The Century Magazine.

delphia, and Boston spawned the venture-somes by the thousands. Whether in companies or as individuals, they came of every conceivable persuasion. Vessels of every imaginable type hit the high seas for California. Drainage of wealth, skilled and valuable manpower, and maritime loss to New England remains incalculable.

But it was not always the big cities that sent their men and ships. Scores of tiny seaport villages along the Atlantic coast, from Maine to the Carolinas, readied a vessel or two. Bangor, New Haven, Long Island, and Charleston were represented in the maritime roll of 1849–51. A company from Fall River made it with the brig *Delaware;* the Sherbourne Company sailed the ship *Henry Astor* out of Nantucket; three companies from Salem reached California in the ships *Elizabeth, Crescent,* and the bark *LaGrange.* The *LaGrange,* incidentally, spent her California sojourn hauled up on the riverbank at Sacramento in indispensable service as a prison for the drunken and criminally inclined gold seekers who resented what they discovered at trail's end.

Three companies originating in the tiny town of Beverly, Massachusetts, were the Essex County & California Company, which sailed on the bark *Metropolis;* the Beverly Mining Company, which voyaged out in the brig *Christiana;* and the San Francisco Company, which left Beverly aboard the bark *San Francisco.* In his book, author Howe includes "The Journal of the Proceedings" aboard the *San Francisco*—an intimate and revealing picture of ship life on the long haul.

Aboard were the forty shareholding members, a cook, a steward, twenty pigs, a dog, a kitten, and a pet crow. Aboard also, for which there were great hopes of profitable sale, were 63,000 feet of planed boards, 10,000 bricks, provisions for two years, and a deck burden of eight house frames. The heavy-laden bark sailed from Beverly on August 15, 1849.

On August 21 the crow committed suicide by trying to fly in the rigging. A week later the dog, having taken savage possession of the longboat, and was disputatious with anyone coming near the vicinity, was "consigned to a watery grave for cause." By September 4 the second pig had been killed, and this one eaten

The bark San Francisco *took 149 days to bring its San Francisco Company from Beverly, Massachusetts, through the Golden Gate. Courtesy the Collection of the Beverly Historical Society, Beverly, Massachusetts.*

by crew and passengers. The first pig had been wantonly murdered by one of the men standing watch.

After a two-month run down the Atlantic, which had just about everything in it for the *San Francisco* company—revelry, disputes, food problems, and the gamut in weather, from calms to shrieking winds—the bark made the Cape Horn passage in "strong gales and a heavy sea." By November 20 they were in Valparaiso. "A beautiful city," declared the journalist. "The harbor is a fine one and is crowded with vessels of all nations. . . . However, San Francisco is the city I most wish to see." It was January 11, 1850, and 149 days from Beverly, before he saw San Francisco.

The company's captain describes the port as "the most degraded, immoral, uncivilized and dirty city that can be imagined." San Francisco was a lot of things to a lot of people. What destroyed the high-minded Salem

and Beverly socialistic societies—what had demolished hundreds of previous groups, and turned so many of their conscientious shareholders into mendicants, peddlers, drunks, and individualistic ore scratchers—was the collision of two mighty armies of gold-hungry men. At Sacramento and San Francisco the legions who had come overland by prairie schooner were meeting headlong the flood of young men who had chosen the attack by sea. Casualties along the prairie trail were matched by the wrecks piled up at Cape Horn and the Straits. Many a dull-sailing old square-rigger was, at the end of the voyage, smashed on the rocks while trying to negotiate the currents and deep fogs so relentlessly a part of the narrow entrance to the Golden Gate. Such sleek clipper ships as the *Flying Dragon, Noonday, Carrier Pigeon, Dashing Wave* all perished practically within sight of their coveted anchorage.

Let it never be imagined that the United

States, and particularly New England, were sole contributors to the white-winged pageant. Australia, New Zealand, the Pacific islands, all sent their share of characters in search of California's beckoning wealth. Chile, the isthmus nations, and Mexico, excited by the strange breed of men who were suddenly their unexpected and itinerant guests, provided their quota of nationals. And no one knows how many gold seekers took voyage from Europe and Asia.

The idea of socialistic companies forming, to head for America's gold coast, was just as lively an issue in England, Holland, and France as it was in New York or Boston. In England public stock was sold to finance willing bands of adventurers. California's gold fever had spread throughout the world.

One of the strangest of all sailings was that of the *Anne Louise,* from Le Havre, France, September 9, 1850. Aboard were three companies, *La Ruche d'Or* (Golden Hive), *La Californienne* (the Californian), and *La Bretonne* (the Bretonne). Abbé Henry-Jean-Antoine Alric, the padre acting as chaplain to the two hundred emigrants, kept a journal of this shipload of French argonauts. "After a mass celebrated at the principal church to put us under the protection of the Queen of Heaven, we left Le Havre toward nine o'clock in the morning." They could never have guessed how they would need that protection.

The three French brotherhoods carried out on the *Anne Louise* have some unique qualities of their own. The company of the Golden Hive, for instance, sponsored by Comte de Pons and a former French Army captain, M. Arnail, offered shares for as low as five francs. Members, however, instead of all sharing alike, were pledged only 40 per cent of the gold profits, though they were to receive "free transportation and medical care." Their contracts were to run three years.

La Californienne was one of the first groups to be founded in Paris, and reputedly capitalized at 1,112,000 francs. By March 20, 1849, it already was operative, and on November 27 of that year had dispatched its first contingent out of Le Havre aboard the *Jacques Laffitte.* The "Californians" aboard the *Anne Louise* constituted the fifth dispatched segment of that huge company.

La Bretonne, a regionally financed and recruited group, sponsored only the one company. The Bretonnes, like other companies, was supposed to depart for California with a doctor, a pharmacist, a chaplain, and three women ("preferably 'sisters of charity'") to mend the workers' clothes. The *Anne Louise,* however, left France with seven women (not listed as "sisters of charity") and the one chaplain, Father Alric, who recorded the story.

After clearing Le Havre "under the protection of the Queen of Heaven," the *Anne Louise,* with Captain Delbecke, and carrying her two hundred French gold seekers, made the run to the Canary Islands without incident. On September 18 she dropped anchor at Santa Cruz, on the most southerly island of Tenerife. The ship, being low on water, made necessary this stop to fill her casks.

"I was invited to celebrate a High Mass at the principal church of Santa Cruz; all the passengers, the French consul and nearly five thousand inhabitants attended," Father Alric proudly recorded. After the churchly duties, Father Alric attended a banquet, held at a local hotel, for the visiting ship's officers and company heads. There were many toasts in wines of local vintage. The crew and ordinary passengers spent the night in their own brand of revelry.

All sobered up once the *Anne Louise* had put to sea. But not until she had crossed the equator was the appalling discovery made that the drunken crew had sailed the ship out without stowing the water casks. While the *Anne Louise* wallowed her way in mid-Atlantic, her casks, filled with precious and essential drinking water, were piled on a wharf in the Canary Islands.

Daily water ration to each passenger was immediately reduced to one-half liter; then cut in half; then by three quarters. Finally the tortured humans were forced to subsist for two months on an incredible allowance of only one-eighth liter of rancid water per day.

The first port they touched upon was the Brazilian city of Rio de Janeiro, and not until October 30 did the thirst-crazed men see it. The stopover at Rio lasted a month, and barely came in time to save the lives of those aboard the ill-starred ship. Eleven of the company members left the expedition, some to settle permanently in Brazil instead of fabled California, others to flee back to France at first opportunity. Remaining passengers made loud protests to the French consular offices. Result was that, before the *Anne Louise* could again put to sea, the necessary equipment for distillation of sea water had to be installed, and repairs and changes made in the passenger accommodations.

On December 4 the *Anne Louise* resumed her southing of the Atlantic. The first ten days proved smooth sailing, "but on the eleventh, because of the wind, the current of the Gulf of La Plata, and the rolling and pitching, we spent a terrifying day and lost all our provision of fowl and sheep." On December 25 they were opposite the Falkland Islands where "we celebrated the feast of Christmas by a Solemn Mass."

On January 7 the vessel made a safe rounding of Cape Horn, the priest, like so many other journal-keeping travelers, making note of the phenomenon of the southern latitudes—days without night; the sun dropping only slightly beyond the horizon for three hours out of the twenty-four.

In February the weary *voyageurs* were in Valparaiso, where nine disgruntled company members made formal charges against the ship's skipper for negligence and inept seamanship. On February 11, by craft and subterfuge, Captain Delbecke managed his revenge by deliberately sailing the *Anne Louise* out of Valparaiso leaving the nine complaining passengers stranded and ashore.

Those aboard ship soon had reason to agree that the captain was a poor choice to guide them to the promised land. Winds were favorable, but the voyage went on interminably. Thinking that his ship was properly northing, the captain gave assurances that they would soon arrive in San Francisco. But week after week went by with no sign of the North American coast. When the Marquesas Islands, 740 miles northeast of Tahiti, hove up on the left, he assured his worried passengers that the land they saw belonged to the Sandwich Islands. Discovering his error, the captain swung his ship into the great circle and when, many days later, that Hawaiian group at last showed dead ahead, he solemnly declared that they were arriving in California.

There was no Hawaii stopping, once it was learned that the islands were not California. After by-passing this most desirable landfall, the *Anne Louise* ran into days of maddening calm. The terrible storm which followed "nearly took us to the bottom. For three whole days we were in grave danger. At each moment the yawning gulf seemed ready to swallow us; and, as a last straw, the cabin passengers not being able, as a result of bad weather, to open the food stores, we found ourselves reduced to two potatoes a day and a glass of water."

Privations and misery of this final leg of the journey proved too much for two of the Frenchmen. By now many of them were too ill to stand erect, and after the storm one of the passengers had to be consigned to a watery grave. The vessel's boatswain died the day before the longed-for voyage end in San Francisco. "On April 26 we cast anchor in the magnificent and impressive Bay of San Francisco. Our first concern in landing was to give a Christian burial to the boatswain; then we went our separate ways, most of us never to see one another again."

The cruise of the *Anne Louise* from Le Havre to San Francisco—seven and one-half months of denial and suffering—is high on the list of California's slow sailers.

That mighty throng of gold seekers who chose the long way to their treasure—that tedious and uninterrupted voyage around the southernmost tip of the Americas—all had one thing in common. No matter how lofty and assiduous the planning, how inspired the motive, how brotherly the concept under which they departed from their home ports—a world of good intentions crumbled in the time they "faced the elephant." The misinformation and lack of information on California was appalling—and in the end it proved disastrous.

Many a disillusioned argonaut took the first available vessel back. A few Jasons got their hands on the golden fleece, a few caught indirect glimpses of it, most settled back to their mundane trades in that land far removed from the towns whence they had fled. Some found new, and not always honorable, ways of coaxing the gold, not from the earth, but from their fellow men. And many who had survived the long voyage perished from the cholera, influenza, and smallpox that scourged the Far West.

It is true that ships were sold, abandoned, and left to rot in San Francisco Bay. In the case of company vessels—purchased and manned by the societies who had loaded their

Abandoned and moored in the mud, the once proud Niantic *becomes one of San Francisco's first hotels.*

hulls with ill-planned cargoes of unsalable merchandise—these were often peddled for any possible price, lined up as storeships, or their contents piled ashore in the fantastic heaps of gimcrack garbage that were salient features of San Francisco and Sacramento in the years 1849 and 1850. And many an unclaimed and abandoned vessel that had faithfully brought her gold seekers around the Horn was added to the hundreds of rotting hulls.

The general belief, even to this day, is that most of the argonaut fleet came to this untimely end in San Francisco Bay. John Goodwin, who has compiled a log and chronology on every vessel that sailed to California in the gold rush, declares that this supposition has no basis in fact.

In the frantic scramble on the waterways west, more than a thousand ships, from all over the world, touched San Francisco in 1849. A percentage of these vessels died, according to the legend, when dreams soured and crews deserted to the mines. But little has been said about those that turned around and sailed out again—often after long delays to dispose of cargo, to find new owners, or to wait until their crews discovered that panning for gold was a tough and laborious endeavor compared to sailing the tall-masted homes they once had known. Many a vessel did die in San Francisco Bay. But not all of them.

After a time, thousands of gold seekers—those disappointed and those successful—began clamoring for vessels to take them home. Another fact, slow to discovery, was that there was increasingly lively opportunity for gain in the Pacific runs—to Asia, to Oregon—and especially to Panama, Nicaragua, and lower Mexico. There was need now to haul homeward those brave young men who were surfeited or homesick—or to bring into California the new thousands of hopefuls who had elected to reach California by disembarking at Vera Cruz or Chagres, crossing Mexico, Nicaragua, or the more popular Isthmus of Panama, and catching anything that floated for the northern leg out of Panama City or other ports on the Pacific side.

13

The Argonauts II: Those Who Chose the "Short Cut"

BY PAUL BAILEY

An almost incredible aspect of the argonaut saga is the fact that Pacific Mail Steamship Company was born April 12, 1848—with no part of this transportation dream even hinting at the sudden demand that would so soon be put upon it to move clamoring humanity to America's West Coast. In the beginning the sole province of the newly organized Pacific Mail was to fill a contract with the United States Government to haul the mail, twice a month, from Panama to Yerba Buena (San Francisco) in California, and to service whatever passenger traffic there might be along the route.

The company started business with three steamers—the *California*, the *Oregon*, and the *Panama*—all to serve the Pacific side of the run. The Atlantic half of this inspired dream would be the province of another firm—the Atlantic Steamship Company. Atlantic's contract was to carry the mail from New York to Chagres, their schedules so timed as to connect with the Pacific Mail steamers at Panama. Passengers and mail were to be moved across the isthmus—from Chagres to Panama City—in forty-eight hours or less. For this a railroad was promised.

The whole concept was a Yankee innovation—one of spirit and imagination—to get a man, or a letter, to California and Oregon at a saving of thousands of miles and monotonous months of travel. Were it not for the discovery of gold, and its paralyzing consequences, the steamship mail would probably have gone down in history as a truly bright and workable epoch.

The *California*, first of the new sidewheel steamers, was, like the others, constructed on the Atlantic coast. She started for California October 6, 1848, under Captain Forbes, who was forced, because of illness, to relinquish to Captain Marshall his post as master during the long voyage around the Horn. Marshall brought her into San Francisco February 28, 1849—in time to experience and share full jolt of the discovery of gold. The steamer's glut of passengers, all the crew, and all the ship's officers but one promptly took off for the diggings.

In November of 1848, one month after the *California's* departure for San Francisco, the equally new *Oregon* took off from New York. She arrived in San Francisco on April Fool's Day, 1849. The skipper of the *Oregon*, faced with the same desertion of crew, managed to hold on to his men only by putting them in irons. The *Panama*, last of the trio of steamers, reached California May 1, 1849.

The Atlantic Steamship Company, teamed with the Pacific Mail in this bold new plan of transportation, dispatched its *Falcon* from New York December 1, 1848, supposedly timed to reach Chagres for proper connection with the *California*, due at Panama, on the Pacific side of the isthmus. But the Pacific Mail's steamers were having extreme difficulty in making schedules. Result was that the *California* was twenty-five days late in reaching Panama, and the *Falcon's* passengers, after the hazard of crossing the isthmus, were forced to dawdle nearly a month in a city of wretched accommodations, where the disease death rate was twelve humans a day, and one could find amusement only in cockfighting, tippling, whoring, and gambling.

To compound the problem, the *California*, having departed New York ahead of any knowledge of California's gold strike, had, on her first northern passage, made stop at Callao. Here everyone was afire with gold fever.

The Pacific Mail ship California. *The* California *was the first of three sister steamships to go into Pacific Mail service between Panama and San Francisco. Courtesy the Peabody Museum, Salem.*

The steamer's captain, recognizing a good stroke of business, had filled her cabins with Peruvians obsessed with the idea of getting to California. Result was that when the steamship finally reached Panama, a deadly riot erupted between the New York passengers, angered by the long delay, and the Peruvians who had pre-empted the steamer quarters already purchased back in New York. Even after the Peruvians were heaved out of their comfortable quarters in favor of the Yankees who had purchased through tickets, the problem was far from solved. The *Falcon* had brought to Chagres more paying passengers than there were accommodations aboard the *California*. The tardy Pacific Mail sidewheeler finally departed for San Francisco loaded to suffocation with nearly five hundred passengers—the Peruvians camping on deck, and 168 oversold New York ticket holders, unable to claim the quarters they had purchased, crowded into the steerage with goats, hogs, cows, and an annoyed and frustrated bull.

Advertising and promotion in New England, plus the unexpected advent of California's gold discovery, had now suddenly made the Panama route a very desirable way to reach the Pacific side of the continent. If everything went right, if proper connections could be made out of Panama, it was definitely the shortest and quickest way. The doubtful side of the venture came in the uncertainty of steamers making proper and timed connections, even for those holding through tickets. To a passenger without a ticket, the Panama route could be a living hell.

Chagres, terminus not only for the Atlantic Steamship Company but many a windjammer sailing the trough, was not only a wretched assemblage of huts and hovels, but possessed a harbor so shallow that steamers and sailing vessel of any normal draft were forced to anchor far out and lighter their passengers and cargoes ashore. It was a place where few travelers seemed anxious to tarry. Its two hotels—the Astor House and Saint

THE
EMIGRANTS' GUIDE
TO
CALIFORNIA,

CONTAINING EVERY POINT OF INFORMATION FOR
THE EMIGRANT—INCLUDING ROUTES, DISTANCES,
WATER, GRASS, TIMBER, CROSSING OF RIVERS,
PASSES, ALTITUDES, WITH A LARGE MAP OF
ROUTES, AND PROFILE OF COUNTRY, &C.,—
WITH FULL DIRECTIONS FOR TESTING AND
ASSAYING GOLD AND OTHER ORES.

BY JOSEPH E. WARE.

PUBLISHED BY J. HALSALL,
No. 124 MAIN STREET,
ST. LOUIS, MO.

Title page from a popular book of its time.

Charles—were second-rate by any standards. Some wayfarers, glad to set foot on land after a rough and tiresome sea voyage, and seeking any accommodations offered, occasionally found them adequate. Some were even thrilled by the tropical atmosphere of palms, orange and lemon trees, and bananas growing in profusion out of their green and wide-leaved nests. Everywhere was jungle, alive with the color of orchids and immense and beautiful butterflies. Monkeys cavorted, shrieked, and chattered from the treetops. If one had money, and did not prolong the stay, Chagres was picturesque and tolerable.

But for the hundreds not so lucky, those who found it necessary to camp, or to share a native hut, Chagres was more often a dank and frightening hell. Bugs and mosquitoes were constant torment. Centipedes and scorpions sought shelter in a man's shoes the moment he took them off. And many an argonaut woke up to find a rattlesnake or fer-de-lance sharing his bed. It took more than tropic beauty to entice a man to tarry in Chagres.

From New York to Chagres the distance was twenty-five hundred miles; from Chagres, across the isthmus to Panama City, an unforgettable sixty; from Panama to San Francisco, thirty-five hundred miles of ocean waterway. Steamer fare for the Pacific leg was high for the times—$350 to $600 for first cabin; $300 for second or less. But with all the mileage totaled, it cut the long journey around the Horn in half. The new sidewheel steamers, however, could not claim monopoly on the Panama route. Gradually, as the chaos of stranded passengers leveled out to some semblance of normality, the windjammers took over a large share of the Panama run. But always it was easier for a traveler to get to Chagres than for him to get from Panama to California—no matter what type of vessel he chose.

Panama City, on the Pacific side, while considerable improvement over Chagres, was old, venerable, and decayed—and usually a tragic disappointment to a man marooned in its cloying heat for weeks or months. The place was an inferior comparison to Rio, Valparaiso, and Callao—so well and lovingly known to those who had rounded the Horn. But after the steamy jungle trip across the isthmus, by boat, muleback, and/or afoot, any look upon a civilized community was pleasing. Panama was a study in decaying magnificence.

Her once splendid cathedrals, dwellings, and public edifices were tumbling into ruinous heaps. Her citizens, for the most part, were apathetic, aloof, undemonstrative, and wretchedly poor. Few could afford shoes to shield their feet from the miasmic poisons of the earth, and nearly everyone walked the streets barefoot.

For the hundreds of men marooned for weeks and months, whatever excitement and amusements Panama possessed lost luster day by day. The street women, their heads shrouded in rebosas, were sad comparisons to the flirting and bright-eyed wonders of Rio and Valparaiso. The lively ones, found in the cantinas, were professionals at separating the invading Yankees from their moneybelts, and so diseased that intimacy with them was a hazard. Stranded argonauts paid dearly for their boredom as they wagered recklessly on cockfights and monte. Even the gory ballet of the bullring wore thin under the depressing ennui of Panama.

The journal of Hiram Pierce, out of Troy, New York, noted by Joseph Henry Jackson in his *Anybody's Gold*, is one of the more graphic accounts, and left by a man who tried the Panama "short cut." Pierce, respected citizen of Troy, owner of a blacksmith shop, former president of the fire department, and elder in Troy's Second Presbyterian Church, was not the usual type of youthful, strong-willed, and fierce-eyed gold seeker. In making his choice for the great adventure, Pierce walked out on wife, family, and kin.

He claimed justification for his decision when, in his failing health, a physician had suggested a long sea voyage as one way to fetch him back to par. The choice was made easy when he threw in with one of those constantly spawning mining companies—one being organized in his home town of Troy. This bolt for freedom apparently had been a desire long suppressed.

Oddly, Hiram Pierce and the Troy Company embarked on the S.S. *Falcon* March 8, 1849, almost exactly one year after the Atlantic Steamship Company had teamed with Pacific Mail to furnish through service to California by way of Panama. From the pathetic journal of Hiram Pierce one can only assume that the service had improved none in its year of operation.

After leaving New York the *Falcon*

Panama City. Sketch from Otis, Illustrated History of the Panama Railroad.

docked at Charleston for its quota of California-bound miners. Next stop was Havana, Cuba, followed by a swing across the Gulf of Mexico to pick up an additional load of gold seekers out of New Orleans, and enough coal to steam them to Chagres. At Chagres the eager passengers were dumped ashore, and Pierce and his Troy Company were left to their own initiative in arranging transportation, not only across the isthmus, but from Panama to San Francisco. Up to now it had been a pleasant, uneventful voyage. At Chagres they, with others of the *Falcon*'s passengers, faced the time of great tribulation.

Pierce's journalistic evaluation of Chagres is sarcastically typical. Fortunately the Troy men were not forced to remain in the town too long, managing to bargain for passage up the Chagres River on the *Orus*, a miniature steamboat recently put into service. While she chuffed safely and comfortably through the Panamanian jungles the Yankee miners gaped

in wonder at the curious green pageant unfolding with every curve of the river—strange trees, lush and tangled jungle plants, brilliant-hued birds who swooped and screeched at every intrusion into their wild, unreal domain. Some of the passengers had commenced to wonder what it would be like to negotiate this jungle afoot.

They were a lot closer to it when the *Orus* dumped them seventeen miles upriver. The watercourse now had become shallow, cut by rapids, and broken by islands. The tiny steamboat, despite her shallow draft, was not able to carry them further. The *Orus* captain obligingly arranged with the natives for five *bungas*—flat-bottomed canoes, hewed out of enormous logs—poled when the water would float them, rope-dragged by the naked boatmen through the rapids and over the shallows. The helpful captain arranged for this *bunga* transportation as far as the village of Gorgona, at $10 cash per head. Not until later did

Up the Chagres River to Bujio Soldado. Sketch from Otis, Illustrated History of the Panama Railroad.

Pierce learn that the native boatman's going rate for the trip was $6.00. The captain had pocketed the difference as his cut.

Now at last the travelers were getting close to nature. In the shallow boats one all but rubbed bottoms with the water, and the naked natives poled slowly, and took their time through the oppressive and cloying jungle. Mosquitoes were a constant plague, the heat enervating, and alligators slithered off the mudbanks as the clumsy boats parted the jungle fronds ahead. Parrots shrieked, and monkeys scolded in simian chatter. Even the bubbles that slowly rose through the slime added their decadent stench as they burst. That first night the company slept under the trees. Hiram Pierce led his little congregation in prayer, and then stood guard for the first four hours.

Toward evening of the second day they reached the village of Gorgona. The boatmen, refusing any more service to the Americans,

balked at unloading the *bungas,* or toting baggage to higher ground. Only more pay could induce them to perform this essential service. Hiram Pierce was not a man to haggle over the performance of duty. He whipped out a pistol as neatly as he had whipped out a prayer. Under this persuasion, the natives brought up the baggage.

At Gorgona they were still twenty-four miles from Panama. And it took three days of bargaining before they could secure help for the difficult journey overland. Time was of the essence because more and more of the Americans were sickening with dysentery and strange fevers. The pack train, assembled at Gorgona, cost them another $250. Meanwhile they had to camp. And Pierce and a couple of his friends scouted the jungle for food. The diary lists his bag as "Two wild Turkeys, one Monkey, one Anteater, some Pigeons and one Iguana."

It was a sorry cavalcade which started that

Native huts near Gorgona. Sketch from Otis, Illustrated History of the Panama Railroad.

last leg to Panama seaport. Company baggage, and those travelers too ill to walk, were the burden of the mules. Behind, and afoot, came the weary and discouraged men. According to Hiram Pierce, the twenty-four miles overland proved far too much for ailing travelers to make without a stop. They attempted another camp in the jungle, only to become sacrificial offerings to the bugs and insects. Cries of birds, beasts, and the nags and chitters of the monkey population denied them the sleep which their weary bodies demanded. Long before sunrise the Americans again were on the move. At eight in the morning, reeling with fatigue, they tumbled into Panama. The ship they had expected to find was not there. All they could do was join the two thousand tattered malaria- and cholera-infested travelers who already had been waiting weeks for transportation.

Thirty-five days of "Panama torture" became the lot of Hiram Pierce and his company before they could coax or bribe passage on any kind of vessel. There was no triumphant entrance into California aboard any of the three Pacific Mail steamers. With hundreds and hundreds of wayfarers being fed into the isthmus funnel from the Chagres side—with cholera, yellow fever, and malaria taking daily toll on the stranded hordes of gold seekers—wisdom dictated that one grab the first possible conveyance. The Troy Company gladly took leave of Panama aboard one of those decrepit, badly sailed windjammers which opportunists had picked up at San Francisco.

Pierce found the ship filthy, overcrowded, and the food worse than anything they had foraged out of Panama. Men were fed from the galley like swine, and forced to snatch their meat or other edibles amid the frantic clawing of hundreds of others of similar intent. As could be expected, there was a lot of sickness among the miserable humans who crowded this ancient hull. The ship's doctor, continuously drunk on medical whiskey, was of little help.

Storms of paralyzing fury beset the ill-starred vessel. Two months at sea, and they still were a thousand miles from San Francisco. With twelve days' rations of water remaining, and the captain estimating at least fifteen more days to the Golden Gate, the illness became frightening. Badly cooked pork and stale water finally put Pierce and many of his companions to the crib with "severe Cholic pain & a Diarea discharging a bloody Slime with Severe Headache." Somehow the doctor kept sober long enough to issue pills of opium and camphor to the sufferers. But there were deaths.

Despite every conceivable hardship, however, this shipload of chastened Jasons finally reached San Francisco on July 26, 1849. The little company from Troy, New York, were soon swallowed up in the great human tide of the waterways west. For them, at least, the Panama route had proven anything but a short cut to California.

All the seaboard states furnished companies who chose the Panama route. They were just as socialistically oriented, just as lofty in concept, and just as well planned as those choosing to go overland, or those who made the long voyage around the Horn. As compared with the latter groups, however, there was a difference. There was no attempt to purchase a ship, to load her with articles of trade in the hope of additional profits. And a more immediate test of brotherhood often resulted when they were dumped at Chagres, endured the abysmal crossing of the isthmus, and too often discovered that getting from Panama to San Francisco was no happy or easy matter. Many a company foundered at the halfway mark. And many an individual who

had chanced it alone was glad to be free of group entanglement and acrimony.

More than a score of organized mining companies sailed out of New York Harbor for Panama. In 1849 Massachusetts alone furnished eleven corporate groups. And from Maine to New Orleans came plenty more. Also a far greater proportion of individualistic gold seekers took the Panama route strictly as venturesome passengers, as compared to the long haul around South America. To the Europeans who sought their fortunes in California gold, the Panama route became especially attractive. In spite of the greater danger of disease, death, and disappointment, thousands upon thousands of future Californians were funneled through the short cut.

One of the earliest starters via Panama was the Boston & Newburyport Mining Company. It sailed from Boston February 24, 1849, on the schooner *Edwin*, and in eighteen days arrived at Chagres. The Bostonians made the usual bargain with native boatmen for the upriver trip to Gorgona, bucked the jungle eighteen miles, camped, and next morning were forced to pay the boatmen $60 additional before they could proceed on to Gorgona. This settlement took care of their baggage, but the men were forced to walk the jungle trail to the settlement. It cost them an additional $300 for baggage portage, on bullocks and mules, into Panama. The men walked.

In their long wait at Panama, the Americans fell victim to the "jungle sickness" and a lot of the well ones, easy prey for Panama's gambling sharpies, lost their money at monte. The result was that when the expected Pacific Mail steamer finally arrived, there was not enough cash to buy passage at the going rate of up to $600 per head.

They considered it luck when the bark *Circassian* put into port and offered to haul them to San Francisco for $200 apiece. To raise the needed passage money they were forced to sell much of their precious supplies and provisions. On May 5 the little 110-ton vessel finally took them out of plague-ridden Panama.

The *Circassian* was probably as well provisioned as most vessels on the Panama run, but she had certainly seen better days. Her leaks were such as to require constant pumping,

Stranded in Panama, the weary argonauts took passage on whatever sea-going vessel came their way. Pictured here, the clipper ship Flying Cloud *and an early-day steamer headed for San Francisco Bay. Courtesy the Mariners Museum.*

and her crew consisted of whatever losers could be induced to sail out of San Francisco in those frantic days. Worse, she no sooner had swung into open sea than she was caught in one of those Pacific gales which blew her far south of the equator. Heat, and bilge leaks which followed, quickly spoiled her store of pork and beef.

The *Circassian's* voyage—more than three months at sea—became a nightmare of sickness and privation. The water supply ran so low in the last three weeks that one pint only per man was allowed in the daily ration of two ounces of wormy jerked beef and four ounces of weevil-infested ship's bread—served up together at 4 P.M. At one time the desperate men stormed the ship's hold, found some salt pork, which they devoured raw. Water, if it could be bribed from a crewman, brought up to $1.00 a pint; salt beef, $2.00 a pound. The decrepit bark reached San Francisco in August with its load of unhappy adventurers.

A group out of Lowell—the Massasoit Mining & Trading Company—sailed March 2, 1849, on the schooner *Harriet Neal*. From Chagres to Gorgona they suffered the same problems as their confederates making the crossing. Being far-sighted and enterprising Yankees, they sent scouts on to Panama to make arrangements for their San Francisco passage. The scouts returned with the dour news that there were no vessels at Panama to take them, that the city was crammed with men of like intent, that it would be weeks, perhaps months, before passage would be obtainable. So the company, instead of wringing hands with grief, built themselves shelter at Gorgona, where they set up a wayside eatery. While they waited, high above the fever belt, they cleared a neat daily profit by peddling doughnuts and coffee to the struggling passers-by.

Eventually they shipped out of Panama on the schooner *Two Friends*. Their voyage to San Francisco—four months—consumed as much time as it would have taken them for the entire journey around Cape Horn.

All through that climactic year of 1849, and for a few years to follow, vessels of every description, and from many nations, dumped their passengers at Chagres to claw, boat, ride, walk, and eventually to railroad across the isthmus—to catch any available transportation to California. Some of the fortunate ones made good connections, and saved time in getting to the promised land. Others found it a bitter experience. Certainly the Panama route was for those with plenty of loose cash. But, no matter how rich one might be, there was no avoidance of the yellow fever, the cholera, the jungle dysentery, which sent many an eager gold seeker to an untimely grave, or a quickest possible return to the homeland.

Howe quotes one discouraged argonaut writing from Panama: "I have no time to give reasons, but in saying it I utter the united sentiment of every passenger whom I have heard speak. It is this, and I say it in fear of God and the love of man. To one and all, for no consideration come this route. I have nothing to say of the other routes, but do not take this."

Even before the traumatic year of 1849 closed out to history, the Panama route had become a two-way street. Panama itself had emerged, to every intent and purpose, an American city—a tenuous appendage to San Francisco. Those who had found frustration and disappointment in California's mines, who had enough of their original grubstake left over, or who had garnered enough gold dust by panning or by slick ingenuity, and longed to go back to the old home town, bought passage to Panama, crossed the isthmus, and headed home. The mail steamers, the windjammers, could now be certain of passengers going both ways. And they profited accordingly.

Those struggling up from Chagres, their dream of fortune in the driver's seat, met streams of embittered pilgrims trudging down from Panama. These sad ones had "seen the elephant" and vocally spilled their frightening tales. There were also the lucky ones, those who were carrying pokes of heavy yellow metal back to New York or Boston—often at gunpoint and with hired guards. These fed a little hope and gave a little courage in that weird and speculative compulsion of the gold rush.

Meanwhile the stranded opportunists, and the hard and wise returnees had almost totally captured Panama. American entrepreneurs soon owned its monte parlors, its saloons, its whorehouses. No longer was it Panamanians who would lift the golden fleece from the twin lines of adventurers who for decades would travel the isthmus. Ingenious Yankees—sharp ones out of San Francisco and New England —now ran Panama.

It wasn't the hard-working native boatmen out of Chagres, or the muleteers out of Gorgona who ended up in control of all transportation across the isthmus. This distinction went to two Americans—William H. Aspinwall and George Law—who eventually decided the fate of every traveler who attempted the short cut. From the time they "took over" the paths, the waterways, and the mule portage, to their eventual building of the amazing Panama Railroad, they milked the traveler for all they could get. When their railroad, which Robert West Howard labeled the "treasure road," became operative in 1855, Chagres and its wicked river had been by-passed as the Atlantic port of entry in favor of the new port of Aspinwall. Here began the steel rails which would serve the traveler as the essential but expensive crossing in years ahead.

Many California-bound wayfarers, hoping to escape the Panama trap, crossed over the higher country of Nicaragua. Some made it, and some did not. Always there was the problem of transportation once they reached the Pacific side.

Some groups, including eight companies from Massachusetts, decided on what was probably the most hazardous route of all— across Mexico. Many of these adventurers had served in the Mexican War, just concluded, and felt they knew the nation to the south "like a book." What they failed to comprehend was that the war experience, instead of being an asset to the traveler, was good and sufficient reason to stay out of Mexico. That nation had just suffered the most humiliating defeat in its history. To any and every Mexican, the *gringo*—especially *Norteamericano gringo*—was his enemy. And many an eager gold seeker, hopefully crossing Mexico, paid the supreme price for his folly.

As planned, it looked like the quickest and surest of all routes. Eighteen sailing days from New Orleans to Vera Cruz; 280 miles horseback, nine days, from Vera Cruz to Mexico City; 980 miles down the hump from Mexico City, twenty days, to Mazatlan on the Pacific side. From Mazatlan to San Francisco required little more than thirty days' sailing time. The entire trip from New York to San Francisco should never exceed four months.

Initially, any route chosen seemed fastest to the traveler, though the opinion usually changed before its finish. One group co-operative, calling themselves the New England Pioneers, and all of them former members of the Massachusetts militia, organized their com-

pany military style. Armed with rifles, re-
volvers, swords, bowie knives, and bulldogs,
they journeyed to New Orleans, via Charleston, took passage on the schooner *Nancy
Bishop*, and arrived in Vera Cruz in late January of 1849. Their plan was to cross Mexico as
a unit of cavalry, but only four of the men
managed to get horses at Vera Cruz. The remainder of the company were forced to hoof
it.

Somehow they reached Mexico City without assassination, and, after seemingly endless
troubles, finally arrived at San Blas on the
Pacific side. There, starting as a cantina brawl,
they fought a pitched battle with the Mexican
townsmen. Cost was one dead and several
wounded. At San Blas the company separated,
some taking passage on the bark *Mary Frances*
for Mazatlan, where they, with other Americans stranded there, purchased the schooner
Diana. After enlisting other passengers at $45
a head, they started for San Francisco.

But the *Diana*, decrepit and leaky, was
forced into San José, where Mexican port authorities promptly condemned the vessel.
There some of the more affluent of the decimated company traded what property remained for horses—and started overland for
San Francisco, 2,300 miles to the north.
When the horses gave out, they continued
afoot, living on the corn in their haversacks.
When this was gone they were forced to a diet
of shellfish, rattlesnakes, and cacti. Days without water, days without food, two of them
trudged seven hundred miles barefoot. It took
them fifty-one days to reach San Diego. With
friendly *gringo* help, they eventually made it
to San Francisco. Surely this was doing it the
hard way.

The remainder of this brash company,
stranded back in San José, were forced to labor
at odd jobs, in enemy country, until they
could earn enough to get back to Mazatlan.
From there some of them eventually gained
passage to California—to melt into that
strange amalgam of nations at the Golden
Gate.

The Rough and Ready Company took the
steamer *Greyhound* for Vera Cruz and practically repeated the journey via Mexico City to
Mazatlan, including many similar incidences
that had befallen the New England Pioneers.
They too broke up at Mazatlan—with every
man for himself.

The Essex Company sailed out of Boston
on the schooner *John W. Herbert*, but was
shipwrecked at Aransas Pass. The nearest city
was Corpus Christi, Texas, twenty-five miles
up the bay from Aransas Inlet. Three men
died on the journey from Corpus Christi to
Laredo. Cholera played hell with the company
as it moved through Mexico, becoming far
more lethal than the threat of assassination.
Three more members were lost to this dread
disease before they reached Mazatlan. But
they had made the thousand-mile march from
Corpus Christi, through hostile Mexico, in
seventy-four days.

At Mazatlan they considered themselves
fortunate to obtain passage aboard a Mexican
schooner, but before the fifty-day voyage to
San Francisco was finished, there was a
difference of opinion. The schooner ran short
of both food and water. If Mr. Chapman, one
of the company members, had not ingeniously
found a way to distill sea water by the use of
tin plates, they all would have perished from
thirst. Their food was locomotive biscuits and
mahogany beef, and half the company had to
sleep on the deck of the tiny 115-ton vessel.
When this decimated group finally stepped to
the soil of California, they were totally convinced that the Mexican route was neither
fastest nor safest.

Sadly, in the matter of actually laying
hands on the golden fleece, few of the thousands upon thousands of Jasons who traveled
west ever realized much on the dream. Those
who already were in California—like Sam
Brannan and the residual troops mustered out
of service in the Mexican War—or the lucki-
est of the first-comers—had surest and best
chance of scoring. But luck's percentages
seemed to dwindle out with time.

On the other hand, California's enrich-
ment from the incredibly vast incursion far exceeded whatever wealth was taken from her
soil. The whole world sent their intellectuals,
their artisans, their tradesmen, their clerks,
and their farmers—every conceivable and
needful skill, backed by young and reckless
motivation. And, because so many remained,
gold or no gold, California—in four years—
stepped forth as the most vigorous and enterprising of American states.

A purview of what came off the argonaut
ships clearly defines what California gained in

Steamboat Grey Hound. *Courtesy of the New-York Historical Society, New York City.*

cultural and material assets in exchange for the gold with which she had set the world afire. John Goodman states that the smallest sailing vessel to enter the Golden Gate in 1849 was the *Breeze*, a New England pleasure yacht of fourteen tons. Also among the mini-vessels was the clipper-built schooner *Toccao*, a twenty-eight-ton wonder, built by five ship carpenters of New Bedford with eyes on California. The largest sailing vessel to make the voyage was the full-rigged ship *Grey Eagle*, out of Philadelphia January 21, 1849. Her burden was huge for that day—1,178 tons; her cargo manifest was valued at $120,000.

And the gold rush steamers? They were both larger and smaller than the windjammers. In addition to the big Pacific Mail sidewheelers, many miniature steamboats, used on eastern rivers for pleasure yachts and towing, ended up in San Francisco Bay or plied the Sacramento River. Some made the journey under their own power; others were dismantled and deck-stowed on larger ships.

And the people aboard this motley parade of vessels? Included were the future prominent pioneers and citizens of the Golden State: doctors, lawyers, professors, printers, religionists. Included also were the broken-down failures in every trade and calling—with above-average share of crooks, loafers, thieves, entrepreneurs, and politicians.

The 580-ton ship *South Carolina* departed New York January 1849, two weeks after the Tom Hyer-Yankee Sullivan prize fight. She not only carried Sullivan, but 162 other pugilistic-minded passengers—including eight committee members of Tammany Hall.

Deckhands and seamen fled to California in such numbers that the maritime world of New England was literally stripped of able hands to man the packets and merchantmen on the Atlantic run. The *Ann Perry*, a 348-ton bark, sailed from Salem to San Francisco with a crew of twenty—all of whom had been masters or mates on other vessels. The 550-ton half-clipper ship *Tarolinta* sailed out of New York with an all-black crew of twenty, a blustering captain, and four mates. Every man exceeded six feet.

The *Albany*, a 473-ton ship, sailed with a

The "graveyard of ships stranded in the Cove," San Francisco Bay. Courtesy Society of California Pioneers, San Francisco Maritime Museum.

company of railroadmen from Utica, New York. Another vessel carried a hundred musicians and actors. Early in 1849 a theatrical group was organized in Philadelphia to go to California as cheer to the souls of the gold grubbers.

A circus arrived with the gold rush. On October 12, 1849, the bark *Tasso* put into San Francisco Bay. Aboard was the famous Olympic Circus of Joseph Andrew Rowe. The wild animals, equestrians, and acrobatic marvels of Rowe's Circus were received with enthusiasm and excitement, and the show played to capacity audiences in San Francisco, Sacramento, and the gold camps.

Two companies, composed entirely of experienced whalers, sailed out on the *Mount Vernon*. They carried aboard harpoons and equipment peculiar to their trade, and took one whale off the Azores—the oil of which they profitably sold in California. One mining group, made up entirely of stone cutters from Pigeon Cove, Massachusetts, traveled out on the ship *Euphrasia*. Fifty German Jews, out of Scotland, arrived in New York August 13, 1849, aboard the British ship *Sir William Molesworth*. There they purchased a vessel, set sail, and became a part of the dynamic human mix which pioneered and built the state of California.

The Grecian Jason, and the search of his original argonauts for the golden fleece, makes pale and insipid incident compared to the drama of '49. The Gold Rush Fleet probably has given us the weirdest, most complex, most exciting maritime adventure in history. It isn't entirely that this water trails epic added so immeasurable to the building of America's West. It's that it happened, mates—and the way it happened—that makes it so far out, and so wonderful.

14

The Sacramento

BY BILL PRONZINI

For most of its 250 navigable miles between Red Bluff and San Francisco Bay, the Sacramento River winds lazily through California's fertile Central Valley. Its waters are slow-moving, mostly unhazardous, and its banks and sloughs are lined with willows and mistletoe-festooned cottonwoods and long stretches of farmland. Alongside such mighty and legendary rivers as the Mississippi, the Missouri, and the Ohio, the Sacramento at first consideration seems tame, unobtrusive.

But in truth it is America's "little giant" of waterways—the most important river in the growth and development of northern California and the port of San Francisco. No other body of water played such a vital role in the California gold rush; no other body of water west of the Rockies is as rich in history, drama, adventure, and tragedy.

Until January 19, 1848, when James Marshall discovered the first treasure of yellow metal in Sutter's Creek, the Sacramento was a sleeping little giant: its significance as a "water trail west" was virtually nonexistent. There was no organized river traffic in northern California, and the Sacramento was used only occasionally for the transportation of passengers and freight. Most of the settlements along its banks—Marysville, Knight's Landing, Poker Bend, Dry Slough, Twenty-Mile Island—were inhabited by but handfuls of hardy pioneers. And San Francisco itself was little more than a sprawling hamlet of shacks and mud flats whose principal landing was a tiny place called Yerba Buena Cove.

No steamboats worked the waters of San Francisco Bay; in fact, the only commercial craft, other than sailing vessels and private freight launches, were a series of short-line ferries operated by an Englishman named William A. Richardson. It was but a few short months before Marshall's momentous find that the first steamer was transported to San Francisco and, ultimately, went to work on the Sacramento.

She was the *Sitka*, which the Russians had been using in Alaskan waters for several years and which was purchased on a whim by San Francisco's leading merchant of the time, William Leidesdorff. Leidesdorff bought her in August of 1847, along with a consignment of smoked fish, gunpowder, spirits, and assorted trade goods, with the general idea of using her to increase business with John Sutter's colony at New Helvetia, where the Sacramento and American rivers joined. Sutter was one of Leidesdorff's steadiest customers.

The Russian bark *Naslednich* brought the knocked-down pieces of the *Sitka* to San Francisco in the fall of 1847. The packet was then assembled on Yerba Buena Island. Only thirty-seven feet long, she was a sidewheeler with limited capabilities; it was even facetiously said that if a man stood on her port guardrail, he would lift her starboard paddle wheel clear out of the water. But Leidesdorff had confidence in her, and after a few trial runs up and down the Bay, he sent her on her maiden voyage up the Sacramento on November 29.

Six days and seven hours later, the *Sitka* crawled into New Helvetia—a distance of approximately 120 miles. After her return trip downriver, the *Daily Alta California*, San Francisco's leading newspaper of the time, reported tongue-in-cheek that she was beaten into the port of Benicia by an ox team, to the tune of four days.

The *Sitka* increased her speed considerably on subsequent runs, but she was destined to meet a premature end: a howling

The "Forest of Masts" panorama—the gold rush fleet in San Francisco Harbor early in 1851. The Smithsonian Institution and the Bancroft Library, University of California at Berkeley. Courtesy the San Francisco Maritime Museum.

norther sank her ingloriously in San Francisco Bay in February of 1848. She was later raised, stripped of her engine, and finished her days as the schooner *Rainbow*.

But she had carved her niche in history, and the era of the "great steamers, white and gold" which plied the Sacramento and San Joaquin rivers had begun. On her heels came the great flotilla of California river steamers, each one finer and speedier than the last, to meet the mushrooming demand for transportation created by the gold rush.

Thousands upon thousands of people flocked to San Francisco in search of wealth and dreams; the city, razed by its first great fire in 1849, grew out of the ashes to become the center of commerce in northern California, and to offer a multitude of enticements ranging from culture and the arts to every imaginable type of sin. Among those who came were men bent on making their fortunes not in the digging of gold but in the transportation industry. Ships set forth from dozens of ports around the globe, many of which failed to make it through the Golden Gate; the ocean floors are strewn with the bones of San Francisco-bound craft that lost their battles with the raging Atlantic and Pacific storms.

The deep waters of the Sacramento attracted ocean-going vessels as well as conventional riverboats. Sloops, schooners, brigs, and even clipper ships competed for business between San Francisco and the town of Sacramento City, the most notable of these being the *Senator*, built in New York for East Coast trade between Boston and New Brunswick. But soon the faster and safer steamboats assumed the bulk of the traffic; the increasing size of sea-going ships and the rapid silting of the river from the hydraulic mining in the Sierras closed the inland ports to all but local craft.

Several of the burgeoning number of packets to operate on the Sacramento came around the Horn from New York. One of these was the famous "stolen steamboat"—the 530-ton sidewheeler *New World*, which Captain Ned Wakeman and his crew, at the behest of the boat's owner, William A. Brown, sailed out from under the literal noses of creditors and deputy sheriffs in New York Harbor.

The chronicle of the *New World*'s voyage to San Francisco reads like a high adventure novel. First of all she endured bravely a number of bad storms and an outbreak of yellow fever. Then she was chased into the harbor at Rio de Janeiro by a British frigate, since she had no lawful papers. Wakeman, however, contrived to fall overboard from a small boat and foxed the American consul into believing he had lost the packet's papers while in the water. Proper clearance was given, and the *New World* set sail again, minus eighteen crew members who had died of the yellow fever epidemic.

In Valparaiso she was ordered into quarantine for twenty days, but Wakeman protested so vehemently, and perhaps greased a few palms so generously, that she was released after eight days. While in that South American port Wakeman had learned that he was to be arrested at Panama by New York Authorities representing the boat's creditors; but he was much too crafty to stand still for that. Instead of putting into Panama, he anchored behind the island of Tabago and then slipped ashore dressed in civilian clothing. Next he sought out several hundred Americans who had drifted across the isthmus and were anxious to get to the California gold fields, and offered them transportation to San Francisco at $300 per man—if they would agree to intimidate the two New York deputies and a guard of ten soldiers waiting in Panama. They were only too eager to oblige.

Faced with bodily harm when the *New World* anchored in sight of Panama the following morning, the two deputies tore up their extradition papers and allowed the steamer to continue on her way. Three months later, on July 11, 1851, she steamed into San Francisco Bay and promptly went to work on the Sacramento.

She was a fixture on the river for the next fourteen years, under the aegis of the California Steam Navigation Company. Then she was sold to the Oregon Steam Navigation Company, spent several years in the Northwest, and finally returned to California to wind up her career as a Vallejo ferry.

Another of the well-known "imports" was the *Antelope*, which had been a Long Island Sound excursion boat. She was a slim, frail single-stack sidewheeler, and some said it was a miracle she had survived the open seas. After her arrival in San Francisco, she maintained a dependable and accident-free schedule on the Sacramento. It was for this reason that she was accorded the honor of being the first California riverboat to carry Pony Express mail from Sacramento City to San Francisco on April 15, 1860; and also the reason why she was later used regularly by Wells-Fargo to transport millions of dollars in gold bullion and dust downriver to its San Francisco bank.

By 1850 there were twenty-eight steamers operating on the Sacramento, and this number increased steadily as the years passed. The competition was fierce, cut-throat; any lowering of tariff by one boat resulted in immediate—and greater—lowerings by others. Passenger fares to Sacramento, which had been as high as $30 per head in the early days, tumbled to one dollar and finally to but a single dime. There was uniform disregard for safety measures; accidents were prevalent, and many a physical altercation resulted in harm to innocent citizens.

Early in 1854 the various owner-captains, as well as those astute businessmen who had built fleets of steamboats, gathered at a peace table to put an end to this pointless warfare, and to curb the growing number of packets vying for business. Among those present were Charles Minturn, who represented the big Sacramento steamers such as the *Senator* and

The sidewheeler New World, *the famous "stolen steamboat" that sailed around the Horn in 1851. Society of California Pioneers. Courtesy the San Francisco Maritime Museum.*

New World, and Richard Chenery, who guarded the interests of several smaller riverboats. Out of this meeting of minds came the birth of the California Steam Navigation Company—the major force in northern California steamboating for the next seventeen years.

Chenery was elected president of the combine, and stock was fixed to sell at $1,000 per share. Tariffs were set to enable the owners of the company boats to recoup some of their early losses. Fares to Marysville were placed at $12 per head, to Sacramento at $10, and to Stockton on the San Joaquin River at $8; freight was $6 per ton to Stockton, $8 to Sacramento, and $15 to Marysville.

The public, of course, was not pleased. Newspapers denounced the monopoly, and leaders of the Marysville community even went so far as to build their own high-pressure steamer, the *Queen City*, and put her on the river at much lower rates. Other opposition lines also developed, but the California Steam Navigation Company was too powerful for these upstarts to proliferate, and they either went out of business or were absorbed by the combine.

There is no question that California Steam Navigation *was* a monopoly, but it nonetheless succeeded admirably in ending chaos on the Sacramento and San Joaquin. Eventually prices went down to a more reasonable level, became stabilized, and transportation on the inland waterways benefited to a major degree. It was only when the golden age of steamboating came to an end as a result of the rapid encroachment of rail lines that California Steam Navigation lost its power and was finally forced to sell out to California Pacific Railroad in 1871.

The company built a number of packets during its time, and one of these was the queen of California steamboats, the *Chrysopolis*. Many of the boats constructed in California and the Northwest closely resembled the traditional Mississippi River pattern, while others blended the features of the types used on the Hudson and other eastern waterways; but the *Chrysopolis* epitomized a new style and flavor peculiar to the West.

The name *Chrysopolis* means Golden City—an appropriate, even a heroic appellation for the slim princess that became the darling of California rivermen. Designed and built by John North in 1860, with lavish care, she was 245 feet long, had a beam of forty and a depth of ten feet, and drew four and a half feet of water. She carried a single-cylindered, vertical-beam engine of 1,357 horsepower; her paddle wheels were thirty-six feet in diameter, with eight-foot buckets. The fact that she was made with speed in mind is borne out by the record she holds for the fastest time from San Francisco to Sacramento City, on a run on the last day of 1861: five hours and nineteen minutes.

The *Chryssie*, as the rivermen affectionately called her, rivaled the Mississippi's "floating palaces" in luxurious appointments. She sported carved rosewood paneling, ogee molding, red plush unholstery, and crystal chandeliers in her Social Hall, Ladies' Cabin, and Gentlemen's Saloon. Her pride and joy was the most sumptuous cuisine on the western frontier, including such delicacies as fresh venison and fresh lobster, oversized oysters, French pastries and wines. "All you can eat for one dollar" was a promotional phrase used in her brochures and advertisements.

Voyage after voyage, the *Chryssie*'s private cabins and decks were jammed with bearded miners and burly roustabouts and sun-weathered farmers; thick-muscled Kanakas and Filipino laborers and coolie-hatted Chinese; sharp-eyed merchants and foppish gamblers and bonneted ladies who might have been the wives of prominent citizens or trollops on their way to the gold fields of the mother lode. Everyone who could afford the luxury took the opportunity at least once during the 1860s of traveling on the slim princess.

Yet another of her attractions was dependability. When she backed down from the landing in San Francisco every second afternoon at four o'clock, she could be counted on to reach her destinations quickly and without incident. Her captain, James Whitney, dis-

The Chrysopolis, *the "Queen of the Sacramento River steamboats," at her dock in* Sacramento *in 1869. A few years later she had succumbed to the competition of the* railroads. Courtesy the San Francisco Maritime Museum.

dained racing, a popular and dangerous sport among a number of the packets and their masters; the *Chryssie* was too elegant a lady to engage in such plebeian pastimes. In her fifteen years of service, she was never late, and except for one relatively minor occurrence, for which she happened to be blameless, she suffered no blemish on her exemplary record.

That one incident has rather humorous overtones, at least in retrospect. It took place on St. Patrick's Day of 1869, and involved a boisterous Irish militia outfit, which had been formed during the Civil War, called the Emmett Guards of Sacramento.

In honor of their patron saint, the guards embarked en masse on the *Chrysopolis* with the intention of joining their adjunct, the Emmett Guards of San Francisco, for a full-scale celebration. Unbeknownst to the leaders of the guards, and to the *Chryssie*'s crew, two of the group managed to smuggle a small cannon and a keg of black powder on board. Just before the steamer reached San Francisco on St. Patrick's Day morning, the two villains set up the cannon at the aft taffrail on the main deck and touched it off. This was intended as a grand salute to their counterparts waiting at the wharf; what it turned into instead was chaos.

It seems they foolishly neglected to remove the powder keg from the immediate vicinity of the cannon, so that when the shot was fired, sparks instantly ignited the keg. The resultant explosion loosened planking, set several red plush seats on fire, terrified passengers, and engulfed the steamer in a cloud of black smoke. Sixteen of the Emmett Guards were injured. The two perpetrators of the act, miraculously enough, were not killed; some people thought at the time that this was more regrettable than fortunate.

With the coming of the railroads, the *Chrysopolis* became less attractive to passengers and shippers of freight, and therefore more expensive to operate. Finally, in 1875, she was sold to Central Pacific and later rebuilt as a ferry on the San Francisco–Oakland run. A rather ignoble end to the undisputed queen of the Sacramento and her benevolent reign.

While such steamers as the *Antelope* and the *Chrysopolis* operated relatively trouble-free, a number of other packets were crippled or destroyed as the result of careless accidents.

Competition among the hell-raising crews led to an undue emphasis on speed, and speed in turn sometimes led to disaster. Captains would undertake to race their packets as sporting propositions or to prove that they commanded the fastest boat; some of the perilous liberties they took with their temperamental steam boilers resulted in the deaths of hundreds of men and women.

One example of the lunacy of steamboat racing is the case of the *R. K. Page*. On her regular run up the Sacramento one day in 1853, she drew abeam of another packet, the *Governor Dana*, and was promptly challenged to race. The challenge was readily accepted. Soon after the race began, the *Page*'s chief engineer entered into a side bet with a passenger, which made him even more determined for a victory. As the two packets steamed upriver, the engineer was told that the *Page* was losing ground. He decided his boilers were not producing enough steam, and without considering the consequences he pitched a cask of oil into the furnace. This built up steam well enough, but to such an unmanageable level that the boiler suddenly exploded with terrific force, bursting loose of its moorings and sailing upward through the superstructure. Three passengers went with it.

This was a minor tragedy, though, compared with such carnages as the eruption of the *Sagamore* near the Stockton wharf in 1850, in which fifty citizens were killed, and the explosion on board the *Secretary* in 1854 which resulted in a death toll upward of twenty. The worst tragedy in California riverboating occurred on January 27, 1855, when the main boiler on the *Enterprise* blew up at the mouth of the American River during a race and ripped through a crowd of passengers. Fifty-six people were killed, drowned, or fatally scalded by steam.

The lessons taught by these early disasters were blithely ignored by most steamboaters. As a result, senseless accidents continued to take place in every year of the following two decades. This, too, was part of the reason for the decline in popularity of the river packets, so that when the railroads offered safer, swifter transportation the people in California were more than willing to embrace it.

When the gold yield from the placer mines began to decline in the late 1850s, San Francisco and the communities of Sacramento

The San Francisco waterfront from Telegraph Hill in 1863. The gold rush fleet had disappeared, as had the forty-niners, but the discovery of silver in Nevada brought new stability to the burgeoning city. Courtesy the San Francisco Maritime Museum.

and Stockton underwent a period of depression and social upheaval. River traffic was severely affected; revenue dropped as fewer passengers and fewer consignments of freight were transported between San Francisco and the mother lode. The situation was not helped by the influx of criminals during the late 1840s and throughout the 1850s; many of them formed gangs and roamed such sections of San Francisco as the infamous Barbary Coast, robbing and killing with impunity. Miners who came down from the diggings on the riverboats were the chief target, and because they could not count on protection from San Francisco authorities, a large number of them ceased making the trip in from the gold fields. The two Committees of Vigilance which were established in the 1850s failed to solve this problem; in fact, they compounded matters since many of the vigilantes were little better than rogues themselves.

It took the discovery of silver in Nevada to bring San Francisco out of the depression, establish permanent order and adequate police

and fire protection, and create a new era and a new prosperity. The city's population swelled to sixty thousand; substantial buildings were erected on its hills and on the fill land below Montgomery Street which had once comprised the waterfront. San Francisco capital controlled the greater number of Nevada mines, and local industry furnished not only necessary machinery for mining and reducing ore, but most of the necessities and all of the luxuries for the residents of the rich silver towns. The steamers again did a booming business in the transportation of equipment, supplies, and miners from San Francisco to Sacramento, from which they could proceed overland to Nevada.

Just as San Francisco was growing, so were its neighbors. There was an increasing need for ferry service between Bay Area communities and between the larger settlements on the Sacramento and San Joaquin. Ferries had been operating continually in San Francisco Bay since 1826, when John Reed built a sloop to carry travelers across the Bay to what is now

Sausalito; Captain William Richardson, mentioned previously, had also made his fortune shuttling passengers between San Francisco and the East Bay. But it was not until the owners of such small sidewheelers as the *Caleb Cope*, the *Hector*, and the *Jenny Lind* recognized the lucrative potential in ferry service, and deserted the Sacramento, that the business of short-distance passenger transportation became large and organized.

Regular service was instituted to Petaluma, Vallejo, San Jose, and dozens of other towns reachable from San Francisco by water. On the Sacramento River small ferries made travel between settlements simpler and less expensive than it had been on the larger packets. Before long the northern California ferries were carrying the bulk of passengers on the inland waterways, and helping to increase the

rapid rate of progress and growth in that part of the state.

By the 1870s San Francisco had grown into a major city and a major port. More than sixteen hundred ships were arriving yearly from United States and foreign locales, carrying import and export goods of every conceivable type. But by this time, too, the railroads had begun to take over the bulk of freight and passenger traffic. Prior to 1869 most passengers and virtually all freight passing in and out of San Francisco went by water; by 1876, however, the interstate and transcontinental rail lines were handling 20,000 tons of cargo per month, and carrying upward of 100,000 passengers each year.

Well before the arrival of the new century, the tracks of the iron horse were everywhere in northern California, with short-line

The riverboat Modoc *loading cantaloupe at Sacramento while her passengers wait patiently for the last few crates to be brought aboard. Courtesy the San Francisco Maritime Museum.*

The riverboat era was reaching its ebb when this photograph was taken in the late 1800s but the ferry service in San Francisco's busy harbor was beginning to boom. The Jack Lowe Collection. Courtesy the San Francisco Maritime Museum.

companies and Southern Pacific spurs serving even the smallest of settlements. The railroads could not, of course, accommodate all of the travelers and all of the freight bound for inland and North Coast locations; what was left was quickly handled by the riverboats at competitive prices. Nevertheless, the number of steamers operating on the Sacramento and San Joaquin declined year by year.

The viability of the river packets was not enhanced by the bitterly contested waterfront strike of 1891, in which members of the Coast Seamen's Union and the Steamshipmen's Union battled management and nonunion sailors for many months. The opposing factions fought with clubs, stones, knives, and even firearms; mooring lines were sabotaged, lifeboats smashed, and other vandalism perpetrated along San Francisco's *embarcadero*. When the bloody strike finally came to an end two years later, passengers and merchants had long since wearied of the struggle and of the cause of the rivermen.

The Alaskan gold rush of 1897 seemed to promise a new life for the steamers. Gold seekers again poured into San Francisco, and the demand for passage north became feverish; several riverboats were turned into ocean-going vessels to accommodate the hue and cry. But the promise turned out to be a false one: the fever waned as reports filtered down the Pacific coast that the Alaska strike was of considerably less than bonanza proportions—and the sudden outbreak of the Spanish-American War in 1898 refocused attention elsewhere.

While the riverboats were struggling through hard times, the ferries continued to flourish. Shortly after the turn of the century, the San Francisco, Oakland & San Jose Railway Company—or the Key System, as it came to be called—was formed. The first of the Key System's boats were the *Yerba Buena* and the *San Jose*, both of which were built in 1903 and both of which were propeller-driven. They operated from the Ferry Building in San Francisco and serviced the long, open-deck East Bay trestle which accommodated electric trains for Oakland, Claremont, and Berkeley, as well as the interurbans of the Oakland, Antioch & Eastern Railway. As the years passed, the Key System acquired several other ferries and grew into a conglomerate that dominated for more

An unidentified sternwheeler at dock in Sacramento, alongside of the barge Yolo, in the waning years of the river's steamboat days. Courtesy the San Francisco Maritime Museum.

than thirty years, until the building of the Bay Bridge in 1936 and the Golden Gate Bridge in 1937.

The Great Earthquake of 1906 had little immediate effect on river traffic, although some ferry boats suffered minor damage. But the city that was reborn yet again from the rubble—the new, modern San Francisco—depended even more heavily on the railroads and the coming Age of the Automobile for transportation and shipping. More and better roads were being built; the emphasis was on speed and large profits, neither of which could be supplied by inland water carriers.

Symbolically, the death knell for California's steamboats was sounded by the tragedy which took place on August 28, 1932. The Depression had rendered more than a dozen packets, barges, and smaller craft unprofitable to operate, and these were being held out of service at Broderick, just across the river from Sacramento. Among them was the *Flora*, which Hollywood film-makers had rented and redubbed *Dixie* for her role in *Huckleberry Finn*. On that fateful August night, a resident of a nearby houseboat heard odd rumbling sounds—and when he came out to investigate he saw smoke and flames gushing from windows on one of the steamers. He spread the alarm, but it was already too late: other boats ignited, oil tanks blew up, and before long the entire fleet was ablaze. Fireman were helpless; crowds of people stood watching proud smokestacks and pilothouses and texas superstructures toppled and consumed. The following morning there was nothing left of the boats except sodden hulks and heaps of glowing embers and the tangled ironwork of engines and walking beams.

In November of 1941 the last of the passenger steamers were withdrawn from the Sacramento, and subsequently sold, like so many other northern California riverboats and ferries, to the federal government during the Second World War. These were the *Delta Queen* and the *Delta King*, constructed in 1926 to much ballyhoo and the claim that they were the "last word" in luxurious inland liners; they were each 1,837 tons, 250 feet long, and as opulent as any of the early packets. But they had been unable to compete with the automobiles and the railroads: they were, sadly enough, doomed to obsolescence from the beginning.

A few freight-carrying steamboats lasted until the late 1940s, but their retirement, too, was inevitable. The nearly one-hundred-year reign of the steamer on the rivers of California had come to an end; as one individual of the time put it, "The rivers have all gone dark."

Today, the placid waters of the Sacramento are the domain of pleasure craft and a few small ocean freighters that transport minor cargoes to and from the port of Sacramento. The river has come full-circle: from anonymity to noble stature and finally back to relative oblivion.

But the "little giant's" part in the progress and achievements of California, the true spirit of the West that exists within its depths, commands for it a permanent place as one of America's great waterways. And if indeed the past is with us always, perhaps there can be heard along its older sloughs and reaches, on hushed moonlit nights, the gentle *Ssoo, hah! Ssoo, hah!* of steam engines, and the soft chunk of paddle wheels, and the ghostly voices of the men and women who created the pages of history.

15

The Columbia: The Great Monopoly

BY ELLIS LUCIA

PART I

When John Comigers Ainsworth arrived in Oregon in 1850, the instant reaction was that he'd beached himself foolishly on a shoal and wasn't going anywhere. In contrast to California, which was teeming with the gold rush, the land of the Columbia River was sparsely settled and largely undeveloped. Portland had "more stumps than houses" and many Oregonians of the wagon trains had abandoned farm and family to answer the call of gold in the south. All this also gave Ainsworth serious doubts about the sound judgment of Lot Whitcomb, who'd talked him into coming here.

Shortly John changed his mind, for first and foremost, this Mississippi River skipper was a steamboat man. And the Pacific Northwest was the greatest steamboat country he'd ever laid eyes upon. The rivers ran in all directions and were virtually the only way to get around this big, rugged territory. But there were almost no power boats, other than the small and inefficient *Columbia*, a makeshift sidewheeler performing spasmodic duty around Oregon City on the Willamette River, and on the lower Columbia. Most people and commerce moved by keelboat, sail, flatboat, whaleboat, raft, canoe, or floating log. Certainly the opportunity was here, but whether the region would ever grow sufficiently was still very much in limbo.

Ainsworth's friends in California, other steamboatmen off the Ol' Mississippi, thought he'd blown a boiler. If a fellow wanted to go to steamboating, ample opportunity was at hand on the Sacramento and San Francisco Bay where the rates were high and there was more business than any self-respecting ship could handle. But Ainsworth was a loner; and it was then that he ran onto Lot Whitcomb buying gear for construction of Oregon's first bona-fide, home-built steamboat which he would—in all modesty—name for himself. Whitcomb believed in the country and talked a good fight. This appeared a rare opportunity, since Whitcomb's knowledge of steamboats and river navigation was obviously limited.

Therefore, when Lot offered Ainsworth the command, John couldn't turn it down, although there were times when he wished that he'd done so. By then it was too late. He was now sold on the green, rain-swept Oregon Country as a place where, with a little bit of luck, a steamboatman could make a fortune, acquire a great deal of power and influence, and help develop the territory. He was young and eager for success. By then, too, he was seriously involved with an attractive young lady who would shortly give him roots by benefit of matrimony. Funny, he mused, how a fellow could get all tied up without even realizing it. Soon he'd placed his lifetime's stake in the Pacific Northwest so that only in later years would poor health drive him from the place.

From the outset, Ainsworth and Whitcomb didn't get along. Whitcomb was envious of the younger man's vast knowledge of steam navigation and river travel, acquired from years of knocking about the Mississippi where he'd spent Tom Sawyer days as a youth, dealt in commerce with an uncle, worked on, skippered, and owned steamboats, and once had as his pilot a fellow named Sam Clemens. Years

Captain John C. Ainsworth, 1864, king of Columbia River steamboatmen, who built an empire with sternwheelers and ruled the big river with his Oregon Steam Navigation Company, reaping a fortune. Courtesy Oregon Historical Society.

Steamboating would never leave him; it was forever in his blood despite his love of power and big money, and his ambition. Many times he longed to return to the simple life at the helm of a gallant riverboat.

The *Lot Whitcomb*, under construction near Oregon City, appeared to be a finely designed vessel. She was a 600-ton sidewheeler, 160 feet long with a twenty-four-foot beam, a hold depth of nearly six feet, 140 horsepower engine, twin boilers, and the promise of making twelve miles an hour on the open river. The *Lot* would need every bit of that power to fight the swift and shifting currents of this challenging waterway, for the Columbia was no placid backwash. Neither would the *Lot* be a shabby freighter, but was fashioned for passenger comfort, with roomy private quarters, a ladies' cabin, spacious dining room, and much of the interior finished in polished wood paneling and rustic pioneer elegance. The river had seen nothing like her, a credit to her owner and a pacesetter for any future vessels invading this river empire.

Young Ainsworth was amazed that Whitcomb had done so well until he met the ship's carpenter, William L. Hanscombe, who knew fully what he was about. But both jealous men didn't want interference, discouraging the future skipper from giving any help at all. Ainsworth felt this was passing strange. He'd arrived too soon, he learned, for the vessel wouldn't be ready until December. It left him with plenty of free time to spend at the nearby farm home of Judge S. S. White with the judge's daughter, Nancy Jane. That caused him almost to miss the boat entirely, for Whitcomb—whom Ainsworth later described as "not entirely reliable"—was maneuvering to replace him with Hanscombe. He suggested Ainsworth might sign on as a supercargo or in some other capacity.

The Mississippi man held his ground, knowing his rights even in this raw land. He had his papers, the deal had been made, and he wouldn't be pushed off the boat. He would take command, he announced firmly, and this resulted "in the formation of a conspiracy against me."

The *Lot Whitcomb* was launched on Christmas Day, 1850, accompanied by a brass band from Fort Vancouver, speeches, the firing of cannon, and a fancy dress ball. A tragedy marred the occasion and forecast events to

later, when he'd become the celebrated author Mark Twain, Clemens presented his former captain with a fine gold watch in memory of their early relationship. Ainsworth could expect no such token from Whitcomb.

Yet sticking with Whitcomb would, for now, give him a foothold in the Northwest. He could readily envision a huge fleet of handsome vessels plying these beautiful waterways where Lewis and Clark had traveled down to the Pacific. His hands were eager for the wheel of that first real steamboat, to feel the pulse of these magnificent waters beneath her hull.

"The sensation to me," wrote Ainsworth in his memoirs, "of entering water that had never before been divided by the prow of a steamer, was beyond description. The excitement and the pleasure were always very great. . . ."

come when a salute cannon blew up, killing one of the celebrants. But now Oregon had a sleek steamboat built for speed and comfort, able to range the rivers from home port near Oregon City to Portland, Vancouver, up to the Cascades in the dark Columbia River Gorge, and one hundred miles downriver to Astoria.

The *Lot* had hardly swung into full service when she hung up on a reef at the mouth of the Clackamas River, where two decades later Ben Holladay would almost be defeated by Ainsworth's forces in the building of the first railroad. But that was well into the future. Right now Ainsworth was being blamed for the *Lot's* predicament. Scuttlebutt had it all wrong. The sidewheeler had been making regular daily runs since her launching, but on Sundays was laid up at Milwaukie. Her skipper spent his day off with the Whites, returning Monday morning. While he was away, Whitcomb and Hanscombe decided to take the boat to Oregon City, a few miles upstream. Ainsworth had opposed such a run, the water being too low at this time of year. But if Whitcomb proved otherwise, it would give him ample reason to dismiss Ainsworth for lack of good judgment.

When the steamer hung up, Whitcomb sent for Ainsworth to get her off. John flatly refused; he wouldn't command again until she was back where he'd left her. Thus, the *Lot* stayed on the reef for two weeks until coffers were built and the water depth improved to float her free and clear. Meanwhile, stories were circulated by Whitcomb and Hanscombe as to Ainsworth's incompetence as a commander, although anyone acquainted with the Captain knew better. Nevertheless, the lies came near to ruining his reputation as a topnotch steamboatman, just as he was getting established in this new country.

Ainsworth was convinced that he couldn't remain very long with Whitcomb. He also reached another conclusion: the sidewheeler was wrong for Oregon. This was sternwheeler country. A good sternwheeler could have crawled off that reef in short order. Meanwhile, John knew he must have his own boat, although as yet he couldn't afford it. He must also convince these Oregonians that he possessed the skill and know-how, and that steamboats were the transportation answer for the potentially rich Columbia country.

After several months Whitcomb and Hanscombe were forced to the financial wall. In the settlement Ainsworth received $3,500 for his time, which he promptly plowed back into the steamboat. Abernathy, Clarke & Co. of Oregon City bought the controlling interest, and Ainsworth was placed in command. He ran the *Lot* until 1854 when she was sold at $40,000 for use on the Sacramento, Ainsworth receiving 10 per cent as his share.

Those intervening years gave John ample opportunity to learn the Columbia in terms of steamboating, making him unique in his field. The *Lot Whitcomb* was an elegant sight plying the broad waters swiftly and efficiently, and Ainsworth felt king-like high in the pilothouse. At times he joined his Indian deckhands, packing sacks of cargo on his shoulders, for he believed that success came only to those who worked hard, and he still longed for his own fleet to serve this Oregon country.

But time was running out. The territory was growing and, as it did, more boats came to the river. Several small craft were operating around Portland, among them the makeshift *Hoosier* built from a longboat and powered by a pile-driver engine. Commerce was still minimal, but Ainsworth feared the day would arrive when someone else, perhaps a Mississippi riverman with the financial force, would read in these rivers what John saw, and launch a fleet which would squeeze him out.

The $4,000 from the *Lot's* sale gave Ainsworth a grubstake to construct his own ship much as he'd run on the Mississippi. He talked things over with Jacob Kamm, another Mississippi man who was a wise engineer and would build many future vessels of the Columbia fleet. They agreed on a sternwheeler and their reasons were sound. The plucky sternwheelers would be versatile, strong, and durable, to deal with underwater shoals, bars, snags, and shallow water on the constantly fluctuating northwest rivers where even the mighty Columbia could go from flood to low water almost overnight. Sidewheelers were difficult to manage in swift water, crosscurrents, and varying channels, while the propeller types, of which there were a few, fouled in shallow water, snapping shafts and breaking blades. Why, the sternwheeler could even stand on its tail, turn around, and crawl across a sandbar, and was as tough as a mustang, able to withstand an astounding amount of batter.

Columbia navigators boasted they could go "anywhere it's damp." Here the Bailey Gatzert *churns through wild water near the Cascades. For many decades, the sternwheeler was the best way to get around the rugged Oregon country. Courtesy Oregon Historical Society.*

ing and patching. Columbia skippers later bragged that they could take their shallow-draw sternwheelers anyplace.

"We can run anywhere it's damp," they boasted. "If it's wet enough, it's deep enough."

The 115-foot *Jennie Clark*, 18.5 feet in the beam, was what Ainsworth and Kamm had in mind. She responded like a well-trained mare, with the rudders close to the thrashing sternwheel, two connected engines for handling by one man, a four-foot stroke and six-teen-foot connecting rod turning the single fifteen-foot wheel. Her boiler was centered. There was only a single cabin. While she lacked elegance and grandeur, she made up for it in speed and efficiency, able to outrace any

boat on the river. She was also highly maneu-verable in tricky situations and landings. Placed in service from Portland to Oregon City in 1855, the *Jennie* quickly showed a profit in freight and passengers and, beyond this, proved to Ainsworth and Kamm that sternwheelers were the way to go—a prototype of the future, clear to the 1970s.

PART II

The legendary River of the West was the aorta of the old Oregon country. Along with its many tributaries, some of them like the Snake and the Willamette sizable arteries of their own, the Columbia stretched for thou-sands of miles, covering a grand and varied land in sweeping, turbulent style. The river knifed through otherwise impregnable country, slicing the jagged mountains and untamed flatlands, and cutting across great distances of arid plains or rolling hills so thick with timber that no man or beast could push beyond them.

White newcomers soon learned what the natives had always known: these rivers, save for sections of maddening white water, were natural highways for the flow of people and commerce. Along them, too, traveled the region's wealth and sustenance, including the Columbia's unbelievable salmon runs and the mighty timber to the lower ports where it was very early shipped to Hawaii, China, and Australia from the Hudson's Bay Company's first sawmill, demonstrating that the river was indeed the Northwest Passage to the Orient.

The Columbia's waters extended far, far inland into what became Idaho and Montana, almost touching fingers with the slight beginnings of the continent's other grand river drainage in the Yellowstone country. Within a few feet, a raindrop might flow west to the Pacific, while a second drop went down to New Orleans, past John Ainsworth's homeland. But by comparison the Mississippi was a sluggish stream; the Columbia was young, virile, and unconquered, a challenge to any steamboatman in each mile and every surprising obstruction. Every day and every season was different, deceptively dangerous and unpredictable. Amid towering bluffs, the broken basaltic blocks of some ancient volcanic explosion would churn the Columbia to death-dealing rapids on one side, and run placid as a country creek near the opposite shore, while a bit farther on, pinnacles of jagged rock thrusting from deep below in mid-river split this surly giant into two or more parts. The shifting waters and seasons combined into the calm riffles of early spring, and then the snaggle-toothed white water of late summer. Steamboatmen needed to learn every foot of this river, and what you learned yesterday might not apply tomorrow. Wind, slanting rain, ice, snow, sleet, blizzards, fog, choppy white waves that swept across the bow . . . the black nights without a single light to indicate where you were . . . sunken logs and huge timbers

The old Columbia, before the dams, was a challenge to steamboat skippers and their crews, with much swift and tricky water. It became sternwheeler country, for this type of riverboat could meet the challenges of northwest waters. Ellis Lucia Collection.

floating downstream, heavy as the boat itself and able to rip out the bottom of a fine craft or knock out the paddle wheels—all these dangers and many more made the Columbia riverman a special breed.

Worst of all were the barricades in the deep gorge of the Cascade Mountains which ran north and south through what would become Oregon and Washington states. Here, if Indian legends may be given credence, and I for one feel that they must, the volcanic peaks fired rock and hot lava and created an earthquake which sent an awesome natural stone bridge crashing into the yawning gorge. For a time it halted the great river, flooding the inland West. But then the river broke angrily through, creating a boiling, swirling, exploding waterway to challenge the best skills of any riverman. The Cascades, they called these rapids, and they divided the river, like Gaul, into three sections—the lower from the sea to the first big rapids; the middle stretching to The Dalles and another turbulent piece of bad water at Celilo; and the upper reaching as far inland as any steamboat could navigate.

Bad rapids were all along the way: the Owyhee . . . Devil's Bend . . . Four O'Clock . . . Umatilla . . . Rock Creek . . . Squally Hook . . . the Indian . . . John Day . . . Preacher's Eddy . . . Biggs Rapids . . . Hell's Gate . . . blinding you with bright sun on white water or sporting evil from winter snow. The skipper was forced to read his calculations with his mind's eye and the echo of his whistle bouncing off the bluffs (no radar or computer guidelines then) to bring boat, passengers, and freight safely to the next landing.

John Ainsworth was exposed to every stretch of that river in all seasons. He thrilled to its high adventure, while steamboating elsewhere, even on the Willamette, could become dull routine. When his hands were on the hand-polished mahogany wheel of the *Jennie Clark* he felt the course of empire—the pulsating rhythm of the Kootenai, the Snake, Clark's Fork, the Clearwater, the Pend Oreille, the Deschutes, the John Day, the Willamette. Yet the key to it all lay in those white-water blockades within the yawning gorge. Control of the portages around these rapids and the one at The Dalles meant control of the river and its commerce. John knew that he must have them, for it spelled survival of the big company he had in mind. And a single company would best serve the Columbia and its people,

he felt, since many small steamboat rivals would only result in constant brawling and rate wars among themselves.

Ainsworth wasn't the only one to recognize the importance of the portages. The Indian tribes had long considered their worth, and the Army recognized their strategic military value. But the portages remained in private hands of greedy men who suddenly realized the potential was better than any gold mine. And, with the success of the *Jennie Clark* and the *Lot Whitcomb*, steamboat fever was spreading as others leaped aboard. The enterprising Bradford brothers, who owned the north bank's portage area around the Cascades, deep inside the main gorge through the mountains and connecting the lower and middle rivers, launched a sixty-foot sidewheeler, *James P. Flint*, on the middle river. The *Flint*'s career was short-lived, however, for she piled up on a rock. The hull was salvaged and fitted with the engine from the pioneer *Columbia* to run to Vancouver as the *Fashion*. Since other steamboats were beginning to operate on the middle and upper river, the competition there was much more spirited.

The Bradfords had a good thing in that north bank, while the south bank cliffs made a portage system far more difficult, if not impossible. F. A. Chenoweth first developed the north bank lower portage in 1852 with a mule-powered tramway running over wooden rails laid on pilings and stilted timbers, crudely transporting settlers and shuttling freight around the white water. Hauling military goods for the growing Indian wars helped the profits considerably. Then Chenoweth sold out to the Bradfords, who built a two-story warehouse and began extending the rickety tramway in the spring of 1856 to service two small steamers now plying the middle river. Meanwhile, on the south bank, W. R. Kilborn wanted a piece of the portage action, so opened a wagon road, operated a wobbly tramway, and erected a substantial warehouse.

The Bradford operation was the more desirable. A small settlement sprang up, as did a military blockhouse. But the portages remained vulnerable to looting by natives when supplies were wrestled around the rapids. Sometimes thievery was very heavy, much to the Army's distress, as this was giving aid and comfort to the enemy, and causing the steamboat operators considerable embarrassment and financial loss. The threat of a major In-

Main trouble spot was the Cascades, inside the yawning Columbia Gorge, where portages on north and south banks were owned by rivals who hated each other. Captain Ainsworth knew that until he got control of these portages, the river would be useless for steamboating. This is the Oregon portage, which in early years was a mule-powered tramway, with wooden rails. Note the rickety tram in the distance through the trees. Ellis Lucia Collection.

dian uprising was growing, for the natives seemed to be stockpiling stolen military hardware, and if the Army's 1856 campaign were to be successful, the portages must be held at all cost.

Meanwhile, Chief Kamiakim of the Yakimas had mastered an ambitious plan to drive the whites from the Oregon Territory with a simultaneous rebellion by all the tribes. To beat the whites, Kamiakim knew you had to bottle up the river. His agents had been working many months co-ordinating everything. Now with spring coming on, Kamiakim was ready; and this spring would come harder than most for people of the Columbia Gorge.

In the early morning light, activity was stirring on the *Mary* and the *Belle* which were tied up near the Bradford store. This late March day would be spent loading military supplies bound upriver; a few days before, the *Mary* had transported a large troop detachment to The Dalles to join the inland campaign of Colonel George Wright. Despite rumors of an uprising, the Army left only nine men guarding the important Cascade portage, feeling the Indians would never attack this stronghold. But within the week the little *Wasco*, churning toward The Dalles close to shore, was sprayed with arrows and gunfire by whooping natives near Dog River. No harm done; the *Wasco* scooted out of range.

Now as men stretched sleep from their muscles and minds, and prepared for a day's work on the tramway, the *Belle* backed from her berth at the lower end, swinging into midstream to head for Vancouver. Then the Indians hit, everywhere at once, swarming over Bradford Island, onto the tramway and into the village. Other forces were spotted on the bluffs where they could fire down upon the stunned and fleeing men, women, and children, all trying to reach the store, the safest building in town.

Kamiakim timed the attack well, with the troopers away and the steamboat tied up at the dock, its boiler fire low. A few minutes earlier and he'd have had the *Belle*, too, which probably was his plan. The fireboats, as the natives called them, were a prime objective; if they could be burned it would keep any alarm from sounding at The Dalles and Fort Vancouver.

Already crew members were turning the

Mary into a fortress, breaking out what few weapons were aboard as arrows and spears plunged into the cabin walls and smashed windows, narrowly missing the men. Two crewmen, who had been ashore raced across the landing with Yakimas in hot pursuit and leaped aboard. But the skipper, Dan Baughman, was trapped ashore and would have to make out as best he could.

Hand-to-hand combat raged over the *Mary*'s deck as the natives cleared the open space between dock and boat. Pilot Hardin Chenoweth, taking charge, yelled orders to get the steam up, for the *Mary*'s only chance was to make it out of there under full power, for the rapids were close below. Scooting low, Chenoweth made it to the wheelhouse with arrows and lead whistling around his ears and piercing his shirt. When the natives saw smoke pouring from the stack, they angrily turned their aim into the wheelhouse. Chenoweth dived to the deck and someone cut the *Mary* loose. Still, she didn't yet have enough strength to fight the swift water; her sidewheeler buckets were merely flopping over.

The shooting continued, but from the floor Chenoweth couldn't see what was going on. He shouted for more steam . . . more steam . . . and for a few moments things hung in the balance, for it seemed the *Mary* couldn't hold against the swift flow and was drifting broadside to the current. Then the paddles began gaining power, but Chenoweth didn't dare come off the deck. Hooking his feet in the wheel, he flipped over and was able to get his head out the door where he could see to maneuver. It was just in time. Now the engines were throbbing steadily as the *Mary* took on life, holding her own in the current and able to get beyond rifle range, guided by Chenoweth's feet. Then he gave a long joyful blast on the whistle, telling those trapped in Bradford's store that the *Mary* was free and rushing to The Dalles for help.

The sidewheeler swung wide to the Oregon shore to pick up wood along the bank, for her fuel supply was down. Meanwhile, the attackers turned their attention to workers trapped along the tramway and people in the store and burning buildings and cabins of the settlement. The siege continued all day and throughout the night, and the whites knew they couldn't hold out for very long. Their only hope of rescue lay with the steamboats, returning with troops to drive the Indians off the island.

Ironically, those aboard the *Belle* were unaware of the attack. But a friendly Indian, paddling all night, reached Fort Vancouver to spread the alarm. The *Belle* was suddenly transformed into a battleship. Forty men—all the fort dared spare—were taken aboard under the command of Lieutenant Phil Sheridan, and also a heavy amount of munitions and supplies. The steamer *Columbia* out of San Francisco lay in the harbor, and Sheridan commandeered a twelve-pound cannon put aboard the *Belle*. Skipper M. F. Farlane couldn't believe his eyes at the sudden importance of his little ship.

Rumors were flying that the entire Cascade riverfront was under attack, and that the natives might hit Vancouver and Portland. Only the steamboats could save the day in what became the one major engagement in the West's history between the natives and the paddle wheels. The rumors put the region's biggest town of two thousand near to panic. In Portland a volunteer force was quickly organized to go up on the *Fashion*. But it was discovered there were no rifles and none of the citizens was about to part with his own fire power, with Indian attack imminent. By scrounging, the volunteers found twenty rifles, but the delay cost them twelve hours while a cursing Captain J. O. Van Bergan kept the *Fashion*'s steam up waiting for them. They picked up more arms and a few men at Vancouver, but by now they were far behind Sheridan and perhaps too late for any action. Even so, the volunteers, cursing the stupidity of their neighbors in Portland, were spoiling for a fight.

A second volunteer force was in the making in Portland. A messenger reached Oregon City to tell Captain Ainsworth they needed his boat. The Captain, rounding up his crew, dashed for Portland, loaded extra fuel and the volunteers aboard, and took off for the Cascades.

Meanwhile, the *Fashion* reached the lower landing of Bradford Island to find Sheridan and his men pinned down, despite the cannon's fire power. Upriver the *Mary* and the *Wasco* were thrashing to the rescue with 250 men, arms, and supplies from The Dalles, having gotten word of the attack to Colonel Wright and his men, who were marching east but only a few hours distant. Wright made an immediate about-face. The steamboats were jammed with gear until the guards skimmed the water, with the captains shouting their anger. So the Army found a flatboat for the horses and more equipment, hitched it behind the *Wasco*, and were under way.

At Bradford's store, the battle appeared more hopeless all the time. The settlers were losing heart; then someone saw smoke signs far in the distance.

"The steamboats are coming . . . the steamboats are coming. . . ."

Their spirits lifted; the trapped whites felt rescue was close at hand. And Sheridan's men broke out of their trap to push across the island. The steamboats were the turning point, but it was far from over yet, with hundreds of natives ranging over the portage site. The *Mary* eased toward shore and the Indians opened up, strafing her decks. The cannon boomed grapeshot, scattering the natives for the moment. But the pilot had misjudged; the *Mary* hung up on a sandbar from her heavy load, and once again Chenoweth hit the wheelhouse deck as the *Mary* thrashed about, trying to work off the bar. Had she been a sternwheeler, she might have crawled off quickly. The *Wasco* was moving closer to protect the stranded vessel, and after what seemed hours she got back afloat, in a zigzagging action to avoid the native fire. Then Chenoweth maneuvered her near the bank, with the *Wasco* nearby, and an avalanche of blue uniforms jumped ashore, sending the Indians into a ki-yiing retreat.

By the time the *Jennie Clark* arrived, the three-day siege was almost over. The dragoons had secured the island and Sheridan was taking captives, some of whom would hang under the auspices of the territorial marshal, Joseph L. Meek, the celebrated mountain man. Most of the natives slipped away, back into the mountains. Left behind were sixteen dead soldiers and civilians, and a dozen wounded.

As expected, the volunteers on Ainsworth's ship were disgruntled at missing the whole damned war. But Ainsworth felt it was just as well, for he didn't yearn to have the *Jennie* burned or sunk. His last dollar was in that vessel, and also his future. Nevertheless, the steamboats had won the day, in all likelihood making the river and much of the sur-

The Cascades' north-bank portage was the scene of much turbulence from floods, the gold rush, and an attack by native American tribes. After he took over, Ainsworth developed the north-bank portage. Note steamboat at dock at far right. Ellis Lucia Collection.

rounding territory safe from future Indian harassment. It demonstrated further that Ainsworth was correct as to the importance of the portages. What was needed now was a single flag. Right then, John Ainsworth turned his attention from the Willamette to the much bigger game on the Columbia. Somehow he had to move ahead before it was too late, to get those portages and build the great steamboat fleet he dreamed about to run far inland, anywhere it was damp.

PART III

Bickering, feuding, and personal greed had long plagued the competitive Cascade portage operators on opposite sides of the river. They hated and mistrusted each other, and each was trying to gain the upper hand in an intense rivalry bidding for steamboat business. The boat owners, passengers, and shippers had to tolerate all this—the changing rates, price squeezing, poor service, delays, thievery, the high-handed attitudes of the portage men—

and longed for something that would eliminate this bottleneck that was ruining the river traffic and holding back development of the region, many of its citizens Americans looking to the day when they could apply for statehood.

All this was as Ainsworth had predicted, and he was about to do something about it. In 1858 he launched the 126-foot *Carrie Ladd*, a sleek sternwheeler with freight deck, "ladies' saloon," combination open parlor and dining room, and a certain beauty to her lines that would set the general mode for many Columbia River steamers. Her engines boasted cylinders sixteen inches in diameter, with a sixty-six-inch stroke. And she could make the eighteen-mile run from Portland down to the mouth and then inland to Vancouver in ninety minutes, and the fifty-seven miles to the Cascades in five hours forty minutes.

The *Carrie* was Ainsworth's third ship; he'd built her for the Columbia, and the future. But shortly he found the portage situation more intolerable than he'd imagined. The portage operators owned some small steamboats now and thus, wielding the whip hand, set the freight fees to The Dalles as high as the traffic would bear, around $30 a ton. On the north side the fees were split four ways among the portage owners, Ben Stark and the Bradfords, and boat operators. The Oregon portage owners, J. S. Ruckel and Harrison Olmstead, were more congenial with each other, and with the steamboatmen. But Ainsworth regarded their operation as "of very inferior character," although they didn't have to split their fees and therefore were encroaching substantially on the Bradford business by offering lower rates.

Ainsworth decided (and he may well have had this in mind when building the *Carrie Ladd*) to break the north portage control. The power of the *Carrie* and the seasoned skill of her skipper couldn't be denied. By-passing the lower landing, Ainsworth rammed the vessel through the dangerous lower white water to the middle landing, thus being able to collect half the freight charge rather than only a fourth. No vessel had done it before and it was devastating, especially to Ruckel and Olmstead, who before long were suggesting some kind of agreement to avoid ruination. It also cooled off the Bradfords and Stark, forcing a combination of "all the interests" to the middle landing under the name Union Transportation Company, which as part of the arrangement guaranteed the Bradfords the upriver business.

The loosely formed company lasted about a year, but Ainsworth saw more rough water ahead due to the continued friction between the portage owners and the steamboatmen, with the latter still at the mercy of the portages. But bringing the various warring factions into line seemed almost impossible, even though they admitted that consolidation was desirable "if terms could be agreed upon."

"This agreement," wrote Captain Ainsworth in his memoirs about the U.T.C., "was the first gun to a battle that waged hot and long. The selfishness and unreasonableness of some of the parties was often beyond endurance, and the whole thing would break up in a row with threats to a steamboat war that should have no end."

John Ainsworth, who became known as "the Captain," remained the strong, steady, patient, and determined hand at the helm. He feared such a war worse than anything, for it would surely ruin this great river system and put an end to his own ambitions. Yet for a long while things were as touch-and-go as running a section of wild water at night in the midst of a blinding snowstorm, with the wind howling, the windows freezing up, and the fuel supply down to the last few sticks. Ruckel and Dan Bradford were particularly obstinate, hating each other's guts and refusing reasonable talk from sheer stubbornness. The others weren't much better, but despite the snags, John was moving gradually toward the kind of organization he envisioned. He also was receiving some wise coaching from his good California friend, financier William Ralston, who'd been instrumental in organizing the great California Steam Navigation Company.

When Ainsworth brought in Robert R. Thompson and his fine *Colonel Wright*, and his interests in the upper river portage above The Dalles, renewed howls of protest came from the lower portage men. But late in 1860 the Oregon Steam Navigation Company was chartered with $172,500 capital and about a dozen steamboats of the lower, middle, and upper river. Ainsworth was president of the board of five, which included Captain Lawrence W. Coe, steamboat builder, former owner of the *Mary*, and partner with Thompson; Simeon G. Reed, Portland financier; and the two rival portage men, Ruckel and Dan Bradford. Six months later Thompson replaced Coe on the board.

Ainsworth hoped this would solve the portage problem, but he was wrong. It might even have enhanced it, with Ruckel and Bradford eyeball to eyeball across the conference table. Yet while they battled like bobcats on the O.S.N. board, the pair would hang together to protect their portages from any encroachment by the navigation company. This was most exasperating to Ainsworth. Making matters worse, the portage owners held a five-year contract with the O.S.N., guaranteeing payment of half the freight cost rate between Portland and The Dalles, to be apportioned no matter which portage was used. And Simeon Reed proved a failure, exhibiting more interest in his own wheeling and dealing in Portland than in the trials of the budding navigation company. Thus, handling the portage deals was left to Ainsworth and Thompson, with the voting often deadlocked "because the other two board members were seemingly blind to everything else except their portages."

The Columbia: The Great Monopoly

Ainsworth and Thompson were determined that the floundering company wouldn't sink.

"It was simply a question of success or ruin," Ainsworth recalled later, "and we had no intention of being ruined."

He mistrusted and feared Dan Bradford worst of all, for he was a very greedy man.

"Bradford was tricky in all that he undertook to do," said the Captain. "If there was an underground way of arriving at any business point, he would adopt it rather than pursue a straightforward course."

Ainsworth was about to exhibit the kind of toughness that would carry him far in the business and financial world. The O.S.N. wouldn't survive long, he knew, under this crushing portage system. The losses were costing the O.S.N. a bundle. Ainsworth watched for his chance—a sign of weakness in either portage operator—and he found it just in the nick of time for the O.S.N. to cash in on a big bonanza.

Gold was discovered in Idaho, and then in Montana and eastern Oregon. In 1862 the rush was on, seemingly everyone in the West and across the world trying to make it upriver. But spring flooding and high water from the annual runoff knocked out the Bradford operation, throwing the bulk of the gold rush traffic to the south shore. Ruckel never had it so good, soon reaping a fortune from the mounting flow of men and supplies.

In a neat bit of timing, Ainsworth and Thompson announced they'd acquired control of The Dalles portage and were planning improvements, including a railroad (the Oregon country had no railroad at this time) around the white water of Celilo Falls, the Indians' famed fishing grounds where Lewis and Clark had such a struggle during their downriver thrust to the sea. The railroad was impressive bait; Ainsworth talked Bradford into supporting him on the O.S.N. board with the enticing hint that such "improvements" might also come his way. Indeed, all the portage men envisioned railroads for their own property, financed by the O.S.N. Maybe this navigation company idea wasn't so bad after all! That was just what Ainsworth wanted them to think.

The Dalles, which divided the middle from the upper river, became a major steamboat center. During gold rushes to eastern Oregon, Idaho, and Montana, this waterfront was a booming place. The portage tramway is seen in the distance, over roof of the wharf boat. Ellis Lucia Collection.

Many sternwheelers of the Columbia system like these, the Governor Grover *and* Senator, *were unpretentious workhorses, primarily for hauling freight, including horses and cattle. In frontier times, Oregon roads were bad and in places nonexistent, and the rivers were the best way to go. Every farm, every hamlet had its dock and supply of cordwood for the steamers that were forever just around the bend. Courtesy Oregon Historical Society.*

In San Francisco the Captain acquired over twenty miles of railroad iron, more than enough for The Dalles operation. He also purchased a tiny steam locomotive, to become known as the Oregon Pony, but failed to say anything about it in his reports sent back to Oregon.

Bradford was eager for that extra rail for his own portage. Then he received a staggering blow when the Pony was dropped onto the wooden-strap iron rails of his arch enemy across the river. This was only temporary to relieve the gold rush congestion while The Dalles line was being built, Ainsworth assured him. What else could they do, with the Bradford system still under high water? But Bradford was very angry and worried, for Ruckel's stock was rising.

Now Ainsworth told Bradford that the only way to beat out Ruckel was to change his thinking—to support the O.S.N. and make it his primary interest. To do this he should sell his portage and railroad franchise to the navigation company. Through the company, Ainsworth suggested, he could wield direct power over Ruckel, bringing him to his knees on whatever terms they might dictate about the portage. Bradford had little choice but to accept.

That settled, the Captain changed course in midstream again, pulling a two-hundred-man crew from The Dalles railroad to work on the north shore line at the Cascades. That put the fear of the Lord into Ruckel and Olmstead. Through hints and deception, coolly playing each side against the other, Ainsworth observed that wherever the O.S.N. threw its support would leave the opposite portage valueless, especially with this gold rush jackpot. Bradford and Ruckel were fit to be tied as Ainsworth swept the deck clean. The navigation company acquired control of both portages and was able to cancel out that terrible five-year contract on the freight rates.

Ainsworth admitted that the trickery was high-handed, but felt it was necessary under the circumstances to go to extreme.

"This was not the style of doing business that was agreeable to me," he declared, "but we had to work as best we could with the material at hand."

Control of all the Columbia and its major arteries had been the skipper's goal right along. Save for the Willamette, he now had it. The O.S.N. could dominate the big river to suit itself. And it did, growing into one of the West's greatest monopolies, more powerful and influential than either Ben Holladay or Wells Fargo on the central plains. But steamboating flourished under the O.S.N. and Ainsworth's guiding hand, and grew more efficient by this single control, as independents and other small companies which threatened the O.S.N.'s domain were run off the river. Only the Willamette, flowing south through the big Oregon valley, and where Ainsworth ironically had begun his Northwest career, remained outside the O.S.N.'s realm, although steamboaters there, too, had to cater to its whims.

The gold rushes of 1862 and 1864 stimulated the O.S.N.'s formative years, as the steamers grew more numerous and elegant, the service and schedules better, although the rates weren't necessarily cheaper than before. The profits were huge. In 1861 the sternwheelers carried 10,500 passengers and 6,290 tons of

The passenger fleet, first developed by Ainsworth's O.S.N., boasted the comforts of the times, including excellent menus and private staterooms. Around the turn of the century the boats became lush and elegant. This sternwheeler, loaded with excursion celebrants, makes its way through the Cascade Locks, perhaps bound for the Pendleton Round-Up. Courtesy Oregon Historical Society.

freight, while a year later these totals more than doubled to 24,500 passengers and 14,500 tons of goods. In the O.S.N.'s first twelve months investors had a $240 return on $500. During the big gold rush of 1864, the company made a clear profit of $783,339, while in its twenty-year history the O.S.N. paid dividends estimated at over $4,600,000. Another barometer was Simeon Reed, whose attitude markedly changed. He began functioning far better on the board, for Reed understood active dollars above everything else.

Still, people cursed the O.S.N. for its monopolistic ways. Rates were as high as the gold rush traffic would bear, close to forcing violence at times, for passengers and shippers had little choice but to pay them. One of the famous stories was how the company figured its shipping rates by the cubic volume. In the case of a wagon, clerks measured the vehicle over-all with the tongue stretched out full length, then moved the tongue to a vertical position to calculate the height. When the rate was established, the tongue would be stoked under the wagon.

At The Dalles an agent was measuring a small military cannon. He kept scratching his head, making calculations several ways. Two soldiers asked what was wrong. The clerk said it wouldn't come out right, since the rates were figured on the basis of forty cubic feet equaling a ton.

"That's easy," a trooper said. He brought up a pair of harnessed mules, hitching them to the cannon. "Now try it."

The happy clerk measured off the length, including the mule span and the height from ground to ear tip, then announced that the figures were now correct. Government people played fast and loose with taxpayers' money, even in those times!

Rates ran $15 a ton to the Dalles (121 miles), $45 to Umatilla (217 miles), $50 to Wallula (240 miles), and $90 to Lewiston (401 miles). A Lewiston merchant received a crated shipment of miners' shovels measuring a cubic ton and containing ninety shovels, costing $90 and thus $1.00 per shovel. All this did nothing to enhance the O.S.N.'s reputation as "your friendly neighborhood company." When a merchant was asked why he charged a quarter for a single darning needle, he replied, "Madam, you forget the O.S.N. freight charge."

The strangle hold the O.S.N. had on the territory seemed impossible to break or even bend in the years before the railroads. The independent Willamette's People's Transportation Company tried to place steamers on the Astoria run, but at once the O.S.N. sent the *Julia* into service at a ridiculously low fare and beat them back, buying out the rival ships and two others. That happened many times; sometimes shoddy boats were built just to pose a threat to the O.S.N. and thereby sell them to the company for a fancy price. The O.S.N. didn't want third-rate boats, but would buy them just to keep rivals off the river.

The O.S.N. would go to any extreme to choke off the competition, with the financial depth to do so, bringing in bigger and faster luxury steamers from California and even the East Coast, making the long journey around Cape Horn. When Captain Ainsworth needed the *Shoshone* on the lower river and located her up in the Boise Basin, he sent his toughest steamboatman, Bass Miller, to bring her down through the wild Snake River Canyon in what became truly one of the great steamboat sagas of all time, only one of two steamboats ever to make the journey successfully.

Freight rates to Lewiston reached $120 a ton. Angry miners and businessmen started freight lines from the Idaho mines across the Nevada Desert to San Francisco. The O.S.N. allegedly stirred up the tribes and sent renegades and toughs to eastern Oregon's barren country to make life miserable for the freighters. Losses were high in goods, treasure, and lives, and thus encouraged travelers and shippers to go the "safe" way down the Columbia—on O.S.N. boats, of course.

Bradford and Ruckel remained bitter over the tricky maneuver the Captain had pulled on them, despite the huge profits being raked in by the company. They convinced Reed that Ainsworth was conniving and untrustworthy, thus forcing the Captain from the board. Ruckel was named president, but it soon became apparent that the situation was impossible. The vast knowledge of the steamboatman was needed to handle the multitude of river problems confronting the O.S.N. At year's end he was reinstated, Ruckel resigning. This resulted in the Ainsworth-Thompson-Reed control that became known as "the Triumvirate."

The O.S.N. expanded wherever it saw opportunity, although it was never able to invade

Blow for the landing . . . a familiar sight for many decades in the Oregon country, well into the twentieth century. This is a latter-day view of the Beaver, showing a car in the right foreground. The railroads and then the automobile dealt the death blows to Columbia-Willamette steamboating. Courtesy Oregon Historical Society.

Puget Sound. People's Transportation continued its checkmate above Willamette Falls. Nevertheless, the navigation company's power and influence were felt everywhere, especially in the destinies of Oregon, where Ainsworth started a major bank (United States National of Oregon) and O.S.N. wealth began famed Reed College, established by Reed's widow. The empire reached to Idaho's Lake Pend Oreille, while the *Mary Moody* was built to run on Clark's Fork in Montana. Sometimes these operations were losers, but they kept any competition from gaining a paddle hold.

For a few years the O.S.N. had everything pretty much its own way. But things never stay the same for long in the United States, and this was especially true on the frontier. Oregon became a state in 1859, and now the

Oregon country had the railroad fever as a way of building up the Northwest and also breaking the O.S.N.'s monopoly. A direct route east appeared unlikely for the moment; a railroad south through the Willamette Valley to connect with the transcontinental line being laid across the plains would serve the region well, especially the valley communities, and would give farmers and other shippers an alternative to the O.S.N.'s brutal freight rates.

Ainsworth quickly recognized the threat; the only way to protect the O.S.N. and continue its power would be to control the railroad. The O.S.N. threw its weight behind a railroad company being formed in Portland, commonly called the West Siders, while people on the east bank and upstate organized a rival company known as the East Siders. Then

Ben Holladay, having sold his Overland stage-coach company to Wells Fargo for a cool $2,300,000 and eager for a railroad, stepped into the fray. Ainsworth and the O.S.N. were now confronted by a formidable adversary, since Holladay had both the wealth and power in depth, not only on the West Coast but in the national capital. He was also as tough and wiley as the Captain. He took over the East Side railroad, winning the franchise to build it through high-handed politics and slick maneu-vering, such as Ainsworth had used against the portage owners.* Then he captured the Peo-ple's Transportation Company for $200,000, by $25,000 monthly installments. Holladay, like Ainsworth, knew he must control both land and water transportation to survive.

Ainsworth had met his match, for Old Ben was thrusting his railroad south at high-ball speed. On O.S.N. prodding, a con-struction company was formed to build locks around the Willamette Falls, which would again give the O.S.N. the upper hand. Bernard Goldsmith, who headed the outfit, managed token financing from the legislature, but was seemingly faced with an impossible deadline as crews chipped away for two years at the west

* For detailed accounting of how Holladay gained the railroad franchise, see "High Iron by Christmas" in *Trails of the Iron Horse* (Doubleday, 1975), companion book to this steamboat volume.

bank's rocky bluff. Meanwhile, Holladay had his own rival locks project under way on the opposite shore, near Oregon City, for other-wise he would be up against the same sort of rate fixing Ainsworth had faced on the Colum-bia.

Goldsmith's crews were out ahead of Hol-laday, coming down to the wire. But a vessel must be put through the locks by deadline to make it all legal, and suddenly Holladay had tied up all the steamboats. Instead of the im-pressive ceremony Ainsworth and his friends envisioned, the company was desperately scrounging around for any kind of ship. The tiny *Mark Wilkins* of Portland was sent scur-rying upriver, going through the new locks just in time. Holladay and People's Trans-portation's reign over the Willamette was now broken; he would be unable to set the rates high-handedly, and rival riverboats would now be on the Willamette in force. It proved the turning point in Holladay's long and colorful career in frontier transportation, and the be-ginning of the final decline of the King of Wheels. Ainsworth was glad to see Holladay's monopoly broken, even though he was re-spected as an adversary. In many ways the two tough Westerners were very much alike and hailed from the same part of the country. Soon the O.S.N. took direct control of the Willamette locks system and its boats at last

Locomotives like this wood-burner took both passenger and freight business from the sternwheelers. When Ainsworth stepped down, his company was reorganized into the Oregon Railway & Navigation Company. But the directors became more interested in the rail traffic than in the water. Ellis Lucia Collection.

began appearing in numbers on this major Columbia tributary.

But the squeeze was on. Roads were improving and there were proposals of railroad construction up the Columbia. The arrival of Henry Villard forced Holladay to the wall. Since the O.S.N. wasn't able to finance railroad construction east, the German railroad builder brought about reorganization into a new corporation, the Oregon Railway & Navigation Company to connect with the Union Pacific in Utah. Columbia River steamboating thereby entered a new age as the Triumvirate bowed out. But while the new outfit seemed more interested in rail than water, the river steamers long remained an important mode of travel and shipment of goods and produce, especially from what became known as the Inland Empire region of eastern Washington and Oregon. Eventually, in 1912, it became unlawful for a railroad company to own a competing boat system, so the steamers had to be sold, truly bringing to an end the single company era of Captain Ainsworth.

EPILOGUE

Hundreds of boats now plied the river and its tributaries in all sizes and shapes, but still the sternwheeler was the predominant design. The work horses that hauled wheat, grain, logs, lumber, livestock, and machinery and would call at any landing where the flag was out (each river farm and ranch had its own landing and supply of cordwood), were rugged, unpretentious, rustic craft, free of fancy trappings yet able to endure most any punishment. The passenger fleet grew more elegant, especially on the lower river running to the coastal resorts; and while they didn't have the plushness, social refinements, and romance of the Mississippi packets, the Columbia's finest rated among the fanciest ships afloat, with beautiful saloons of plush furnishings, Brussels carpet and crystal chandeliers, exotic dining with silver plate and white linen on the tables, entertainments and musicians, spacious game rooms and bars that were busy all day, private staterooms for those who could afford them "finished in a delicate tint of lilac . . . and the floors covered with mosaic oilcloth."

It was a day's journey from Portland to The Dalles, negotiating the portage and later, the locks at the Cascades. Most passengers spent the night at the famed Umatilla House, built by the O.S.N. and ranking among the most elegant hostelries on the Pacific Coast. The steamboats remained a popular mode of travel well into the twentieth century. Many people are yet living who traveled the sleek steamers that blew for the landing and sported their name plates proudly on the pilothouses . . . the *Telephone* . . . *Telegraph* . . . *Georgiana* . . . *T. J. Potter* . . . *Henderson* . . . *Hassalo* . . . *Georgie Burton* . . . the *Bailey Gatzert* on which Portland's first Queen of Rosaria for its famed Rose Festival arrived in 1914. In the early years of this century the steamboats were a particularly popular way to reach the beaches north and south of the Columbia's mouth, where on the north side they docked beside the terminal of a narrow-gauge railroad, which ran up the Long Beach peninsula. To accommodate its passengers it adjusted its schedule daily according to the tides.

Ainsworth left his Oregon empire when his steamboat days were done, largely for reasons of health, settling in the Bay Area where he established the Central Bank of Oakland. He was also instrumental in developing the resort of Redondo Beach in southern California. But his name remains well implanted in the Oregon country as one of its stalwart founders, with a Portland school, street, and river park named in his honor, and his home near Oregon City a refurbished historical landmark. And in the bank he founded are proudly displayed detailed models of the steamboats that figured in its beginnings.

The sternwheeler—indeed all other types of river steamboats—has faded from the Columbia River country. The great river isn't the lively challenge of Captain Ainsworth's day; it's now a chain of lakes behind huge hydroelectric dams. Diesel tugs dominate the scene, pushing heavy barges up and down the busy waterway, through locks of the many dams. The last passenger vessel, the tiny *America*, ended its Portland-Astoria voyages ($1.25 round trip!) a quarter century ago.

One fine sternwheeler remains, and she's a live one. The 219-foot diesel-steam *Portland* works the harbor daily for the port of Portland. She's the only bona-fide working sternwheeler in the country that is neither excursion boat nor plaything. The harbor's peculiar conditions and the unique maneuverability of

While steamboating has long since faded from the Columbia system, one sternwheeler still remains active. She's the Portland, *operated by the port of Portland, Oregon, and the only bona-fide working sternwheeler left in the country. The* Portland *is used primarily as a harbor tug to maneuver big ocean-going vessels in the tight Willamette River. As Captain Ainsworth saw a century ago, the sternwheeler was just right for Oregon, being highly maneuverable. Ellis Lucia photo.*

the steam sternwheeler, recognized by Ainsworth over a century ago, have kept this singularly colorful vessel afloat.

And she has class; Portlanders feel about her as San Franciscans do about their cable cars, for she's a part of the Pacific Northwest heritage. When the *Portland* is working the harbor, swinging huge ocean vessels in the narrow river, near its many bridges, employing her four main rudders and three monkey rudders, she puts on quite a show. Her huge thrashing red wheel, laboring hard, backing and moving forward, gently nudges big ships many times her size, while the water churns to a white foam. You can hear the warm sound of her steam whistle all over town, as once you could the steam locomotives—a song out of the past. And since she has a certain style, every so often the *Portland* makes goodwill trips up the Columbia as far as Lewiston, the only sternwheeler—indeed, today the only steamboat—to ply Captain Ainsworth's big river of what was once mighty sternwheeler country.

16

Steamboat Through Hell: River Traffic on the Colorado of the West

BY DONALD H. BUFKIN AND
C. L. SONNICHSEN

There was no excuse for putting a river there —it was completely out of place. The country on either side—the California-Arizona Desert —was a howling wilderness for four hundred miles upstream, to the head of "navigation." The channel of the Colorado wound through burning sands and barren hills, past rocky slopes and waterless washes. The vegetation was sparse. The few Indians who lived along its banks were hard-pressed to survive and as primitive as they came. The idea of important commerce on this cantankerous and capricious stream seemed laughable, and steamboat traffic at that! Who would believe it?

And yet it happened. The military garrisons and the early settlements of a young territory were supplied by a sea route from San Francisco around the peninsula of Baja California, through the gulf to the mouth of the Colorado River, and thence up the temperamental stream to ports incredibly far north, almost to the Utah line. Near the point where the river meets the gulf, freight and passengers were transferred in the early days to sternwheelers for the last and most perilous lap of the journey.

A unique combination of economics and geography made the traffic necessary. It was all the United States Government could do to get the mails overland to the Pacific coast in the years before the railroads spanned the continent, and stagecoach companies bridged the gap only at irregular intervals and under extreme difficulties. Freight and passengers had almost as much trouble coming in from California to the West. For many years it was the

river or nothing as miners and soldiers and settlers had to be transported and supplied in northern and western Arizona.

The result was a fantastic chapter in the history of the West. The nature of the stream, the adaptive design of the river craft, and the adventuresome character of the men who operated them combined to create a kind of transportation unlike any other in the annals of the nation.

Start with a stream in which the main channel was constantly shifting and for which no detailed charts could be compiled because changes were so frequent and so constant. Add a breed of river pilots who developed an instinct for the vagaries of the fickle stream— men who could command Indian crewmen, haul a boat over the ever-shifting sandbars when the situation demanded it, bear heat, mosquitoes, and the primitive life of a frontier territory, and cope with the limitations of the region to keep their steamboats running. They had to have boilers which could take the silt- and mineral-laden waters and which could be fired by the soft, pulpy desert woods growing close to the river's banks. They had to have boats which would draw less than two feet of water under a full load. It was said that a good captain in the "Arizona fleet" could make six knots an hour upriver on little more than a heavy dew.

No other system of river transportation had to contend at the river's mouth with a tidal range of from twenty-two to thirty-two feet. No other American river was subject to a tidal bore which swooped some forty miles upstream, traveling hundreds of yards in a few seconds, sometimes damaging and even capsizing the frail riverboats. This phenomenon, occurring with varying intensity on a lunar cycle, was the result of a strong incoming tide encountering and finally over-riding in a wall of water the full discharge of the Colorado. It is no exaggeration to say that steamboating on the river was a unique American experience accompanied by pains and perils encountered no place else on the continent.

Traffic on the Colorado lasted only fifty years, but three hundred years of preliminary exploration and investigation were necessary before it could begin. The adventurous Spaniards in Mexico pushed farther and farther into the unknown lands to the north. Ulloa, Alarcón, and Díaz, beginning in 1539, probed the mysteries of the Sea of Cortez—the Gulf of California—and the remarkable river which discharged a flood of red, silt-laden waters into its upper reaches. Was California an island? Nobody was sure until the intrepid Father Eusebio Kino presented convincing proof in 1701 that it could be reached by land from the internal provinces of New Spain. The years passed and more people arrived. Father Fernando Consag visited the Colorado Delta in 1746, Father Francisco Garcés in 1771. In 1774 Juan Bautista de Anza pioneered a land route through the future site of Yuma to the California coast, bringing 250 colonists to Monterey the next year.

This was the beginning of important events at the Yuma Crossing of the Colorado River, most of them involving natives resident in the vicinity. Father Garcés established two missions there, both of which were destroyed in an Indian uprising in 1781. Garcés and his priests and soldiers, clubbed to death, were the first of many who were to die at the crossing.

During the Mexican War, Major Stephen Watts Kearny, on his way to California, followed the Gila in its westward course and reached the crossing in 1846. The Mormon Battalion was not far behind. By the Treaty of Guadalupe Hidalgo the area came under the jurisdiction of the United States, just in time for the great migration of 1849.

Thousands of gold seekers converged on Yuma ferry in the rush to the California gold fields. Many of them arrived exhausted and out of supplies and with equipment desperately in need of repair. To protect them and to provide for at least part of their needs the U. S. Army established a military garrison in October of 1849.

As travelers crowded in and a chance for profit arose, the business of ferrying men, animals, and supplies attracted a variety of ambitious characters to the river. Intense competition was the result. At first the Indians and Mexicans operated crude rafts and barges. When Dr. Abel B. Lincoln and the infamous John Glanton tried to muscle in, there were several bloody outbreaks which culminated in another Indian uprising.

It seemed obvious that something would have to be done. The post at Yuma was a key point on the transcontinental route and it had to be maintained and supplied. Access by land, however, was extremely difficult. San Diego lay 150 miles due west across the most forbidding stretch of country on the North American Continent. The Colorado Desert, with its extensive sandhills and its below-sea-level sink, contained few reliable water holes. The cost of freighting across this barrier, combined with the impossibility of delivering supplies with any regularity, turned attention to the river itself as an alternative to the overland route. The 150-mile meandering course of the stream between Yuma and the gulf was unexplored and unknown, but the makers of the Treaty of Guadalupe Hidalgo had the foresight to insert a provision which guaranteed access to the newly acquired lands by way of the Gulf of California and the Colorado River, tacitly assuming that the river was a navigable stream.

The supply difficulties which forced reductions in personnel and occasional temporary abandonment of the Yuma post finally induced the Army to order a reconnaissance of the water route. Lieutenant George H. Derby of the Topographical Engineers was instructed to explore and map the Colorado upstream to the mouth of the Gila and determine its navigability. In December of 1850 he began his task. His report, submitted months later, gave assurance that the gulf-and-river route was a practical means of supplying the military posts upstream. Prophetically, he suggested that the most practical craft for the purpose would be a shallow-draft stern-wheel steamer.

The Derby survey opened the way for the entrance of Captain George Alonzo Johnson, who played a major role in developing the river into the principal supply route of the raw

The utilitarian Yuma ferry prepares to transport a lone passenger from Arizona to California. The ferry cable can be seen stretching across the river to the stanchion on the California side. The buildings of Fort Yuma appear on the skyline.

young territory. Johnson was an industrious, ingenious, persistent New York Stater who had put in some time on Great Lakes steamboats and had resolved to try his fortunes on the West Coast. For a while he was involved in a ferryboat venture at the Colorado Crossing but in 1850 he and his partners sold out and in 1851 he secured a contract to transport military supplies by sea and river to the port at Yuma.

His first attempt was a failure. With his contract in hand he left San Francisco on the U.S. transport *Sierra Nevada* with A. H. Wilcox as captain and a cargo of supplies on board. The plan was to sail the ship as far up the Colorado as possible, and the crew actually managed to work her to within seventy miles of Fort Yuma before Johnson moored her to the bank for transfer of cargo. He constructed two flatboats, loaded them, and tried to pole them upriver but had to give up the attempt when one was swamped and the other was barely able to make it to Yuma. The experiment convinced him that flatboats were not the answer.

While he meditated on his mistakes, the Army awarded another supply contract to Captain James Turnbull, who had previously operated steamboats on the Sacramento River in California. Turnbull came up with what looked like an improvement on Johnson's ideas. He had a sidewheeler steam tug constructed in sections in San Francisco and shipped to the mouth of the Colorado in the U.S. transport *Capacity*. On the lonely and desolate mudflats of the delta, late in 1852, the *Uncle Sam* was assembled and launched. The first steamboat to operate on the Colorado arrived at Fort Yuma with whistles blasting on December 3, 1852. The effort had been great, but it had proved that the treacherous Colorado could be conquered and that it was feasible to supply the isolated outposts along the river by sea in conjunction with specially designed steamboats. For the next half century river craft would play an important role in the development of the Territory of New Mexico (which until 1863 included present-day Arizona). After the creation of Arizona Territory, the steamers nurtured the military, commercial, and social development of the young commonwealth.

The *Uncle Sam* proved that small or medium-sized steamboats could navigate the Colorado, but there were important drawbacks. A ship sometimes took more than two weeks to negotiate the 150 miles of meandering river channel between the estuary and Fort Yuma. A California newspaper (the *Alta California*) reported humorously that at one point a passenger found himself eight miles from Yuma by land, but as the boat followed the river's windings for another sixty miles, he discovered that he was twenty-five miles from the town.

Obviously a single small riverboat would have to make several trips upstream to transport the cargo of an ocean-going vessel, and it could not do so in a reasonable length of time. Discouraged temporarily, Turnbull was in San Francisco looking for a more powerful engine for the *Uncle Sam* when he learned that she had been lost on the river.

Now it was George Johnson's turn again. With Captain Turnbull out of the picture, he and several important partners organized the George A. Johnson Company in 1853. Following Turnbull's lead, the new company had a sidewheeler built in sections in San Francisco and shipped to the estuary. In January 1854

The early Yuma waterfront as viewed from Fort Yuma on the California side of the river. The railroad bridge (right) is downstream and on the left. The steamer Gila is tied up to the bank. Arizona Historical Society photo.

the *General Jesup* was assembled and launched. This ship proved to be more powerful and successful than the *Uncle Sam* and began the efficient transportation of passengers and large tonnages of freight brought by deepwater vessels around Baja California from West Coast ports.

Finding that the *General Jesup* was a success, Johnson had another river steamer assembled at the river's mouth. Late in 1855 the *Colorado No. 1*, larger and more powerful but still designed for shallow draft, became the first sternwheeler to operate on the river. As Lieutenant Derby had foreseen, such vessels were better adapted than sidewheelers to the operational realities of the silt- and sandbar-clogged channel.

A regular pattern of service began. Shipment was from West Coast ports, notably San Francisco, by ocean vessel, and cargoes were transferred to riverboats at the mouth of the stream. A growing fleet of shallow-draft steamers, specially adapted for use on the Colorado, carried passengers and freight upstream from there.

At first the major effort involved getting supplies to Yuma, but as the new territory began to develop, riverboats probed farther north. New military posts were established, new mining discoveries were made, and people entered the territory in greater numbers. The river was their link with the outer world. George Johnson proposed that he be authorized to explore upriver by steamboat under contract with the War Department. A more aggressive man, however, took the initiative away from him.

Lieutenant Joseph C. Ives of the Army Topographical Engineers did it by maneuvering successfully to extract an appropriation from the Secretary of War for a Colorado River expedition which would determine the character of the little-known stream upriver from Yuma. He had a small iron-hulled steamboat built at Philadelphia, divided into eight sections, and shipped by sea to Panama. *The Explorer*, as he called it, was transported across the isthmus by rail, shipped to San Francisco, loaded on the government-chartered schooner *Monterey*, and deposited in 1857 on the mudflats at Robinson's Landing at the mouth of the Colorado. There it was laboriously reassembled and launched just before the place was flooded by extreme high tides.

George Johnson, meanwhile, was making his own plans, which involved beating Ives at his own game. He was determined, with or without government contract, to determine how far upstream the Colorado could be traveled by steamboat. In the *General Jesup* he left Yuma on December 20, 1857, and reached El Dorado Canyon (which he is reported to have named) seventy-four miles above Fort Mojave and 360 miles above Yuma.

Eleven days after Johnson's start, on December 31, 1857, Ives began his own voyage north from Robinson's Landing. Eventually he reached Black Canyon, some forty miles north of Johnson's Ultima Thule, but paid for his victory by running hard against a barrier which is still called Explorer's Rock. The Johnson-Ives rivalry gave no final answers to anything, but it did demonstrate that the Colorado was a practical water highway through almost four hundred miles of rough country which could not be economically supplied by any other route. A new era had begun.

Business was stimulated by a series of mining booms inland and along the river, beginning with the discovery of rich placer gold deposits at Gila City in 1858. Additional placers were found in 1862 at numerous locations adjacent to the river between Pot Holes and La Paz. Ledges were located in Johnson's El Dorado Canyon, reportedly by soldiers from nearby Fort Mojave, in the 1860s. Inland, the Rich Hill, Lynx Creek, and Walker District discoveries were made near the future site of Prescott. Each one generated more excitement, attracted more men, and involved more capital, and the demand for economical transport and convenient accessibility generated more river commerce. Military supplies and troop rotation, initially the major inducement to the traffic, took second place to mining as newer and more efficient river craft were acquired, more warehouse capacity was provided, and more service and repair facilities were created.

Between 1858 and 1865 three new steamers were placed in operation bearing names which became famous on the river: the *Cocopah No. 1*, the *Mojave No. 1*, and the *Colorado No. 2*. Others, worn out from the brutal bruising of river service, were retired or scrapped.

Profits were high enough to induce other determined men to challenge George A. John-

UTAH

NEVADA

Lee's Ferry

CALLVILLE   RIOVILLE

VIRGIN RIVER

COLORADO RIVER

GRAND CANYON

Black Canyon

EL DORADO CANYON

RIVER

HARDYVILLE
FORT MOHAVE
The Needles

LIVERPOOL LANDING   PRESCOTT

AUBREY CITY

CALIF.

COLORADO

ARIZONA

LA PAZ
EHRENBERG

NORTON'S LANDING
CASTLE DOME LANDING

FORT YUMA   GILA RIVER

YUMA   TUCSON

MEXICO

PORT ISABEL

SCALE IN MILES
0   50   100

GULF OF CALIFORNIA

The Colorado River Ports

D.H.B.

The Colorado river ports.

Colorado steamers and a barge, laid up during a period of slack river business, are awaiting cargoes and assignments.

son's monopolistic grip on the business. His firm had been reorganized in 1864 and incorporated as the Colorado Steam Navigation Company—usually called the C.S.N.—at Sacramento, California. It was suspected that C.S.N. was a subsidiary of the powerful Combination Navigation Company which operated on California rivers and now sought to extend its dominance to the Colorado. This ambition, if it existed, was frustrated when the first real competition developed. Samuel "Steamboat" Adams formed the Union Line, which in June of 1865 combined with the Philadelphia Mining Company to form the Pacific and Colorado Steam Navigation Company (P.C.S.N.). The new lines brought to the river two more steamers, the *Esmeralda* and the *Nina Tilden,*

and a first-class riverman, Captain Thomas Trueworthy, already famous on the California streams. For a few brief years in the mid-1860s spirited competition for business continued at fever pitch.

In addition to supplying the mines, the P.C.S.N. proposed to provide Mormon Utah with an outlet to the sea by way of the Colorado. The Mormons were more than willing. In 1864 they sent out a group who located a point on the river north of Black Canyon near the entry of the Las Vegas Wash into the river, built warehouses, and established a river landing which they named Callville after Anson Call, leader of the expedition. It was above George Johnson's El Dorado Canyon and Lieutenant Ives' Black Canyon—commonly regarded as the farthest points which steamboats could reach—but venturesome captains began looking for a way to reach the new river port. They used ring bolts anchored into vertical rock walls to aid in winching the boats up and over the rapids, managed to reach the place, and established service in 1865.

The days of Callville as a river port, however, were numbered. Difficulties with the seasonal rise and fall of the river, coupled with the completion of the first transcontinental railroad at Promontory, Utah, in 1869, ended the short-lived Utah trade. Thereafter El Dorado Canyon was the point farthest upriver to be reached regularly by river craft.

The failure of Callville, combined with the up and down cycle of the mining industry along the river, brought to an inevitable end the competition between the two steamship companies. The Colorado and Pacific firm, in an effort to revive its corporate vigor, was reorganized in 1867 as the Arizona Navigation Company. A few months later, however, it was absorbed by the C.S.N., which enjoyed another decade of profitable service without challenge.

An important result of the boom times in the mid-sixties was the birth of Port Isabel in 1865. This was a shipyard and drydock built by the C.S.N. on a deep-water slough reaching inland from the channel where ocean-going ships anchored while preparing to unload cargoes. This unique community, named for one of the early schooners calling at the river's mouth, provided a harbor for the riverboats where they could be protected from the violence of the open sea and the menace of the tidal bore, at the same time using the extreme range of tidal rise and fall to operate the drydock basin. Some of the craft that worked the Colorado were built at Port Isabel and many of the boats ended their service there, their machinery removed and salvaged and their hulls transformed into wharves and warehouses.

Port Isabel was unique in many ways. Lying some seventy airline miles south of Yuma (150 by river), it was actually in Mexico, but it was for a moment in history Arizona's one and only seaport. During its brief existence the shipyard at the river's mouth was home to the Arizona fleet of river steamers and home of a sort to possibly a hundred persons who kept them operating. Another point of interest was the fact that, although it was on Mexican soil, it functioned as an American community. Mexican customs were not collected upon goods transferred from ocean vessels to riverboats in the estuary off Shipyard Slough, and Port Isabel operated, as far as is known, without benefit of Mexican title.

This does not mean that Port Isabel had all the comforts and amenities of towns on the other side of the continent. If there was ever a jumping-off place, Port Isabel was it. We know what life was like from a series of poignant letters sent to her family back in Maryland by the young wife of Captain David C. Robinson, C.S.N. local superintendent, from this lonely spot out on the mudflats near the mouth of the river. "Just imagine," she wrote on October 17, 1870, "a place where there is not a tree nor a stone as large as a pea, not a bit of anything green as far as the eye can reach, excepting a little salt grass along the very edge of the river."

There was a row of one-story buildings—a cook house, meat house, mess room, and storeroom. At the end, she said, was

> our house; that is as soon as Mr. R. can get the carpenters at work. Then Mrs. Dougall's. Then in front of this is a carpenter shed and piles of lumber, while still further, first is a drydock, to build and repair boats, and a blacksmith shop—and you have Port Isabel . . . an old steamboat . . . is used for lodging for the men and a good house it makes.

Even for someone not condemned to live there, Port Isabel was a soul-shattering experience. What a shock it must have been, after a long ocean voyage, to anchor in the estuary at the head of the gulf and look out upon those hundreds of square miles of tidal mudflats! Martha Summerhayes, wife of an Army officer, was one who experienced the hell on earth of the lower Colorado. A sensitive eastern lady, she came to Arizona with her husband and a boatload of soldiers in the sweltering month of August 1874 on the steamer *Newbern*, which had to anchor for three days off Port Isabel before the sea was calm enough to permit the troops to go aboard lighters for transfer to the riverboat *Cocopah*. "The wind was like the breath from a furnace," she remembered. "It seemed as though the days would never end,

The steamer Gila *was one of a number of paddlewheelers built at Port Isabel. It was launched in 1873 and reconstructed in 1899 and renamed the* Cochan. *Here it is shown moored to the riverbanks near the Yuma Quartermaster Depot.*

and the wind never stop blowing. Jack's official diary says: 'One soldier died today.'"

Two more soldiers died before the river voyage began and were buried on those desolate flats at the end of the world. Returning from the funeral, the band played "The Girl I left Behind Me." Jack explained to his incredulous wife:

"It would not do for the soldiers to be sad when one of them dies. Why, it would demoralize the whole command. So they play those gay things to cheer them up."

Seven days at Port Isabel were followed by three on the river before the *Cocopah* reached Fort Yuma. It was hotter there, and Martha heard a story about a soldier who died at the fort and came back from hell for his blankets, "having found the regions of Pluto so much cooler than the place he left."

During the 1860s and early 1870s the steamships were the answer to military and ci-

vilian supply problems in western Arizona. Then the tide turned and the riverboats faced their last and mightiest foe, the Southern Pacific Railroad. In 1877 the rails reached the west bank of the Colorado and gave the *coup de grâce* to traffic from the mouth of the river to Yuma. Port Isabel was dismantled and abandoned in 1878 and sank slowly into ruin on its muddy flats, unvisited and unremembered. The steamboats through hell continued their hazardous progress upriver, however, for a good many years. The names of the ships and the operating companies changed but the character of the snags and sandbars never varied.

Meanwhile legends of the river and the hardy men who fought it flourished and multiplied. Arizona still remembers those captains. They were a unique breed, at home on water that contained almost as much red silt as moisture. Men like George A. Johnson, Jack Mel-

lon, David C. Robinson, and Isaac Polhamus
spent the full span of their productive years on
the river and would not have considered
spending them anywhere else. Others like
James Turnbull and Thomas Trueworthy,
while involved only briefly, nevertheless made
significant contributions to the development
of steamboating on the Colorado. Whether his
term of service was short or long, a captain
had to be resourceful, courageous, unflappable,
and indomitable. One day was never like another. Each predicament called for a new solution. The risks were enormous, the hardships
were unbelievable, and the rewards were, relatively speaking, minimal, but it took a special
man to captain a Colorado River steamboat,
and these were not just superior men. They
were supermen. Captain Jack Mellon was perhaps the most remarkable. He was better

educated than the rest, had a phenomenal
memory and the strength of a giant. If tales
are true, he was capable of digging up a three-
hundred-pound anchor buried in a mudflat
and carrying it single-handedly back to his
ship. Men are still alive who remember him
and tell these stories for true.

Even for the best of captains navigation
of the river was difficult in the clear atmosphere and bright sun of day. It was impossible
at night, and the boats always tied up at the
bank during the hours of darkness. Casting off
as soon as he could see, the captain spent half
his time aground working his boat around,
over, or through the inevitable sandbars, and
the other half seeking to keep moving in the
center of the elusive channel. Captain Jack
Mellon described two of the standard river
navigation techniques as "crawfishing" and
"grasshoppering." When his boat went hard
aground on a sandbar, as it was destined repeatedly to do, the captain followed one of
these two procedures. An anchor was walked
out, or lines were made fast to tree trunks on
the banks; then the deck winch was used to
pull the boat over the bar. This was grasshoppering. If the occasion called for another
technique, the captain backed his boat into
the sandbar with paddle wheel churning and
chopped his way through it. This was
crawfishing.

On a river as shallow and unpredictable as
the Colorado the captains had to be independent, resourceful, and innovative in dealing
with the situations that arose, many of them
unprecedented and unexpected. During the
summer runoffs the river became a raging
flood and the captain's problems were multiplied. In dry times sandstorms hurled desert
dust and filled every cranny of the boat with
gritty yellow powder. In the winter there were
piercing winds and freezing temperatures.
Captain Isaac Polhamus wrote in his log on
Christmas Day, 1879, "It blew North West
Gale and verry cold—froze all day in the
shade. Pipes all froze last night—have been repairing pipes all day today. River this morning
full of floating ice."

Passengers suffered incredible hardships.
The boats were primarily cargo carriers and accommodations for people had to take second
place. Cabins were few, small, and simply
furnished with wooden bunks, thin mattresses,

*Isaac Polhamus, last of the Colorado steam-
boat captains, stands near the bow of one of
his ships for this characteristic portrait. Yuma
Territorial Prison State Historic Park photo.*

and straw-filled pillows. When the steamer tied up at the bank for the night, the traveler could choose between staying in his cubicle, hoping a breeze would stray through his single window, or going on deck with his bedding to contend with the mosquitoes. Since the insects were large and voracious, most of the passengers sweltered in their cabins. The only man who was obliged to stay out was the night watchman and, according to the Yuma *Sentinel*, he had to take extraordinary precautions:

> He wore close-fitting canvas trousers and jacket, fisherman's boots, a wire helmet and masque covered with fine gauze and buckskin gauntlets. In the sole of each boot was a hole plugged with a cork. When the inside man

felt that his boots were about full of perspiration, he pulled the corks.

There was a single privy, located at the rear of the boat next to the paddle wheel. To get to it, one had to walk the length of a deck covered with galvanized iron which absorbed the heat and burned through the thin soles of ladies' shoes.

Eating was another ordeal. The metal knives and forks in the furnacelike dining room were almost too hot to handle. The chairs were so hot that a diner had to keep changing his position to relieve his harassed body. Sometimes the cook was Chinese and the food was bearable. Otherwise the fare was limited to boiled salt beef, potatoes, canned vegetables, and canned butter for the biscuits,

This remarkable view of commerce on the Colorado River of the West shows the latter-day craft Aztec proceeding upstream through the swing span of the railroad bridge. In the background the buildings of Yuma Penitentiary occupy Prison Hill. Just beyond, the Gila River flows into the Colorado. Reynolds Collection, Arizona Historical Society photo.

Two citizens of Yuma visit the steamboat landing to inspect the Cocopah II, *and across the river, the twin-stacked* Mohave II. *Yuma Territorial Prison State Historic Park photo.*

unless some enterprising passenger could stage a successful hunt for game birds while the steamer rounded a bend.

These old river monsters resembled each other in ways besides their Spartan accommodations for passengers. Since they all faced the same obstacles, their design was also similar. They were stern-wheel wood-burning steamboats running over a hundred feet in length and twenty-five in width. They were able to haul a vast tonnage of freight, towing a loaded barge at the same time, without drawing two feet of water. The standard craft had three decks—a boiler deck for machinery, fuel, and cargo, a passenger deck with cabins, and a wheel deck with a wheelhouse forward of the

stacks. In no way did these ships resemble the palatial structures on the Mississippi and the Missouri. Such amenities as railings and paint were often dispensed with and the word "shipshape" was never used on the Colorado.

Nevertheless they had their own magnificence. The largest and most graceful of them was the *Mohave II*. A twin-stacked sternwheeler, she was built at Fort Isabel in 1875 and worked the river for a quarter of a century before retirement. With an over-all length of 175 feet and a thirty-two-foot beam, she ran to approximately 190 tons while drawing less than the regulation two feet of water. In later years, when she was used for picnics and excursions, she was a colorful sight with

The Gila, *later reconstructed and named the* Cochan, *worked the river for almost forty years before being dismantled. Arizona Historical Society photo.*

her three-tiered superstructure decked out in bunting and her rails lined with a holiday crowd out for a cruise.

The latter years of paddle-wheel river craft saw the gradual replacement of steam-powered boats by gasoline-driven contraptions. The new models tended to be smaller and more specialized than their predecessors, and a good deal more unsightly. Steam remained in use, however, until the early years of the new century. The *Searchlight* aided in the fight to close the breach in the banks of the river south of Yuma during the years 1905–7, when diversion of the Colorado for irrigation of the Imperial Valley got out of hand and the entire flow emptied into the Salton Sink, creating an inland sea. The *Searchlight* is credited with being the last steamboat to operate on the river, seeing final service in 1916. The construction of Laguna Dam, completed and dedicated in 1909, ended significant commercial river traffic after fifty-seven years of activity.

The river itself entered a new era. With passage of the Reclamation Act shortly after the turn of the century, the agricultural potential of the "Arizona Nile" began to be realized. Construction of a series of dams tamed the wild river, provided electric power, and utilized water reserves to change the nature of life along its banks. Older towns grew and prospered. New communities sprang up and attracted new people and new industries. The desert traveler approaching the Colorado today is likely to see water skiers and power boats gliding across the smooth surfaces of a series of lakes into which the unruly river has been transformed.

An enterprising operator near Blythe, California, has constructed a small paddle-wheeled boat which carries passengers on river tours. With the aid of a rich imagination and a slip of cardboard from the ticket booth, one may retreat through time and tread the hot deck of a river steamer again, but nothing will bring back the sight of the *Mohave II* or the mighty *Gila* steaming majestically upriver trailed by obsequious barges and convoyed by clouds of curling smoke.

17

Puget Sound

BY LUCILE MCDONALD

It took ships to discover the Puget Sound country. The vast waterways of western Washington and coastal British Columbia were unknown until an Englishman, Captain Charles William Barkley, sailing off the Pacific coast in 1787, saw a large opening in the coastline which he concluded was the mysterious Strait of Juan de Fuca. Captains Charles Duncan and John Meares looked at the same mouth of water the next year and so did Robert Gray, of Boston, a little later, but it remained for the Spaniards to be the first to venture inside the strait. They explored it by degrees in 1790 and 1791, and in 1792 they attempted to establish a settlement inside the entrance at Neah Bay on land claimed by the fierce Makah tribe of Indians.

That outpost was doomed to failure partly because of a ship's officer's appetite for wild berries. He was First Pilot [Mate] Antonio Serantes of the frigate *Princesa*, which was anchored in the bay for the purpose of founding a Spanish stronghold on the south side of the waterway. This was in case Spain were forced to give up everything north of there in face of the growing British activity in the area.

The commander of the vessel, Lieutenant Salvador Fidalgo, had supervised erection of a palisade of upright stakes and a thatched structure like those of the tropical coast of Mexico. His men unloaded bricks and constructed an oven to supply bread for others of the Spanish fleet in the strait. Not much more had been accomplished when Serantes, hungry for fresh food after the monotonous shipboard diet, went strolling in the woods, nibbling at wild blackberries. An Indian beckoned him farther for better fruit. That was the undoing of Serantes. He failed to return to the *Princesa*

and search revealed his body in the woods a few days later.

Fidalgo, apprehensive of further murders by the Indians, fired upon a canoeload of Makahs with fatal results. Then he became terrified at the prospect of bloody retaliation and sent word to Spanish headquarters at Nootka, located on the west side of present-day Vancouver Island, to get him out of there quickly; his ship wasn't safe any longer.

Although the Spaniards hung on at Nootka several more years, they abandoned Neah Bay at the end of summer and the site of Fidalgo's meager establishment disappeared under the lush growths of the rain forest. The bricks of its oven were dug out many years later beneath the blackberry briars.

British explorers, with two ships under Captain George Vancouver that same summer of 1792, penetrated farther into the strait than the Spaniards and it became a question as to who owned the country, although Spanish names already were plastered on the map. Between the two nations' investigations the general extent of the numerous waterways was determined and the explorers were satisfied that none led to the much-talked-of Northwest Passage, which all early comers were seeking. Spain's dreams of far-flung northwestern boundaries to her empire faded after her settlement on the Nootka Sound failed. She abandoned the port and for the next forty years this portion of the coast was frequented only by fur traders.

As Puget Sound and the Strait of Juan de Fuca were not the haunt of the much-desired sea otters, even the fur traders' ships stayed away and only Indian canoes were seen on the inlets.

Makah war canoe, and the Spanish vessels Mexicana, Sutil, *and* Princesa *at Neah Bay, the first Spanish settlement in Washington. Courtesy Biblioteca Nacional, Laboratorio Fotográfico, Madrid.*

Then, in 1832, employees of the Hudson's Bay Company, which had fixed its headquarters eleven years earlier on the Columbia River, noted a patch of fertile soil at the mouth of the Nisqually River and chose it as the site for a trading post and farm which became Fort Nisqually. It was serviced by company boats, also calling at newly founded Fort Langley near the mouth of the Fraser River. Sheep and cattle were raised at Nisqually, and beef, butter, and cheese produced there were shipped to the Russians at Sitka, Alaska, and to the Hawaiian Islands. Cedar shingles were sent to California and hides, tallow, and wool were loaded on company boats bound for England.

After 1849 the company established another post at Fort Victoria on Vancouver Island. Besides its four sailing vessels regularly visiting the three company forts at Langley, Nisqually, and Victoria, there appeared the Pacific coast's first steam vessel, the *Beaver*, a sidewheeler that came out from London in 1836. In addition to its coastal trade the company sent ships with supplies from England, most of which went direct to the Columbia River and were distributed from there.

Although no one beyond the British company appeared interested in the Puget Sound country, the year 1841 was marked by the visit of Lieutenant Charles Wilkes with his United States Exploring Expedition, which prepared maps and made rough surveys of rivers and harbors, giving names to many landmarks. Among other places, Wilkes examined the San Juan Islands, which the Spaniards had partially explored, christening various channels and isles.

In spite of the rush of Americans by wagon train to the Oregon country in the next few years, newcomers were discouraged by the uncertain political situation from seeking land north of the Columbia River. As a consequence Hudson's Bay employees were the only whites on Puget Sound and the two little strongholds at Nisqually and Victoria were isolated in the vast timbered expanse that was still the domain of Indians. However, with the threat of increasing immigration, the company took the precaution to designate Victoria as its main depot.

Ownership of land in Washington was a big question and Americans were uncertain about their rights, reasoning that the British might regard the territory between the Columbia and Canada worth fighting for. To bear out their fears, England sent a fleet of three warships to the Sound to make a show of protecting British interests. The vessels lay off Fort Nisqually for some weeks while a threat of war hung over the Pacific Northwest. However, Washington's status as an American possession was established by the treaty of 1846, fixing the forty-ninth parallel as the international boundary.

Before that happened a Kentuckian named Michael Simmons traveled overland with a small party and explored the Puget Sound country. Included was a canoe trip to spy out land for possible settlement. He liked the water-power possibilities of Tumwater Falls at the southernmost end of the Sound and decided to stop there. His group was short of funds and paid for its first supplies obtained at Fort Nisqually by splitting cedar shakes and delivering them in canoes. The Hudson's Bay factor required the Americans to pledge not to engage in the fur trade or pay Indians more than they received from the company for wild game or labor.

Early in 1846 four more men joined the little community at Tumwater and in the fall they had a grist mill in operation. Timber offered a better business outlook, as at Nisqually the only boards were cut in saw pits by two Hawaiian employees. Therefore the American settlers purchased a saw blade from the Hudson's Bay Company at Vancouver and set up a "muley" type mill. They rafted the lumber to Nisqually, 25,000 feet at a time. The *Beaver* was the first vessel to carry away some of their product.

During the period when ownership of the country was still in doubt an Oregon provisional government had been formed and Hudson's Bay employees represented their areas in the territorial legislature and as justices of the peace. The first voting places included Michael Simmons' establishment at Tumwater and the store at Fort Nisqually.

Olympia was platted in 1850, and in 1848 the first land claim was taken on Whidbey Island, which was soon destined to attract several sea captains (one of whom founded Coupeville in 1852). From the time of the treaty Americans and Hudson's Bay employees were sharply suspicious of each other's intentions. The treaty had allowed the company possessory rights to the land it occupied north of the Columbia until such time as the two governments could reach a mutually agreeable evaluation of the properties. Everyone knew that when the British were paid off by the United States the grazing and agricultural lands would be open to settlement. More Americans were coming in and some were inclined to jump the gun and appropriate choice areas for themselves. Only the California gold rush and its exodus south served to stem the tide to a certain extent.

Indian trouble broke out at Fort Nisqually, causing an appeal to be registered for protection against the tribesmen. A small unit of federal troops was sent north and Fort Steilacoom was founded in 1849 in buildings that belonged to the Hudson's Bay Company.

As long as possessory rights remained in force the treaty provided that trade and navigation privileges of the two nations were to be on an equality basis. However, for the first time duties would have to be paid on goods imported from England. Appearance of the customs service on Puget Sound furnished a surprise for British ship masters, who until then had been free to do as they wished and had known few laws.

On December 21, 1849, the British schooner *Albion* cast anchor in Discovery Bay and commenced a strange logging operation. Her supercargo, Captain William Brotchie, had been skipper of the *Beaver* and, being familiar with these waters, had persuaded the owners of the vessel to obtain a contract for supplying mast timbers to the British Navy. Supposedly they were to be cut on Vancouver Island and Indian labor was to be paid with clothing, tobacco, ornaments, clasp knives, files, fishhooks, and needles. The *Albion* was also to explore for timbers on the American side and if suitable land were found cheaply Brotchie was authorized to buy a square mile of it and leave someone in possession. It was understood the best spar timbers were on the American side of the strait, but since the treaty the only way for the land to be acquired legally was for an American citizen to stake out a claim.

Brotchie arranged with the chief of the Clallam Indians to log the big trees near Discovery Bay. Masts varied in length from seventy to ninety feet and had to be cut twenty-four to thirty inches square at the butt and

Indian canoes beached at a Hudson's Bay trading post. Washburn Collection.

nearly the same thickness halfway up. Great difficulty was encountered in cutting them under the direction of the ship's carpenter. There were no oxen or horses to haul them to the water and the work was done by a hundred or more Indian men and women, all pulling together, aided by a four-inch hemp hawser that snapped many times.

If the Indians encountered an obstruction they would rest the log until Brotchie or the carpenter shouted, "Nah, *shookum kanaway* [Strong all together]."

Then they would heave in unison, the nearly naked Indians straining at the cable in the dark wintry forest.

Seventeen timbers had been loaded in this tedious fashion and four months had been expended at the task when on the morning of April 22 a little company of American soldiers from Fort Steilacoom and Customs Inspector

Eben May Dorr, of Astoria, appeared at the ship's side and informed the captain they were seizing the vessel for various infractions of the law. Dorr had done the same thing a few days earlier at Nisqually Landing, seizing the *Cadboro*.

Americans were extremely vindictive with regard to the Hudson's Bay people and some aggressive characters squatting on the cleared and improved lands close to Nisqually were heartily in sympathy with the customs collector's determination to stop any trade in British goods and produce. It did not matter that most items on the *Cadboro* represented the normal supply of stores for the post on which Dr. W. F. Tolmie, the factor, said he would willingly pay duty. Dorr seized not only the *Cadboro*, but the storehouse on the dock. Tolmie went off by land to Fort Vancouver on the Columbia River to protest and receive legal counsel from his superior; meanwhile the Nisqually establishment was short of supplies because such items as sugar, salt, and flour had been locked up.

A month later the collector of customs came from Astoria in person and received duties paid on the goods, which were released to Tolmie, but not until after he had been considerably inconvenienced by their detention.

The situation with Brotchie was somewhat similar. He insisted he had not known of the creation of a customs district anywhere in Oregon Territory (it had only been created in January).

Dorr inspected the stock of trade goods on the *Albion* and concluded some must have been sold to two or three settlers on the Sound in addition to the amounts paid the Indians for labor. The soldiers boarded the ship and ordered her moved to Steilacoom. Although the officers repeated their statements that they would have been willing to make a proper entry, obtain a clearance, and proceed in any lawful way to buy the timber, a decree of forfeiture for violation of the revenue laws was entered and the *Albion* was sold at a riotous and hasty auction.

"It was a scene of great jollification or dissipation to the settlers," a contemporary related, "for what remained of the *Albion*'s fine liquors and wine were dealt out with no niggardly hand."

The fortunate bidder got the ship for $1,450, loaded her with piling, potatoes, and fresh beef and sent her to San Francisco, where the cargo was sold at a good profit. Then an attempt was made to sell the vessel, but there was a surplus of ships in the harbor and she wound up as a lodging house, later being filled with stones and sand and sunk to create waterfront property. Thus ended the career of a schooner valued at nearly $50,000 by her original owners. She was the subject of much diplomatic correspondence between the United States and Great Britain, but when a release order came through it was too late to save her.

Trouble of this sort was still going on as late as November 1851 when two company vessels anchored off Fort Nisqually and sent passengers ashore without first reporting to the collector, whom the British had no idea was anywhere near. Simpson P. Moses, the new man assigned to the Sound, was itching to exercise his authority, so he seized the *Beaver* and the brigantine *Mary Dare*, which had brought out the year's supplies for Fort Nisqually from England. Wanting a substantial charge to hold the *Mary Dare*, he discovered a cask of refined sugar that he said violated a congressional act of 1799. It was Dr. Tolmie's personal allotment and the latter got busy, appealing to an American judge to prevent forfeiture and sale of the goods aboard ship.

When court opened, the judge held the ship's captain responsible and subject to fine and imprisonment. He had already been warned and fled to Vancouver Island in a canoe paddled by ten Indians. The *Beaver* was to be detained until the captain was captured, but Dr. Tolmie put up bond on the *Mary Dare*, paid duty on her cargo, and appealed to the Secretary of the Treasury for remission of any fines. These were returned, the bond was remitted, the American Government paid damages for the unwise decisions of its frontier officials, and the case against the captain was stricken from the docket.

It was time that American vessels ventured into these waters. The first was the U.S. steamship *Massachusetts* in April 1850, bringing a joint commission of Army and Navy officers delegated to select sites for lighthouses, fortifications, and Navy yards on the Pacific coast. The *Massachusetts*, designed to travel either under power or sail, was an object of curiosity wherever she appeared. She examined the shoreline to the forty-ninth parallel and, after calling at Vancouver Island for coal, she rounded the north end of the island and returned south. It would be four years before she was again on the Sound.

When the gold fever in California tapered off, some of the argonauts headed back to their lands around Olympia, purchased the brig *Orbit*, abandoned in San Francisco Bay, and brought her north with a speculative cargo including four ready-to-assemble buildings. She was the first American ship to penetrate to the head of the Sound. Michael Simmons bought most of the ownership of the vessel, having decided to dispatch timber in her to San Francisco. With proceeds of the sale of a cargo of spars, he founded a trading store at Olympia. The *Orbit* ran into considerable hard luck, so after several voyages, mostly from Nisqually to Victoria with livestock, Simmons sold her. She started for Hawaii with a cargo of fish and spars, but again ran into trouble in a gale and limped into Victoria for repairs. There the new owners disposed of her to the Hudson's Bay Company and thus disastrously ended the first American shipping venture on the Sound.

Among the American settlements which sprang up was Steilacoom, founded in 1851 a few miles from Nisqually and the military post. This was started by Captain Lafayette Balch of the brig *George Emery*, a thrifty Yankee from Maine. He desired a location for a store and, having been refused a site at Olympia, he laid out a town for himself. He put his trade goods and a manager ashore and began carrying piling and other timber in his ship to San Francisco. He brought back loggers and as his settlement grew he attracted other persons to the town by donating land for public enterprises.

More and more vessels were drawn to Puget Sound by the timber trade and by reason of having passengers who wished to take up homesteads. Among them was the *Exact* in November 1851, bringing Seattle's founders, the Denny party, who first chose a site on a sandy point west of the present city, dubbing it New York, to which they appended the Indian term "Alki," meaning "by and by." It has retained the name of Alki Point to this day. Early the following year several members of the party explored Elliott Bay to the north, going in an Indian canoe and taking along a clothesline borrowed from a housewife and horseshoes for weight so that they might sound the depth of the water. Finding it deep all along the shore, they decided to stake claims on the east side and move their families.

Carson Boren built the first house. Others with him were Arthur Denny and his son, David, William Bell and a newcomer, Dr. David Maynard, who was looking for a place to pack salted salmon, another product in demand in California. Chief Sealth of the Suquamish tribe showed him a desirable spot where his people often camped in the fishing season, so the other settlers moved their stakes and made room for the doctor. Shortly afterward Henry Yesler appeared on the scene, hunting a sawmill site, and the original claim-

An early steamer towing a log raft on Puget Sound. From the Harrison Eastman sketchbook.

ants again obligingly shifted stakes to give him space at what became the foot of Seattle's Yesler Way, America's first Skid Road. (From oxen dragging logs down it in early days it became a street catering to loggers.)

Other American vessels that appeared on these waters in the first years of the 1850s were the *Georgiana*, which carried away some of the Steilacoom and Nisqually settlers to a quickie gold rush in the Queen Charlotte Islands. It ended disastrously and the Hudson's Bay Company was obliged to help ransom part of the argonauts from the Indians.

Then there was the little *Leonesa*, which provided income for the Alki Point settlers by buying timbers from them for reconstruction of San Francisco's wharves after the destructive fires in that city. The Coast Survey vessel *Active* brought the initial marine surveyors to the Sound. Men were placed ashore to set up astronomical stations, but the Makah Indians, belligerent as ever, made life difficult for them.

At the end of the season's work the surveyors buried a bottle to mark the place where their instruments had stood, but that winter the Indians of Cape Flattery suffered a smallpox epidemic and half of them died. They believed the white men had bewitched them and, to counteract this imagined curse, they dug up the bottle, took it in a canoe far out of sight of land, and threw it in the ocean.

Whatever progress was achieved in the new country, it was mainly through the medium of water travel. A group arrived by boat and founded Port Townsend, which for some years was the main port in the area. Discovery of coal on the shore of Bellingham Bay gave impetus to settlements there. By canoe more land seekers arrived on Whidbey Island and by 1853 it had forty white inhabitants, enough to found a county government. The men made their living salting salmon and cutting piling and spars.

If any excitement occurred in those days it was usually near the shores of the Sound, for the hinterland was still Indian country. Thus when war broke out against tribesmen east of the Cascade Range of mountains eventually it reached Puget Sound, first in attacks on scattered farms in the White River Valley, southeast of Seattle.

Washington had broken away from Oregon in 1853 and had become a territory with the seat of government at Olympia. If military aid was to be sent to the Seattle area it had to come from the new capital. Residents of Seattle had erected a stockade for defense and frightened settlers rushed to it from outlying districts. By the time the Indians mustered strength enough to attack the community in January 1856 a small warship, the *Decatur*, was anchored in the harbor and responded to the raid by firing a howitzer shell at the tribesmen. The Indians, alarmed by this type of warfare, set fire to two houses, killed two whites, and then disappeared in the forest. That was the total action in the battle of Seattle.

Many lumbermills were springing up around the Sound and ships came from long distances to load their product. Mail ceased to be carried by canoe and a contract went first to the *Major Tompkins*, then to a larger boat, the *Eliza Anderson*, in 1859.

The *Anderson* was slow but dependable and remained on the Sound for forty years. Faster steamboats became her competitors, but her owners countered with rate wars. In time she won fame for another gimmick, a steam calliope which could be heard for miles. One Fourth of July, while she was at the Victoria dock, the calliope rendered loudly United States patriotic airs, thus disturbing the quiet Canadian night. The steamer was ordered to

The reconstructed British blockhouse at Garrison Bay.

cease the racket or leave. whereupon she moved into the harbor and continued to blare out the same brand of offensive American music until 3 A.M., sailing time.

Getting back to the year 1859, it went down in history for its Pig War scare. The question at stake was in which of three channels adjacent to the San Juan archipelago the international boundary should be fixed. While the Hudson's Bay Company had by then withdrawn from all American-claimed territory, ownership of the islands had not been definitely determined. The company maintained a sheep farm and fishing station on San Juan, one of the largest in the group, staunchly contending that everything west of Rosario Strait, where Vancouver had passed by, was British. The Americans held out for placing the line at Haro Strait, the deepest waterway. Ships of the joint boundary commission were in the area all that season, British members favoring, as a compromise, an alternate line of demarcation which would place all of the islands except San Juan, the westernmost, in American waters.

However, Yankee squatters had moved in on the island; sixteen or more of them had staked claims on the company's sheep pastures, much as their compatriots had done around Fort Nisqually.

Affairs reached a climax when another Kentuckian, Lyman Cutler, living in a tent not far from Hudson's Bay farm buildings, shot a company pig rooting in his potato patch, which was fenced only on three sides. Cutler and his friends regarded the porker as no better than a common razorback, so he offered to replace it or pay $10 at most for the animal. Charles J. Griffin, who was in charge of the farm, retorted that the deceased hog was a valuable breeding boar and he would accept no less than $100 for it. Cutler departed in a huff and Griffin wrote a letter to the company complaining about the outrage and asking that legal steps be taken to punish the American squatter.

The letter was barely on its way by canoe to Victoria when the *Beaver* arrived, bringing two company officials on their way from Nisqually to Vancouver Island. They paid Cutler a visit and warned him that if he refused to pay he would be arrested and tried.

The Americans rallied to Cutler's support and, as the Fourth of July was almost at hand,

they raised the stars and stripes on a pole three hundred feet from Griffin's house. The flag was flying there July 9 when the U.S.S. *Massachusetts* passed with Brigadier William S. Harney, military commander of the Department of the Columbia, on board. He was inspecting defense posts in the area because of the threat of Indian attacks from the north.

Harney landed on the island and was greeted by a delegation of squatters with their recital of grievances against the company. The tale of the lately departed pig, with retelling, grew considerably in proportion to the incident's importance. The Americans insisted they needed a company of soldiers for protection because Cutler expected a gunboat to be sent to take him to Victoria for trial.

Immediately upon Harney's return to the mainland he mobilized a force to occupy San Juan. On July 27 the *Massachusetts* landed Captain George E. Pickett (later of Civil War fame) and sixty-eight men from Fort Bellingham on the island and they had an orderly camp set up by the time the British corvette *Satellite* (assigned to the boundary survey) arrived later the same morning. The *Satellite* was bringing a justice of the peace to try the Cutler case. Its commander chose to regard the landing of American troops as trespass on British property and requested them to leave. Pickett stood firm and posted a notice that no laws other than those of the United States would be recognized on the island.

When word of this reached Victoria, several hours distant, Governor James Douglas ordered the fifty-gun frigate *Tribune* to join the *Satellite*. They lay broadside in front of Pickett's camp with fires banked and ready for action. The American captain refused to permit British troops to land and sent an urgent request to Harney for instructions. His reply came in the form of more Army units, which were landed out of sight of the British warships and marched to Pickett's camp. Heavy cannons were moved ashore from the *Massachusetts* and Colonel Silas Casey from Fort Steilacoom commenced construction of a redoubt.

In the final line-up five infantry and four artillery companies on the island were theoretically facing five British vessels mustering 1,940 men and 167 cannon. Not all of the ships were at San Juan at any one time, but they were available if needed.

Thus Cutler's war on the pig had grown to highly magnified proportions, although thus far his was the only shot fired. Suspense hung over the island while more American adventurers thronged in to stake land.

Militant as Harney's intentions were, his troops faced a reluctant adversary. Admiral R. L. Baynes in Victoria told that colony's legislative assembly that he had no intention of plunging two nations into war for possession of a sheep pasture in a remote part of the world. His ship captains were ordered to observe a policy of watchful waiting while their commander sent to London for instructions.

Governor Douglas, less patient, wrote the British minister in Washington about the affair and when the letter arrived on September 3 it caused consternation in government circles. A message went out at once, censuring Harney for not consulting his superiors before acting. This was followed two weeks later by another communication saying that President Buchanan saw no objection to a plan for temporary joint occupation of the island, which had already been proposed to Pickett. General Harney was reminded that he should not have interfered with the Boundary Commission's business. General Winfield S. Scott was sent

to the Pacific coast and it was agreed between him and Douglas that one small detachment of troops would be left on the island and the British were to be entitled to the same privilege, neither force to exceed one hundred men.

Thus before the year was out San Juan Island boasted two military camps; the British blockhouse still stands today at Garrison Bay. Cutler left the island, but other settlers arrived, both British and American, and for thirteen years ownership remained in doubt, as the Boundary Commission never came to an agreement on it. Finally both governments consented to have a disinterested nation umpire the question and Emperor Wilhelm I was chosen to pass judgment. Guided by the opinions of a historian, a geographer, and a specialist in international law, he agreed that the entire archipelago should go to the United States. The joint occupation, which had become a friendly exchange of social activities on the part of the troops, ended in November 1872. San Juan Island was the last American territory from which the British withdrew.

Long before then there had been many changes on Puget Sound. One event was the arrival of a cargo of brides from the Atlantic seacoast. A dearth of wives, schoolteachers,

The earliest known photo of Seattle, 1860. Courtesy Washington Historical Society.

Asa Shinn Mercer. Courtesy Mary Lou Pence.

and women in general had existed in that timbered country and along the rambling waterways where bachelors were endeavoring to farm lonely land claims.

A young man, Asa Shinn Mercer, came to Seattle in 1861 to assume the duties of president of the territory's embryo university and at once perceived that his student enrollment was doomed unless the population increased. Without women, he reasoned, this could not be accomplished, so he took it upon himself to go East in 1864 and recruit a few, escorting nine of the fair sex to Washington by way of the Isthmus of Panama. Elated by the moderate success of his first venture, he proposed to make another trip and bring out five hundred more women. He wrote about his plan to President Lincoln, with whom he was acquainted, endeavoring to enlist the executive's support. Unfortunately the day Mercer arrived in the national capital almost coincided with the President's assassination. Although this was a severe blow to the project, Mercer did not give up. For almost eight months he journeyed through New England expounding his patriotic plan—widows and sweethearts of the Civil War dead would have a chance to regain the love they had lost by becoming part of the future development of a wilderness which was in dire need of teachers, musicians, nurses, dressmakers, and housekeepers.

Mercer encountered difficulties on all sides and it was only with the aid of General Ulysses S. Grant that his venture was rescued. In the end the California-Oregon Steamship Co. agreed to buy a ship and transport Asa's feminine cargo around Cape Horn to Washington Territory. When he brought the women to New York to embark the newspapers attacked his project, branding it a diabolical scheme to fill western houses of ill fame with the flower of New England womanhood. This frightened many away and Mercer ended by escorting less than one hundred aboard the steamer *Continental*, instead of five times that number.

It was a voyage of four months before the ship reached San Francisco, where the party was further depleted when some left to accept employment. Mercer was by then flat broke and the owner of the company refused to permit the *Continental* to complete the journey. As a last resort Asa sold a quantity of wagons and machinery he had shipped from New York to start a business. Taking the money, he paid the remaining passage on coastal steamships to Esquimault on Vancouver Island and then by the barque *George Washington* to Seattle. His much-anticipated petticoated cargo, reduced to only forty-six, arrived at its destination June 1, 1866, and was greeted at the wharf by a large crowd of expectant swains. It was not long before the Mercer girls were assimilated into the pioneer community. They found employment at once and some promptly married, including Annie Stephens, whom Asa took as his own bride.

By 1869 the population on Puget Sound had so greatly increased (to be sure, not as the result of Mercer's efforts) that the "mosquito fleet" was born to carry traffic across the water from the little towns that sprang up on the many inlets. Small steamboats ranging from twenty to eighty feet in length, pushed by crude engines assembled in local shops and by sternwheels or sidewheels, chuffed their way up secluded arms of water and gave homesteading farmers an outlet for their produce. Cutting wood to supply the fireboxes of their boilers was the mainstay of any number of settlers.

If not on regularly scheduled mail or passenger runs, the captains eked out a precarious existence towing log rafts or barges laden with bricks, delivering farm animals, and escorting sailing ships from wharves to where they could catch a breeze in the Strait of Juan de Fuca.

The "Petticoat Cargo" afloat as drawn by Waud for Harper's Weekly. Courtesy Mary Lou Pence.

The small craft would stop anywhere to pick up a farmer's family from a rowboat and pull them aboard by hand if a rickety ladder did not serve. Pursers and captains ran errands in town, aided the sick to reach a doctor, acted as bankers, called for newspapers, and carried shopping lists to stores.

Some of the mosquito fleet were as large as the ocean vessels of that day; the term signified all craft confining their runs to the inland sea. It was customary for the smaller boats to tie up at the head of an inlet in order to make an early morning start for the market in Seattle, as this was important to farmers. The first vessel out of some of these miniature ports skimmed the cream of the trade; frequently two rival captains left at the same time and raced from dock to dock.

In those days there were almost no roads around the Sound, just steamboat stops at wharves and floats. From each landing a dirt road might extend five to fifteen miles inland, never joining another route. To go from place to place one hiked to the dock and caught the boat to another landing.

Toward the western end of the strait some skippers engaged in piloting and towing ships from the Pacific Ocean. All sorts, from great four-masters down to lowly schooners, arrived to pick up timber cargoes for South America, Australia, the Orient, Mexico, and California. With so much activity centering on the water routes, a shipyard was opened, revenue cutters assumed duties, and lighthouses were built.

Another era was on the way. In December 1873 the Northern Pacific Railroad opened its line from the Columbia River to Tacoma, but it stopped there and boat travel continued to thrive. Vessels competed on regular scheduled runs from the rail terminus to other parts of the Sound, particularly Seattle, which was growing apace. By 1889 more than two thousand persons were being ferried daily between Puget Sound ports, and that year over four hundred lumber and grain ships were loaded.

The Great Northern Railroad reached

Seattle in 1893, but the little ports and mills were still isolated and dependent upon water transportation. Port Blakely, opposite Seattle on Bainbridge Island, for instance, had one of the largest sawmills in the United States, and its wharves were flanked with sailing ships taking on lumber.

Before the Alaska gold rush there had been little shipping out of Puget Sound to the north. The first Alaskan traffic had been from Portland, beginning with monthly sailings after the United States purchased the territory from Russia in 1867. Soon ships were being dispatched from the Columbia River and San Francisco to open canneries. A tourist service was initiated in 1881 by the Pacific Coast Steamship Co., its vessels sailing from California and stopping at Port Townsend and Victoria to take on mail and freight. From there they put to sea again, following a course in the open ocean because the Inside Passage was considered too perilous. It was not until 1894 that a group of Puget Sound steam-

boatmen inaugurated the Alaska Steamship Co., sailing direct north from Seattle. It was already in business when the big news reached the outside world of gold discoveries in the Yukon. All available shipping was mobilized, Seattle became a supply point for the argonauts, and the city was hoisted out of the great depression of '93.

While water transportation has changed greatly in the twentieth century, one phase continues to thrive in the region and that is the state ferry system which links the islands and Olympic Peninsula towns with the mainland cities. Of great importance is the route between Seattle and Bremerton, site of the Puget Sound Navy Yard. When the choice of location was made in 1891 by a congressional commission there was little traffic to Port Orchard, then the nearest community, and boats on the run to Seattle did not exceed forty feet. By 1892 the dry-dock location began to be called Bremerton after James Bremer, who platted the town site. When the battleship

Seattle welcomed the Mercer girls with a July Fourth celebration in their honor. Courtesy Washington Historical Society.

Iowa was brought into the dry dock in 1901, sight-seers were attracted to the Navy yard—many had never seen so large a craft. Other warships were soon to follow it and boat service to Bremerton expanded. The town boomed and as the years went by as many as twenty-two round trips were made daily from the Seattle ferry terminal.

Of the scores of boats in this service none ever became as famous as the *Kalakala*, placed on the Bremerton run in 1934. The first streamlined ferry in the world, she was newly built on the burned-out hulk of the Oakland-San Francisco Key Route ferry *Peralta*. Boeing Company engineers designed the superstructure of lightweight steel plate, electrically welded throughout. She was given a shiny aluminum paint job, a very short stack, and large doors enclosing the ends of the automobile deck, suggesting the snub nose of an airplane. Her name was taken from the Indian equivalent of "flying bird."

Each evening after her six round trips daily she cruised Elliott Bay with a dance band on board. During the Second World War she was drafted for weekend excursions to Victoria.

The ferries had changed from private ownership to Washington State when the *Kalakala* was finally retired in the fall of 1967. She had made 47,700 round trips to Bremerton, to say nothing of her summer runs to Victoria. She had traveled all told 1,411,532 nautical miles. With changing conditions she was less efficient for handling motor trucks of increased size, her big doors had been removed because of new terminal requirements, and the wind passed through her auto deck instead of around the streamlined structure. There was also an annoying vibration. The *Kalakala* was no longer needed—newer vessels had taken her place—and she was sold for use as a crab-processing plant in Alaskan waters. Today she is a cannery at Kodiak, a strange end for the world's first and only streamlined ferry.

Highways and automobiles have not ended water travel on Puget Sound, but rather have increased it, as indicated by figures showing the state-operated ferries hauled 13,700,000 persons and 5,600,000 vehicles and made 160,000 landings in 1975. They constitute the largest mass-transit ferry operation in the United States.

Formerly it was an adventure to travel Puget Sound ferries in fogs and on dark nights, when captains were dependent on whistle echoes as an aid to navigation. Now modern equipment enables them to see marine obstacles under any conditions. Also there is a definite Coast Guard guided course laid down for all shipping entering the Strait of Juan de Fuca. The days of lumber schooners and barkentines are gone, and oil tankers, container ships, van ships, and barges carry the wheat and timber products, oil, and all the sustaining foods and materials that are sent across the Pacific Ocean or to the most northern arctic shore of Alaska. The glamour years are gone and efficiency prevails, but water routes are still a vital part of life in northwest Washington.

18

The Yukon River

BY ARCHIE SATTERFIELD

The history of the Yukon River might be summed up as total ignorance by white men followed by fifty years of intensive use, followed by virtual neglect. It was the first major North American river discovered by man, yet the last discovered by the white man. And today it is still a free-flowing river for most of its two-thousand-odd-mile course.

From Whitehorse, Yukon, to its broad, shallow estuary in the Bering Sea, the river is unhampered by dredges, pile dikes, or levies. Its channel wanders back and forth at will across canyon floors from season to season, sometimes creating islands overnight where before there was deep water. If you camp near the edge of a bank that is being undercut you can hear the soil plop, plop off into the water all through the night. Otherwise the river is silent for most of its passage through the scrub spruce and willow forests, and the sound of those grand old paddlewheelers that once echoed through the canyons is gone forever.

Today the river that once was the freeway of the North is used only for recreational purposes. Ore from the mines along its course is hauled by truck and railroad; tourists go by airplane and tour bus, and residents use their own automobiles. The towns that once lined its shore are now abandoned, and the woodcutters' camps that served the elegant old paddlewheelers are grown over by the prolific fireweed and wild rose.

It was gold that opened the Yukon to navigation, not fur or the search for personal freedom or scientific curiosity or even the concern for the savage soul. The Russians were first with their search for fur, and they followed the river into present Canada from the Bering Sea. The Hudson's Bay Company discovered its eastern headwaters, established trading posts, and discouraged the search for gold. They knew they could control the fur trade but could not control the prospectors who could pick out the scent of gold a thousand miles away.

The first mention of gold on the Yukon tributaries was most likely from a Hudson's Bay employee who could not keep a secret. It is known that some wrote home about finding "colors" easily on some of the hundreds of feeder streams, and one historian says it was a missionary who broke the news. Slowly the prospectors worked their way north. Most went by way of Alaska, working their way into the unknown land of short, intense summers and long, dark winters. They wintered over in southeast Alaska towns, usually Sitka, the territorial capital, but later farther north. It wasn't until the first traders arrived on the Yukon that permanent towns, such as Circle City and Fortymile, were established to save them the long trek over Chilkoot Pass to the headwater lakes, then a long float trip downstream that had to be reversed before winter set in.

The trips had to be made between the first or second week of June, when the ice cleared from the river and lakes, and the first of October, when the freeze returned. The prospectors simply could not carry enough staples with them to survive a long winter.

But the traders arrived shortly behind the first discoveries and fought their way upriver in rickety steamboats from the Bering Sea. The first steamboat on the river of any consequence was aptly named the *New Racket* and was originally owned by Ed Schiefflin, the discoverer of silver mountain at Tombstone, Arizona. Schiefflin already had more money than he could ever spend, but he was a prospector, not a businessman. The search was life, the

Chilkoot Pass, the early gateway to gold in Alaska. Courtesy of the New-York Historical Society, New York City.

discovery anticlimactic and the signal to move on.

Schieffin poked around on the river awhile, then left after selling his small paddle-wheeler to some traders. They took it farther upriver where prospectors had found gold in the great bend of the Yukon and set up shop. They thought they were above the Arctic Circle and named the town Circle City. They were actually below the line, but it made little difference.

Gradually the trickle of prospectors grew into a stream, and after the discovery of gold at Fortymile in the winter of 1886–87, the traders and prospectors gave up their diggings and buildings—and the hot springs—of Circle City and moved up the Yukon to build Fortymile near the international boundary.

Perhaps it is best to interrupt here and explain the nomenclature of Alaskan and Yukon towns and rivers during that period. The three major traders during this exploratory period were Arthur Harper, Al Mayo, and Leroy Napoleon ("Jack") McQuesten. They had a franchise arrangement with the Alaska Commercial Co. for trade upriver from the estuary town of St. Michaels, and they divided their time between supplying the other prospectors and the local Indians with goods and searching for the big strike themselves.

Their first post was called Fort Reliance, ironically only a couple of hours' paddle downstream from where the strike was finally made on the Klondike River. Since no system of naming rivers was established by the white man, who could not pronounce or spell the Indian names, the streams were simply named for their distance from Fort Reliance; thus the Twelvemile, the Sixtymile, and the Fortymile rivers, names that still stand on all maps.

From the mid-1880s until the big strike in 1896, the Yukon mining camps were scenes of great eccentricity. The miners were isolated from the rest of the world by months of travel and thousands of miles by water. They could have been on the far side of the universe and felt no more isolated. They set up their own system of justice, which seemed to work very well for them, and held court over offenses in saloons. Violent crimes were seldom, and most cases were settled by requiring the convicted party to make restitution, or buy a round of drinks. There was a scattering of wives in the camps plus a few hardy prostitutes from no-body is sure where, and some of the men took Indian wives. A notable case was McQuesten, who married a woman of the wilderness, took her to Berkeley, California, where she became a popular member of local society and managed the family affairs after McQuesten's death.

One of the other men who married an Indian woman was a wanderer, tall-tale teller and pseudo-scholar named George Washington Carmack. He had jumped ship to try his luck in the Yukon drainage, and built his cabin near the town that now bears his name in the Yukon Territory. Carmack was a restless soul and traveled the river hundreds of miles a year. His wife, Kate, was from far upriver on the headwater lakes; a town originally called Caribou Crossing because that was where the woodland caribou crossed between Lake Bennett and Tagish Lake. Each year Carmack wandered up and down the river, often in the company of his wife and her relatives, sometimes covering more than a thousand miles in a season, drifting downstream, then poling the craft back up the swift river or just abandoning a crude raft and walking home for winter.

Carmack had a distinct knack of being at the right place at the right time, and he was on Lake Bennett when the U. S. Army sent Lieutenant Frederick Schwatka to explore the Yukon River in 1883 and he helped Schwatka arrange for packers among the Indians. But Carmack wasn't widely respected among the white population. He was a ne'er-do-well by their standards, a wanderer, and certainly a liar. In fact, some called him "Lyin' George."

In the summer of 1896, Carmack was on the river as usual, this time with Kate, her brother Skookum ("Strong") Jim; a cousin, Tagish Charley, and Carmack's daughter, known to history only as "Graphic Gracey" because nobody could pronounce her name.

At any rate, the party was headed to the small river that enters the Yukon upriver six miles from old Fort Reliance. Nobody could spell or pronounce the river's name either, and the closest they could come was "Throinduick," which to Indians meant "hammer water" because the river was teeming with salmon every August and September, and they went there to drive stakes into the water to trap them.

Another white man was in the area prospecting, and it has been a source of argument for three quarters of a century whether this man, Robert Henderson, was the true discoverer of the Klondike gold or if the honor definitely belonged to Carmack and his in-laws. But it is known that Henderson, something of a hard-luck case, had found "colors" on one of the streams ("pups") that fed into the Klondike River, and that he and Carmack's party met near where the strike was made. Carmack's version, never denied by Henderson, was that Henderson refused to give tobacco to the Indians. This, apparently, was sufficient cause for Carmack to break the unwritten prospectors' code and not bother telling Henderson when he did make the discovery. At any rate, while they were taking a rest, someone in Carmack's group found gold —lots of it—in a stream called Rabbit Creek, and the strike had finally arrived. Carmack was to insist years later that he had had a dream prophesying the strike, but nobody believed it. They knew George.

They staked the stream according to prospectors' rules and headed downriver as fast as they could to record the strike at Fortymile.

That August of 1896 started the last great gold rush.

Of course it was too late in the season to get word "outside" about the strike, so all fall and winter the prospectors up and down the river left their meager diggings and headed to what had now become Bonanza Creek. A trader and sawmill owner, Joe Ladue, was established upriver at the Sixtymile River, but he loaded his sawmill onto a scow and headed to the Klondike to become, almost overnight, a millionaire by operating the sawmill and selling lots for what would become Dawson City.

But it was a stampede in a vacuum. It wasn't until the following summer that the world heard of it. The miners returning to the States, who now were wealthy beyond their wildest midwinter dream, first had to take one of the two or three steamboats down the Yukon to St. Michael, Alaska, then catch the coastal steamers that ran between San Francisco and Seattle and the Alaska Territory. They stowed their sacks and boxes of gold on the steamboat decks with no fear of theft,

Raven's-eye view of Klondike City, and Dawson City downriver, in 1899, about three years after the start of the last great Alaskan gold rush. Courtesy Asahel Curtis, Washington State Historical Society.

then boarded rusty, nondescript steamers at St. Michael to head for home.

The first load of miners arrived in San Francisco on July 15, 1897. There was some excitement, of course, but nothing extraordinary happened after the *Excelsior* docked there. News stories went out, but the chemistry wasn't right.

Two days later, when the *Portland* docked in Seattle, the chemistry had changed. First, there was a race between the newspapers to get the story, and one chartered a tug to meet the *Portland* as it cleared customs at Port Angeles, Washington. When the reporters returned to Seattle ahead of the steamer, the miners arrived in town with newspaper headlines screaming that the "gold ship" had a ton of gold aboard. That was very true, but for a change the newspapers guesstimated on the side of safety; there were actually almost two tons aboard.

Thus, within minutes after the *Portland* landed, the Klondike stampede was off and running.

The strike couldn't have been made at a better time in history. The United States was in the depths of the worst depression in its history, and there apparently was no sign of relief from the economic collapse that had struck six years earlier, in 1893. The nation was in a shambles, with no hope in sight. In Seattle, which became the premier jumping-off place for the Klondike, it was said that the residents ate so much seafood that their stomachs rose and fell with the tide. There had been riots throughout the country, and a ragtag group of desperate men and women, called Coxey's Army because it was led—and miserably mismanaged—by General Jacob Coxey, had marched on Washington, D.C., to demand jobs. As an aside, during the Klondike stampede, Coxey was to again distinguish himself with an invention, a combination sled, bicycle, and sailboat that stampeders could use to haul their gear to the Klondike. It didn't work, either.

The *Portland* had hardly docked before its passenger complement was sold out for the return trip. Other ships were pressed into service, and Western Union's wires hummed with messages to friends and relatives all over the country as groups were organized, men pleaded for loans from back home, and businessmen frantically ordered more merchandise for the "argonauts," as they liked to call themselves.

Ships and boats were resurrected from the boneyards all over the West Coast to haul men, horses, dogs, and equipment to the North. A rickety old coal collier, the *Willamette*, was hastily transformed into a passenger ship with bunks for a thousand. Men made fortunes stealing dogs and selling them as trained sled dogs. The unscrupulous sold "hydraulic hay compressors" that didn't work, and would have been useless had they worked. A man in Kalamazoo, Michigan, sold tickets on a hot-air balloon that would take passengers to the Klondike, if, one suspects, the promoter could find it on a map. One ship ran aground because the skipper couldn't see over the pile of cargo on the deck. Some ran aground without ceremony before leaving sight of Seattle. Others sank. For everyone, it was *caveat emptor*.

One isolated example of the Klondike madness gives a good idea of the whole event, and that involves the mayor of Seattle at the time, W. D. Wood. He happened to be in San Francisco at the time of the stampede, and he immediately wired his resignation to the city council and struck out for the Klondike in his own fashion. He chartered a ship from San Francisco and sold space aboard it for all comers. He was almost lynched before they pulled away from the dock because he tried to leave without bothering to load some fifty thousand pounds of passengers' gear.

The package deal he sold them consisted of steamer transport to St. Michael, then up the Yukon River by steamboat to the Klondike. He neglected to tell them, though, that when they arrived at St. Michael, they would have to help build the boat. That didn't please them, of course, but they were virtually stranded and had no choice. Thus, the passengers helped complete the unlikely looking paddlewheeler, *Seattle No. 1*, which they dubbed the *Mukluk* for the simple reason it looked like an Eskimo's footwear.

Another paddlewheeler was under construction at the same time, named the *May West*, and the Wood charter cruise members at least were able to stimulate themselves by racing with the *May West* group to see who could get under way first. The *May West* won by a day, but it was a hollow victory; both were halted by the onset of winter more than

One of the most difficult passages on the Yukon River was upstream through Five Finger Rapids. Here, the paddlewheeler White Horse *makes it through. Courtesy University of Washington Special Collections.*

eight hundred miles downriver from the Klondike.

Where the two boats stopped for the long winter became something of a shack city. Wood had loaded his boat with food and other supplies to sell at a handsome profit in Dawson City, and he tried to sell them to his passengers at the same rate. They not only rejected his inflated prices, but also simply took what they fancied. Feeling unwanted,

and disappointed too, Wood soon left by dog sled back to St. Michael, mushing through the frozen wastes in a terrible snit.

The *Seattle No. 1* and *May West* passengers sat out the winter—which wasn't a complete waste because two couples were married before spring breakup—and eventually reached Dawson City.

But the winter of 1897–98 was one of recklessness, madness, murder, suicide, epidemics, and occasional heroism. Those who took the all-water route, the "rich man's route," had it very easy compared with those who headed north as the crow would fly. The travelers by land soon learned that the shortest distance between two points may be a straight line, but not if there are miles and miles of hills or valleys on that line. Nowhere was this more apparent than the most popular route to the gold fields—the Chilkoot and White passes.

On maps it looked simple. They could take a coastal steamer up the Inside Passage from Puget Sound to Skagway, Alaska, then walk thirty-five or forty miles, get on a boat, and drift the remaining six hundred miles down a chain of gorgeous lakes to the Yukon River. A boat trip, a walk, and a river trip. Great!

Of course it wasn't that simple at all. The trip to Skagway was bad enough, what with the rickety ships that were pressed into service and the exorbitant rates they charged for standing room. But once they arrived in Skagway, they had to fight their way through the con men, thieves, and murderers who found their way to the bottleneck of the stampede. The events around Skagway during the two years of the stampede alone are worth a hefty volume.

The stampeders then had a choice to make: Chilkoot or White Pass. Chilkoot was the shortest at about thirty-four miles, but the forty-mile White Pass was over more level terrain. Chilkoot soon became the more popular because it started about ten miles away from Skagway at the instant town of Dyea.

The braver ones with a little money to spare often took the White Pass route because it was possible—just barely—to use pack-horses. In all, more than three thousand pack animals were killed on the trail, and contemporary photos show piles of dead horses in gullies and beside the trail, giving it a distinct battlefield appearance. White Pass was also marked by continual battles over a toll road, a conflict that wasn't resolved until the White Pass & Yukon Route railroad was begun in 1898 and the toll road bought out.

Chilkoot Pass was another story. Pack animals were not practical there, so men had to carry their belongings over on their backs, or backs they were able to hire among the local Chilkat Indians or other stampeders who were

broke. Soon the businessmen and engineers arrived and aerial tramways came into the crazed scene. There were a total of three tramways built during the spring of 1898, one of which was eleven miles long, from the head of canoe navigation up the Taiya River at the new town of Canyon City over the summit to the first lake in Canada, Crater Lake.

For most, Chilkoot Pass is the symbol of the Klondike gold rush, and one short stretch of the trail, the last few feet up the summit, is the visual symbol although the Klondike is nearly six hundred miles away.

Chilkoot is a scene from a frigid Hades that only a Dante of the North could conjure up. It could be the symbol of the madness, the paranoia, that some historians believe was typical of the last decade of the nineteenth century. Thousands of men, women, and children hiked the trail repeatedly hauling their goods from cache to cache, some walking more than a thousand miles back and forth over the rough trail, then up the last stretch to the summit and into Canada. There were numerous murders, at least one impromptu trial followed by a public whipping, epidemics of spinal meningitis, avalanches that killed up to sixty people, suicides, cases of insanity.

The Canadian Government made no attempt to keep stampeders out of the country, but they were required to have a year's supply of food with them, plus their normal clothing and tools. A detachment of Royal Canadian Mounted Police (then called the North West Mounted Police) was stationed at the summit of each pass to collect duties and ensure that the required food allowances were brought in. Each stampeder thus carried roughly 1,150 pounds into Canada, and those who did not have the duty on their equipment frequently worked for wages a few days as packers to earn it.

If the stampede had heroes, it was the North West Mounted Police. They huddled in tents and crude shacks at the summits through all kinds of weather and took turns shoveling snow off the roofs during those periods when up to six feet fell in a single day. Seldom were the stampeders able to slip past the Mounties under cover of darkness or blizzard because they were *always* on duty.

Those who survived the passes and stumbled down to the headwater lakes of the Yukon then had another task ahead of them:

Chilkoot Pass, the symbol of the Klondike gold rush.

building some kind of vessel to get them the rest of the way to Dawson City. For many, this was the worst task of all.

They built shacks or pitched their wall tents on the shores of lakes Lindeman and Bennett and began felling the scrawny, tough spruce that lined the shores and sawing them into rough boards, using whipsaws that caused the end of more friendships and partnerships than any other event. The whipsaws were used on platforms with one man above, the other below with sawdust falling in his face and down his shirt constantly.

Others worked at mining the miners, and complete sawmills were hauled piece by piece over the passes. One enterprising old riverman had a small steamboat hauled over the passes and spent the remainder of the winter reconstructing it. There were doctors and dentists, missionaries, prostitutes, lawyers, and newspapermen with their type and presses waiting for the breakup.

When the ice at last cleared at the end of May 1898 more than seven thousand craft were launched in those two lakes to follow the ice down to Dawson City. There were rafts, scows, barges, sloops, canoes, rowboats, sailboats, and the occasional paddlewheeler in the crazy-quilt armada.

From Lake Bennett they went through the broad, mountain-ringed Tagish Lake where the customs post was set up to catch those missed on the passes, then Marsh Lake, and finally into the Yukon at the north end of that broad, shallow lake. From there, the stampeders thought, it was simply a matter of sitting back and watching the scenery flow past. Not so.

Only a few miles downriver was the fearful Miles Canyon, a narrow gash through basalt where the broad river was forced into a channel less than fifty feet wide, where the water had a three-foot crest in the middle, and little backwashes scattered here and there and no way out once the canyon was entered. Then, where the canyon emerged into the broad river again, there was a pair of whirlpools, one on each side of the entrance, either of which could capsize a boat.

The Mounties licensed pilots to take

During the Klondike gold rush of 1897–98 more than seven thousand boats of all kinds were launched on the headwater lakes of the Yukon River to sail, row, or often sink en route to the gold fields some five hundred miles downstream. Courtesy E. A. Hegg, University of Washington Special Collections.

boats through the canyon and would not permit women and children to make the trip. At the same time, another businessman made his fortune by building a wooden-railed tramway five miles around Miles Canyon and the rapids below and hauling boats and equipment around them.

The stampeders who survived the trip to Skagway, then the passes, and finally the river, arrived in Dawson City to find that their victory was empty. All the good claims had long since been staked, and the labor market was so glutted that jobs were difficult to find. Some simply boarded one of the steamboats headed downriver for St. Michael and headed home. Others hung around Dawson City through the rest of 1898 and into 1899, when the Spanish

American War and the gold rush to Nome, Alaska, began.

Dawson City came into existence in 1896 and by 1898 it was the largest city west of Winnipeg and north of San Francisco. It became the epitome, and the last, of the great gold rush towns, and is one of the few to survive beyond the rush. It collected some of the most fabulous characters of the 1890s, and probably had the best press of any such city in the history of gold rushes. Jack London, Rex Beach, Joaquin Miller, and correspondents of all major magazines and newspapers came and wrote. It was at once a wide-open town, yet one under the thumb of the Mounties. Gambling, prostitution, and boozing were permitted. But come Sunday, everything closed

After the stampeders arrived in Dawson City and found the good claims taken, many boarded the steamboats back to civilization. Courtesy Asahel Curtis, Washington State Historical Society.

down. Gunplay was virtually unknown, and theft, as it was throughout the Old North, was tantamount to murder.

In a few years the Klondike stampede became a memory and the Yukon Territory settled down to serious mining along the creeks that feed the Klondike River. The businessmen weren't far behind and soon corporations owned most of the claims along Bonanza Creek, Hunker Creek, and the others. They imported the gigantic dredges, constructed them along the creeks, then built artificial lakes to float them and the old stampeders now worked for wages either supplying wood for the steam-powered dredges, inside the dredges themselves, or out on the stream beds with high-powered water hoses breaking into the permafrost and tearing loose the gravel that bore the gold. Originally this job was done with "steam points," which were pipes driven into the ground through which steam was shot, but just plain water did a better job.

The gold rush and steady ore shipments

that followed it brought dozens of old-time rivermen to the Yukon to ply their trade. At the height of the stampede, shipyards in Seattle built boats "by the mile and cut them off when necessary." The rivermen took them up to the Yukon across the Gulf of Alaska and around through the Aleutians and into the estuary near St. Michael.

The Yukon taught them new tricks. Since the river is noted for its shallows and shifting sandbars, the sidewheelers and deep-draft ships that would work on the Mississippi and the Columbia were of no use. New boats had to be built for the river, and this meant big ships that virtually sat on top of the water with paddle wheels that barely skimmed the surface. Since a very shallow draft was required, regular keels would not work and each Yukon paddlewheeler was trussed up and braced along its bottom to keep it from becoming sway-backed.

Each was equipped with a winch on the bow and it wasn't unusual for one to run aground on a bar, then pull itself over it with the winch pulling and the paddle wheel slapping and pawing its way through the gravel. The paddles were adjustable and could be raised or lowered according to the depth of the water.

A complete transportation system was soon established by White Pass & Yukon Route using the railroad that was punched through the Coast Range over White Pass to Whitehorse, at the downstream end of Miles Canyon and the rapids. From there, cargo and passengers went by steamboat down to Dawson City. A few, but very few, steamboats ran on downriver from Dawson City to St. Michael and back.

However, in 1901 a steamboat named the *Lavelle Young* played an important, if accidental, role in establishing one of Alaska's major cities. A trader named Captain E. T. Barnett chartered the *Lavelle Young* to take him down the Yukon to the Tanana River, then up it some four hundred miles to establish a trading post for Indians. But only halfway up the river the paddlewheeler "ran out of water" as the saying went, and Barnett had to unload in the middle of the wilderness. He was furious and his wife was terrified and crying because they were faced with the prospect of wintering over with no shelter built. He had 125 tons of trade goods for the Indians, and there wasn't one in sight.

However, two prospectors saw the smoke of the paddlewheeler and came out of the subarctic bush to investigate. One of them was named Felix Pedro, who a year later discovered gold on a nearby stream. The two prospectors soon began to spread the word of Barnett's supplies and an improvised trading post was established. When the rush began, Barnett renamed his trading post Fairbanks and he grew rich. The town became the largest along the Yukon system and the terminus during World War II of both the Alaska Highway and the Alaska Railroad, which had been completed in 1923.

The steamboats created communities all along the river between Whitehorse and Dawson City, and people depended on them as much as they do trucks, buses, and airplanes today. Stationed at roughly thirty-mile intervals were the woodcutter camps where the boats stopped to take on cord after cord of four-foot-long spruce that had been dried a year before use. Many of these woodcutters

were remnants of the Klondike stampede, men who failed to strike it rich but became either enamored with the Yukon or simply didn't know what else to do with themselves. They lived lives almost as monastic as monks and some went for years without seeing a town. They usually had one or two horses for snaking trees out of the timber and into camp, and some kept a small dog team for both companionship and for running trap lines during the winter. When they cut over one area, the company would move them to another, and before the wood supply was depleted and White Pass & Yukon Route converted to oil, the woodcutters had supplied some 300,000 cord of wood.

The steamboat season was about four months long in that northern latitude. Often the first trip of the season was delayed by ice in Lake Laberge, just below Whitehorse, so a dam was built on the river above Miles Canyon ·to store water in the spring. When the river ice cleared above and below Lake Laberge, the dam's floodgates would be opened to send a wall of water rushing downstream past Whitehorse and into the lake to flush out the ice. Then the armada of paddlewheelers loaded with passengers and freight would make a grand journey downriver, passing hundreds of small boats and rafts of logs bound for the sawmills at Dawson City, called "float-me-downs," and each town along the route and each woodcutter's camp would celebrate the day as though it were New Year's Eve.

The following September or October, the procedure would be reversed as the last steamboats left Dawson City headed upriver on the low water. Big parties would be held that last night in Dawson City, but it was a sad time because it meant the town was going into the isolation and almost hibernation of the long, dark winter. The residents knew they would be alone until the following May or June, when they would gather at the top of a high hill above town, called Midnight Dome, and watch for the first steamboat around the bend.

Some of the paddlewheelers were pulled up onto banks during the winter for overhauls and to protect them from the dangerous spring breakup when anything could happen. Sometimes ice jams created vast lakes, and if the steamboats were frozen to the bottom—a common occurrence—they would become inept submarines. Sometimes the ice rushing downriver would tear holes in them, or rip out an entire side. Some genius came up with the

The burning of the steamships Casca *and* Whitehorse. *Yukon Government photo.*

idea of partially flooding the steamboats just before breakup and shooting steam into the water to thaw the water around the boat and to free it from the bottom if it were touching. If it was not on the bottom, the crews would chop the ice loose around it so it could float free when the ice began moving.

The steamboat era lasted just over half a century on the Yukon, but everyone knew its days were numbered when the Alaska Highway was punched through the wilderness during World War II. The highway ran across the bottom of the Yukon Territory through Whitehorse on its way to Alaska, but the spur

highways weren't far behind. Finally, the highway was completed from Whitehorse to Dawson City with others making crooked lines on the map to Ross River, Keno Hill, Mayo, and other towns which were built around new mines.

Where there once were more than two hundred steamboats on the river, suddenly, it seemed, there were none. What few were left sat high and dry on the banks. A few were accorded museum status—the *Keno* in Dawson City, the *Klondike* in Whitehorse, and the *Tutshi* in Carcross. Two others, the *Whitehorse* and *Casca*, were on the bank at Whitehorse for a quarter of a century, always just a step ahead of the demolition crew. When at last it was decided to make them into museum pieces too, an arsonist climbed the high fence surrounding them and turned them into a bonfire. Sadly, the old-timers of the river gathered to watch as the tinder-dry wooden vessels became ash heaps. Ironically, photos of the fire show smoke billowing from the stacks for the final time.

After the early 1950s, the river was virtually abandoned. The towns became ghost towns overnight, and cabins were left unlocked, with stoves, cupboards filled with dishes, beds and books. It simply was too expensive to ship the material out. Little Salmon, Big Salmon, Yukon Crossing, Fort Selkirk, Thistle Creek, and the other towns remained but they were ghost towns. Only a handful of trappers stayed on, still using the river as their highway.

Thus the river remained until the late 1960s when the wilderness became an "in" place for people to go on vacations, and the Yukon River was discovered all over again. Now, each summer a parade of canoes, inflatable boats, flat-bottomed riverboats, and rafts make the trip between Whitehorse and Daw-

son City. The river in Alaska isn't used much by vacationers, except an occasional hardy soul who intends to follow the whole river system to the ocean. Few make it because the two-thousand-mile course is simply too much wilderness for one summer. Those few who do complete it usually sell or give away their boat to the Indians near the estuary and fly out, wondering if the trip was worth the effort.

More dams on the Yukon seem inevitable, although it seems unlikely that the Ramparts Dam project will be revived for some time to come by Alaskan power officials. There is constant talk of building more hydroelectric dams in the Canadian Yukon, but this scheme has vocal opponents. And there is also talk of building a steel-hulled paddlewheeler to run between Whitehorse and Dawson City each summer for tourists, and pulling it up on the bank at Whitehorse during the winter for use as a restaurant.

Whatever happens to transportation on the Yukon River, nothing is likely ever to replace the romance of those old paddle-wheelers. Now that it is no longer a transportation corridor other less colorful uses will be found for it.

The end of the steamboat era on the Yukon. Courtesy Archie Satterfield.

Index

Index

Index

Index